# The Speaker's Sourcebook

## Quotes, Stories and Anecdotes for Every Occasion

# The Speaker's Sourcebook

## Quotes, Stories and Anecdotes for Every Occasion

Glenn Van Ekeren

**PRENTICE HALL**
Englewood Cliffs, New Jersey 07632

Prentice-Hall International, Inc., *London*
Prentice-Hall of Australia, Pty. Ltd., *Sydney*
Prentice-Hall Canada, Inc., *Toronto*
Prentice-Hall of India Private Ltd., *New Delhi*
Prentice-Hall of Japan, Inc., *Tokyo*
Prentice-Hall of Southeast Asia Pte. Ltd., *Singapore*
Editora Prentice-Hall do Brasil Ltda., *Rio de Janeiro*
Prentice-Hall Hispanoamericana, S.A., *Mexico*

© 1988 *by*

PRENTICE-HALL, INC.
Englewood Cliffs, N.J.

10 9 8 7 6 5 4 3

**Library of Congress Cataloging-in-Publication Data**

Van Ekeren, Glenn.
  The speaker's sourcebook : quotes, stories and anecdotes for
every occasion / Glenn Van Ekeren.
     p.  cm.
ISBN 0-13-824608-4          ISBN 0-13-824590-8 (pbk.)
  1. Quotations, English.  I. Title.
PN6081.V36 1988
082--dc19                                              87-29192
                                                          CIP

ISBN 0-13-824608-4

ISBN 0-13-824590-8 {PBK}

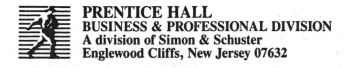
**PRENTICE HALL**
**BUSINESS & PROFESSIONAL DIVISION**
**A division of Simon & Schuster**
**Englewood Cliffs, New Jersey 07632**

Printed in the United States of America

# Introduction

An effective anecdote packs a powerful punch. Real life or fictional, funny or not, a well-placed anecdote makes a lasting impression. Some stories or quotations bring back memories of days gone by. Others help us see the present a little clearer, and still others inspire us to envision the future. It's no secret—quotes and anecdotes make it possible for teachers, preachers, authors, and speakers to make your point.

My first paid public speaking engagement was accidental. The organizing agency had contracted with a well-known speaker who was forced to back out at the last minute. (What an ego booster to be chosen in a last ditch effort to find a speaker. It is a great story to tell now, several years later.) I quickly prepared my motivational speech (inadvertently leaving out the motivation part). It was a clean, one hour, three-point outline.

Standing before my audience of two hundred secretaries brought me face to face with a grim reality. Their eyes were open (barely); however, their minds were closing fast. Fortunately they were polite enough not to leave physically, but it was apparent they were lost in their own thoughts. Suddenly I thought of an unplanned personal story. Should I share it or not? I did.

The transition from boredom to interest occurred immediately when the audience heard the words, "That reminds me of a story from my own personal struggles." The pressure lifted. The intensity of the audience turned to visible concentration and receptivity. The rapport between speaker and listener was now established. As a result, a factual message was embellished and enhanced by a note of personal experience and victory. Those in the audience were able to put themselves into my shoes and to grasp my message.

Although the engagement was accidental, what I learned from that experience set the stage for this book. I made a decision that night to never be without an applicable story, a fitting quotation, or a humorous one-liner. In fact, no preacher, teacher, seminar leader, or author can afford to be without a repertoire of supportive material in the form of quotes and anecdotes.

Thousands of speakers every year enter a room full of people waiting to hear them expound their wisdom. The expectations of the audience range from a desire to be entertained to a wish to hear a message that will change their lives. In either case, the listener is expecting quality. Pure, factual content is not enough.

Perhaps an illustration can best represent my thoughts. When I was a young child, my parents were faithful churchgoers. Although the morning sermon never meant much to me, I still recall the opportunity it presented to gather in front of the sanctuary for a special children's message. Children's sermons captured the attention of a young audience. Why? Because they were laced with threads of remarkable yet believable stories. Our little minds could suddenly envision the minister's words. The major point of each short speech was better understood through the application of these illustrations to our young lives. The quotes and real-life stories remained in our memories long after the rest of the children's sermon was forgotten.

Therein lies the test of quality. Does the anecdote clarify the speaker's point? Does it cause a light to come on in the listener's mind providing a better understanding and application of the speaker's intended message? Simply put, does it make an unforgettable impact?

Quotations and anecdotes provide a tasty seasoning to an otherwise bland menu. Unseasoned speeches, like unsalted popcorn, fail to impress those who indulge. Without tasteful quotes or anecdotes, speakers may find themselves talking in someone else's sleep. That's right. People will mentally fall asleep, and they will leave a presentation, wondering what it was they were supposed to remember.

Allow me to interject a word of caution. As an excess of seasoning can ruin an otherwise delicious meal, a needlessly tasteless joke can ruin an otherwise effective speech. Unrelated stories, anecdotes with little relevance to the topic, or an extraneous real-life experience can become diversionary rather than complementary. Thus, the theme of a message gets lost in inappropriate material. People may then walk away with a bad taste in their mouths. However, carefully chosen quotations, stories, or personal examples can support the theme rather than distract from it.

This book provides an extensive list of tasteful resources. Anecdotes, stories, and vignettes can inspire, reinforce, make believable, and add value to the speaker's or author's ideas. Each topic is addressed in such a way that beginners and veterans alike can feel comfortable making personal adjustments and application to fit their needs. Quotations should be used in their original form and not rearranged or distorted to address one's theme.

Speech makers, classroom teachers, aspiring and seasoned authors, preachers, small-group leaders, executives, and seminar leaders can learn from two men who lived long ago. Aesop was at one time an unrespected, uneducated slave. However, he was able to develop and communicate an entire ethical system through the use of fables and stories. In fact, present-day philosophers continue to reflect not only on the wisdom but on the practicality of Aesop's fables. Jesus taught the multitudes two thousand years ago. It was not a series of three-syllable words, or profound theology, or the latest statistics that silenced the crowds. He spoke, and people listened because Jesus mastered the use of parables. *The Speaker's Sourcebook* is simply a collection of tools that effective communicators will want to master in order to get the attention of the multitudes.

Every attempt has been made to give credit to the originators of the material in this book. Where I have failed to give proper credit, future publications will include credits that are brought to the publisher's attention. I have collected, screened, revised, and categorized a comprehensive resource. The contents have been drawn from a variety of sources and from my experiences. They can be adapted to a diversity of audiences and purposes. One thing remains consistent, however. No story, anecdote, or personal experience is sufficient in itself. Remember to make your point through a well-balanced menu of substance and seasoning.

# Acknowledgments

Any major project involves the contribution of many people. *The Speaker's Sourcebook* is no exception.

Thank you to the hundreds of speakers, authors, and friends who willingly shared of themselves by passing down stories, anecdotes, and personal experiences over the years. Though I have faithfully tried to give credit where due, this was often difficult, and I apologize if I missed anyone.

Thank you to Lois Baartman, Jill Vanden Bosch, and Twilla Wynja for their cheerful typing and retyping of the manuscript.

A special thank-you to Jan Fertig for her valuable input, revisions, and undying support.

Then, of course, there's my family, whose willingness to tolerate some intolerable demands on our time together—combined with their loving support and encouragement—has made this book a reality.

To the other members of our staff who contributed through their support and encouragement, thank you.

# Contents

# Ability

*Men are four:*
*He who knows and knows not that he knows. He is*
*asleep;*
*wake him.*
*He who knows not and knows not that he knows not.*
*He is a fool;*
*shun him.*
*He who knows not and knows that he knows not. He is*
*a child;*
*teach him.*
*He who knows and knows that he knows. He is a king;*
*follow him.*

CHINESE PROVERB

1

Our duty as men is to proceed as if limits to our ability did not exist.

*Teilhard de Chardin*

We judge ourselves by what we feel capable of doing, while others judge us by what we have already done.

*Henry Wadsworth Longfellow*

They are able because they think they are able.

*Vergil*

Every man has three characters—that which he exhibits, that which he has, and that which he thinks he has.

*Alphonse Karr*

I expect to pass through this world but once. Any good therefore that I can do, or any kindness or abilities that I can show to any fellow creature, let me do it now. Let me not defer or neglect it, for I shall not pass this way again.

*William Penn*

For they can conquer who believe they can.

*Vergil*

If a man writes a better book, preaches a better sermon, or makes a better mousetrap than his neighbor, the world will make a beaten path to his door.

*Ralph Waldo Emerson*

Men acquire a particular quality by constantly acting in a particular way.

*Aristotle*

## CAPITALIZE ON YOUR STRENGTHS

Thomas Alva Edison was almost deaf. But he didn't waste valuable time trying to teach himself to hear. Instead, he concentrated on the things he did best: thinking, organizing, and creating. And he became great because of it.

*Anonymous*

2

## KNOW THE KEY TO YOUR TALENTS

You may possess unlimited talents, but if you don't know how to unlock those talents, they are worthless to you and to those around you.

A perfect example is the true story about the Apaches in the time of the Old West. The Apaches attacked a cavalry unit and captured the army paymaster's safe. The Apaches had never seen a safe before, but they knew it held a large amount of gold. However, they had no idea how to open the safe. They pounded on its knob with stones, whacked at it with their tomahawks, roasted it in a hot fire, soaked it in the river, and tried to blast it open with gunpowder, but nothing worked.

Finally, the Apache chief had an idea. He suggested they throw it off a cliff. It would surely pop open with such a powerful jar when it hit the rocks hundreds of feet below the cliff. Much to their disappointment, however, it did not work. All that happened was that one of the wheels broke off the safe. Totally frustrated, they gave up and left the treasured safe in the ravine. Members of the army later found the safe, with the gold still inside. Within a few minutes, they opened the safe with the correct combination.

*People are very much like that safe. Find the right combination to open the treasures that are stored inside and those involved with that person will also benefit from those unlocked treasures and abilities.*

## UNNOTICED VALUE

The United Press International carried this story: "For several years a 14-inch statue was used as a doorstop in the home of Leo Carey of Green Township, Ohio. It was not until his estate was appraised that someone recognized the item as a replica in miniature by Rodin of his classic sculpture *The Thinker,* a masterpiece created in the 19th century. When art dealers evaluated the find, they estimated its worth at $16,000."

*You and I are like this statue. Latent within us are skills, talents, and abilities that are invaluable. They will never be worth anything, however, unless we are willing to assess their value in our lives. Unlike the statue, the special characteristics within us are original. They will increase in value as we use them to achieve our goals.*

## IT'S WHAT'S INSIDE

Several years ago an elderly gentleman tried to make ends meet by selling balloons on a Chicago street corner. His business had its ups and downs. Whenever business got a little slow, the salesman would release a few of his helium balloons. First a pink one, then a blue one, and later a white one. Children would notice the colorful array of balloons, and suddenly business would pick up. One day a little black boy sat across the street watching the balloon salesman. He was intrigued with the flying balloons.

Toward the end of the day, the little boy walked over and tugged on the man's coat sleeve. Looking the balloon salesman in the eye, he asked, "Mister, if you let go of that black balloon, would it go up?" Touched by the boy's sincerity, the balloon salesman looked at the little boy and responded with compassion and understanding. "Son, it's what's inside these balloons that makes them go up."

*It's no different for you and me. What's on the exterior has little to do with how successful we are. It's the spirit within us.*

## TAKE THE CAP OFF YOUR ABILITIES

In 1904, a Beaumont, Texas, farmer was going broke. His farm had suffered from lack of rain, from poor crops, and from diseased cattle. In desperation he made a deal with a large oil company. The oil company wanted him to drill for oil because they believed there might be oil on his land. The deal stated the farmer would set up the oil rigs and drill for oil, financed by the oil company. If the farmer struck oil, he would receive a percentage of the profits from the oil.

The Texas farmer had no choice. He was deep in debt and trying to scratch out a living from his crops and livestock. Much to his elation, he struck oil within a few months. Large quantities of oil had been there all the time. During all those years, he and his family were starving to death trying to farm the land.

*The farmer became instantly wealthy. But did he really? The oil had been there all the time. Your abilities are much like the farmer's oil treasures. Have you taken the cap off your abilities?*

## DON'T LET OTHERS STOP YOU

Others can stop you temporarily, but you are the only one who can do it permanently.

Consider this: An elephant can easily pick up a one-ton load with its trunk. How is it then that, at the circus, these huge creatures stand quietly tied to a small wooden stake?

While the elephant is still young and not so strong, it is tied by a heavy chain to an immovable iron stake. It tries to break the chain but soon discovers that no matter how hard it tries, it cannot break loose. As the elephant grows and becomes strong, it never again tries to break loose because it thinks it cannot.

*Many intelligent adults behave like the circus elephant. They remain restrained in thought and action all their lives. They never move further than the boundaries of their self-imposed limitation.*

## MUST EVERYONE FIT THE SAME MOLD?

Once upon a time, all the animals in a special advanced animal kingdom became very excited about the new school that was being formed for all the animal children. Modern administrators organized the school and adopted a curriculum of activities consisting of running, climbing, swimming, and flying.

All the animal parents flocked to the school, eager to enroll their children in this new progressive school. After all, they wanted the very best for their offspring.

Mr. and Mrs. Duck enrolled their son, Denton Duck, and expected great things from him because he was an excellent swimmer. In fact, he was better than the instructor. However, Denton had been in school only one week when the administrators discovered that he was quite poor in running. So they made him stay after school and practice running. He also had to drop swimming in order to work more on his running. Finally, Denton's webbed feet became so badly worn that he then was only average in swimming. But average was acceptable in this school, so no one worried about this except Denton and his parents.

Now, Ronnie Rabbit was at the top of the class in running but ended up having a nervous breakdown because of having to do so much makeup work in swimming.

And Sammy Squirrel was excellent in climbing until he developed cramps from overexertion and got a "C" in climbing and a "D" in running.

Ernie Eagle was a problem child and was severely disciplined. In the climbing class, he beat all others to the top of the trees, but he insisted on using his own way to get there.

At the end of the year, Earl the Eel could swim exceedingly well and could also run, climb, and fly. Earl had the highest average and was valedictorian of the class.

The prairie dogs stayed out of school and fought the tax levy because the administration would not add digging and burrowing to the curriculum. They apprenticed their child to a badger and later joined the groundhogs and gophers in order to start a successful private school.

*Anonymous*

# Acceptance

*I have no methods; all I do is accept people as they are.*

DR. PAUL TOURNIER

2

The best position is one of noninterference with another's peculiar ways of being happy, provided those ways do not interfere by violence with yours.

*William James*

Oh, the comfort, the inexpressible comfort of feeling safe with a person; having neither to weigh thoughts nor to measure words but to pour them all out, just as it is, chaff and grain together, knowing that a faithful hand will take and sift them, keeping what is worth keeping, and then, with the breath of kindness, blow the rest away.

*George Eliot (Mary Ann Evans)*

Look at people; recognize them, accept them as they are, without wanting to change them.

*Helen Beginton*

Brides remember three things about their weddings: the aisle they walk down, the altar where they kneel, and the hymn they sing. Is it any wonder they approach marriage with an "I'll-alter-him" attitude?

*Anonymous*

At the heart of personality is the need to feel a sense of being lovable without having to qualify for that acceptance.

*Maurice Wagner*

## SLAY YOUR ENEMIES

Love is experienced by those who live with people as they are. True enjoyment and the building of trust comes in our relationships when we learn to accept the faults in other people and love them as they are.

Two great American leaders exemplified this process of unconditional acceptance.

During the Civil War, an aide approached Lincoln and said, "You have got an enemy, and somehow you must get rid of him. Slay him!"

Lincoln responded, "If I turn my enemy into a friend, have I not slain my enemy?"

Also, during the Civil War, Jefferson Davis, president of the Confederacy, asked General Robert E. Lee's impression of a certain officer. General Lee responded, "I commend and hold him in high regard."

"You can't be serious," replied an aide. "Why, that man habitually savs unkind things about you."

Patiently Lee replied, "I understood the president to ask my opinion of this officer, and not the man's opinion of me."

These two scenarios have the same underlying message. Two great men, in difficult times, were determined to accept others without being accepted. That's unconditional acceptance.

On April 10, 1865, Abraham Lincoln addressed an excited crowd gathered to celebrate Lee's surrender. An excerpt from that speech illustrates Lincoln's continued desire to make friends of his enemies. "I see you have a band," Lincoln said. "I propose now closing up by requesting you to play a certain tune. I've always thought 'Dixie' was one of the best tunes I've ever heard. I respectfully ask the band to give it a good turn upon it."

## A SIMPLE GESTURE

History was made in the baseball world in 1947. It was in that year that Jackie Robinson became the first black baseball player to play in the major leagues. The Brooklyn Dodgers' owner, Branch Rickey, told Robinson, "It'll be tough. You are going to take abuse, be ridiculed, and take more verbal punishment than you ever thought possible. But I'm willing to back you all the way if you have the determination to make it work."

In short order, Robinson experienced Rickey's prediction. He was abused verbally and physically as players intentionally ran him over. The crowd was fluent with their racial slurs and digging comments. Opponents ridiculed Robinson as well as the Dodger team.

Around midseason, Robinson was having a particularly bad day. He had fumbled grounders, overthrown first base, and had an equally disastrous day at the plate. The crowd was celebrative in their boos. Then something special happened. In front of this critical crowd, Pee Wee Reese walked over from his shortstop position, put his arm around Jackie Robinson, and indicated his acceptance of the major league's first black baseball player.

Robinson later reflected, "That gesture saved my career. Pee Wee made me feel as if I belonged."

*Consider the number of newcomers who happen into our lives every week. They too are waiting for the displayed acceptance from the crowd. But more important, they need to feel as if they belong in our world and are considered an important contributor. We can have a significant impact on the lives of others by simply letting them know we accept them.*

## AMY'S FAVORITE DOLL

One very special Christmas day, little Amy unwrapped a beautiful golden-haired doll given to her by her grandmother. "It's such a pretty dolly," Amy squealed excitedly, hugging her new doll. "Oh, thank you, Grandma!"

Amy played with her new doll most of the day, but toward the end of the day, she put down her golden-haired doll and sought out one of her old dolls. Amy cradled the tattered and dilapidated old doll in her arms. Its hair had come off; its nose was broken; one eye was gone, and an arm and a leg were missing.

"Well, well," smiled Grandma. "It looks as though you like that dolly the best."

"I like the beautiful doll you gave me, Grandma," said little Amy. "But I love this old doll the most, because if I didn't love her, no one else would"

## ACCEPTANCE: A PRACTICAL CHALLENGE

Dave Galloway shares a heart-rending story about a high-class couple who enjoyed their parties and social eliteness. It was the holiday season, and of course, a festive time for the socialites. Just as they were leaving for one of many parties, the phone rang.

"Hello, Mom," the caller said. "I'm back in the states with an early release from my army duties in Viet Nam."

"That's wonderful, son," his mother replied. "When will you be home?"

The young man said, "That all depends. I would like to bring a buddy home with me."

"Sure, bring him home with you for a few days," the mother replied.

"Mother, there is something you need to know about my buddy. Both legs have been amputated, one arm is gone, his face is quite disfigured, and one ear and eye are missing. He's not much to look at, but he needs a home real bad."

The mother stammered, "A home? Why don't you bring him along for a few days?"

"You don't understand," the young man pleaded. "I want to bring him home to live."

"I think that is asking a lot, son, but you get home soon so we can spend the holidays together. As for your friend, I'm sorry about his condition, but what would our friends think? How would I explain it to the people at the club? And it would be just too much for your father and—" The phone went dead.

Later that night, the couple returned from their party with a message to call the police department in a small California town. The mother placed the call and asked for the chief of police. The man at the other end said, "We have just found a young man with both legs and one arm missing, his face is badly mangled, and one eye and ear are missing. He shot himself in the head. His identification indicates he is your son!"

This "once-upon-a-time" fairy tale does not have a happy ending; and, unfortunately, it is not really a fairy tale. Unconditional acceptance is a reality many people have difficulty comprehending.

How about you? Would you have received the young man with open arms?

# Achievement

*The heights by great men reached and kept*
*Were not attained by sudden flight,*
*But they, while their companions slept,*
*Were toiling upward in the night.*

HENRY WADSWORTH LONGFELLOW

3

Well done is better than well said.

*Benjamin Franklin*

Four steps to achievement: Plan purposefully. Prepare prayerfully. Proceed positively. Pursue persistently.

*William A. Ward*

What I can do, plus what God can do, equals enough.

*Free Methodist*

Getting something done is an accomplishment; getting something done right is an achievement.

*Anonymous*

Doing little things well is a step toward doing big things better.

*Anonymous*

The reward of a thing well done is to have done it.

*Ralph Waldo Emerson*

The secret of achievement is not to let what you're doing get to you before you get to it.

*Anonymous*

All mankind is divided into three classes: those that are immovable, those that are movable, and those that move.

*Benjamin Franklin*

The most rewarding things you do in life are often the ones that look like they cannot be done.

*Arnold Palmer*

If you have accomplished all that you have planned for yourself, you have not planned enough.

*Meggido Message*

Every great achievement was once impossible.

*Anonymous*

Self-achievement is no guarantee of self-acceptance.

*Sidney Harris*

## BREAKING RECORDS

To a certain little boy the Cleveland Browns were more than just a football team. The Browns had on their roster the great running back Jimmy Brown. The little boy who idolized him stood waiting at the locker room door for the Cleveland Browns to finish their game with the Los Angeles Rams.

Suddenly his idol appeared. Bigger than life or his appearance on TV, the little boy was awestruck. Nervously he blurted out, "Mr. Brown, Mr. Brown, you're my football hero!"

"Sure, kid," Brown responded.

Intent on getting his attention, the little boy persisted. "Mr. Brown, I've collected all your pictures, know your records by heart, and watch you whenever I can."

Brown, somewhat disturbed by the boy's persistence, grunted back, "Great, kid. Keep me in your dreams."

Finally, the little boy tugged on Jimmy Brown's jersey and said, "Mr. Brown, I not only know your records by heart but plan to break every one of them."

Jimmy Brown stopped, kneeled down, and looked the little kid squarely in the eyes. "What's your name, kid?" Brown respectfully asked.

The little boy knew he had Jimmy's attention. "My name's Simpson, sir. My friends just call me O.J."

*Great accomplishments, fulfilled dreams, or breaking records begins with a burning desire to see it happen. As a young man, there was no doubt in O. J. Simpson's mind that he would enter the record books. The rest of the story is, of course, history.*

## "I CAN MAKE IT HAPPEN"

History abounds with tales of experts who were convinced that the ideas, plans, and projects of others could never be achieved. However, accomplishment came to those who said, "I can make it happen."

The Italian sculptor Agostino d'Antonio worked diligently on a large piece of marble. Unable to produce his desired masterpiece, he lamented, "I can do nothing with it." Other sculptors also worked this difficult piece of marble, but to no avail.

Michelangelo discovered the stone and visualized the possibilities in it. His "I-can-make-it-happen" attitude resulted in one of the world's masterpieces—*David*.

The experts of Spain concluded that Columbus's plans to discover a new and shorter route to the West Indies was virtually impossible. Queen Isabella and King Ferdinand ignored the report of the experts.

"I can make it happen," Columbus persisted. And he did. Everyone knew the world was flat, but not Columbus. The *Nina*, the *Pinta*, the *Santa Maria*, along with Columbus and his small band of followers, sailed to "impossible" new lands and thriving resources.

The Scotsman George Sweeting was often teased about his hard-working attitude and positive life-style. "Scotty, don't you know that Rome wasn't built in a day?" his friends would tease. "Oh, I know," he would answer. "But I wasn't foreman on that job." George Sweeting held the belief, "I can make it happen."

Even the great Thomas Alva Edison discouraged his friend, Henry Ford, from pursuing his fledgling idea of a motorcar. Convinced of the worthlessness of the idea, Edison invited Ford to come and work for him. Ford remained committed and tirelessly pursued his dream. Although his first attempt resulted in a vehicle without reverse gear, Henry Ford knew he could make it happen. And, of course, he did.

"Forget it," the experts advised Madame Curie. They agreed radium was a scientifically impossible idea. However, Marie Curie insisted, "I can make it happen."

Let's not forget our friends Orville and Wilbur Wright. Journalists, friends, armed forces specialists, and even their father laughed at the idea of an airplane. "What a silly and insane way to spend money. Leave flying to the birds," they jeered. "Sorry," the Wright brothers responded. "We have a dream, and we can make it happen." As a result, a place called Kitty Hawk, North Carolina, became the setting for the launching of their "ridiculous" idea.

Finally, as you read these accounts under the magnificent lighting of your environment, consider the plight of Benjamin Franklin. He was admonished to stop the foolish experimenting with lighting. What an absurdity and waste of time! Why, nothing could outdo the fabulous oil lamp. Thank goodness Franklin knew he could make it happen.

You too can make it happen!

## It Couldn't Be Done

Somebody said that it couldn't be done,
But he with a chuckle replied
That maybe it couldn't, but he would be one
Who wouldn't say so "till he tried."
So he buckled right in with the trace of a grin
On his face. If he worried, he hid it.
He started to sing as he tackled the thing
That couldn't be done, and he did it.

Somebody scoffed: "Oh, you'll never do that;
At least no one ever has done it."
But he took off his coat and took off his hat
And the first thing he knew he'd begun it.
With the lift of his chin and a bit of a grin,
Without any doubting or quiddit,
He started to sing as he tackled the thing
That couldn't be done, and he did it.

There are thousands to tell you it cannot be done,
There are thousands to prophesy failure;
There are thousands to point out to you, one by one,
The dangers that wait to assail you.
But just buckle right in with a bit of a grin,
Then take off your coat and go to it;
Just start in to sing as you tackle the thing
That cannot be done, and you'll do it.

*Edgar A. Guest*

## KEEPER OF THE SPRING

The late Peter Marshall was an eloquent speaker and for several years served as the chaplain of the U.S. Senate. He used to love to tell the story of the "Keeper of the Spring," a quiet forest dweller who lived high above an Austrian village along the eastern slope of the Alps. The old gentleman had been hired many years earlier by a young town councilman to clear away the debris from the pools of water up in the mountain crevices that fed the lovely spring flowing through their town. With faithful, silent regularity, he patrolled the hills, removed the leaves and branches, and wiped away the silt that would otherwise have choked and contaminated the fresh flow of water. The village soon became a popular attraction for vacationers. Graceful swans floated along the crystal clear spring, the mill wheels of various businesses located near the water turned day and night, farmlands were naturally irrigated, and the view from restaurants was picturesque beyond description.

Years passed. One evening the town council met for its semiannual meeting. As they reviewed the budget, one man's eye caught the salary figure being paid the obscure keeper of the spring. Said the keeper of the purse, "Who is the old man? Why do we keep him on year after year? No one ever sees him. For all we know, the strange ranger of the hills is doing us no good. He isn't necessary any longer." By a unanimous vote, they dispensed with the old man's services.

For several weeks, nothing changed. By early autumn, the trees began to shed their leaves. Small branches snapped off and fell into the pools, hindering the rushing flow of sparkling water. One afternoon someone noticed a slight yellowish-brown tint in the spring. A few days later, the water was much darker. Within another week, a slimy film covered sections of the water along the banks, and a foul odor was soon detected. The mill wheels moved more slowly, some finally ground to a halt. Swans left, as did the tourists. Clammy fingers of disease and sickness reached deeply into the village.

Quickly, the embarrassed council called a special meeting. Realizing their gross error in judgment, they rehired the old keeper of the spring, and within a few weeks, the veritable river of life began to clear up. The wheels started to turn, and new life returned to the hamlet in the Alps.

*Source Unknown*

*Never become discouraged with the seeming smallness of your task, job, or life. Cling fast to the words of Edward Everett Hale: "I am only one, but still I am one. I cannot do everything, but still I can do something; and because I cannot do everything, I will not refuse to do something I can do." The key to accomplishment is believing that what you can do will make a difference.*

## SEIZE THE MOMENT

Achievement comes to those who look for opportunities and then seize the moment with unwavering zeal.

In the days of our Founding Fathers, Andrew Bradford held an enviable business contract. Despite its shoddy work, his company was endowed with the responsibility of doing the public printing for all of Pennsylvania. One day Bradford was asked to print an important address the governor was planning to make. Bradford put the document together in his usual careless, unimpressive manner.

Realizing this sloppy product was the opportunity he had been waiting for, another young printer decided to seize the moment. He elegantly prepared and printed the speech, then forwarded it with his compliments to the governor and to each member of the assembly. The rest of the story is history. This unknown printer—Benjamin Franklin—was soon awarded the contract for all of Pennsylvania's public printing.

Benjamin Franklin not only seized the moment but gave special attention to the quality of his work. These characteristics were the foundation for a long list of Franklin's further achievements.

## STUDY THE RIGHT THINGS

One of the first steps to accomplishing great things in your life is to cease dwelling on the negative things in your past. Carefully assess your present strengths, successes, and achievements. Dwell on those positive events in your life, and quit limiting your potential by constantly thinking about what you have done poorly.

Alice and the Mad Hatter in Wonderland had a conversation that illustrates this concept:

*Alice:* Where I come from, people study what they are not good at in order to be able to do what they are good at.

*Mad Hatter:* We only go around in circles in Wonderland, but we always end up where we started. Would you mind explaining yourself?

*Alice:* Well, grown-ups tell us to find out what we did wrong, and never do it again.

*Mad Hatter:* That's odd! It seems to me that in order to find out about something, you have to study it. And when you study it, you should become better at it. Why should you want to become better at something and then never do it again? But please continue.

*Alice:* Nobody ever tells us to study the right things we do. We're only supposed to learn from the wrong things. But we are permitted to study the right things other people do. And sometimes we're even told to copy them.

*Mad Hatter:* That's cheating!

*Alice:* You're quite right, Mr. Hatter. I do live in a topsy-turvy world. It seems like I have to do something wrong first, in order to learn from what not to do. And then, by not doing what I'm not supposed to do, perhaps I'll be right. But I'd rather be right the first time, wouldn't you?

*Lewis Carroll*

## GET OFF THE POT

In our fast-food, quick-buck, go-get-em world, it is easy to become caught up in activity without experiencing any accomplishment.

The French entomologist, Jean-Henri Fabre, conducted a wonderful experiment that beautifully illustrates this predicament. The experiment used processionary caterpillars—wormlike creatures that travel in long, undulating lines, at the same pace and cadence, giving no thought to their final destination. Without forethought, they simply follow the leader.

Dr. Fabre placed a group of these caterpillars onto the thin rim of a large flowerpot. The leader of the group was nose to tail with the last caterpillar in the slow, nonending, deliberate procession. Even for Dr. Fabre, it was impossible to determine which was the leader and which were the followers.

In the center of the flowerpot, Fabre placed an abundant supply of food. The caterpillars paraded around and around, day after day, night after night, until after seven days and nights, the caterpillars began to die off one by one. They died of starvation and utter exhaustion. The abundant supply of food was only a few inches away but slightly outside the path they traveled. Their source of life was visible but not available unless they altered their habitual and instinctive processionary process.

*Mankind too needs to eliminate the processionary activities that get us bogged down in activities without accomplishment.*

## "JUST TEN MINUTES LONGER"

Ralph Waldo Emerson said, "A man is a hero, not because he is braver than anyone else, but because he is brave for ten minutes longer."

People don't become heroes because of their knowledge or their good intentions nor by the things they hope to someday achieve. Heroes are people who get things done because, as Emerson said, "They stick with it ten minutes longer."

Heroes don't dillydally through the day doing things that make no lasting impression. Henry Ford said, "The number of needless tasks that are performed daily by thousands of people is amazing."

Here is a list of tasks Henry Ford considered detrimental to a person's ability to become a hero:

- They make too many telephone calls.
- They visit too often and stay too long on each visit.
- They write letters that are three times as long as necessary.
- They work on little things, neglect big ones.
- They read things that neither inform nor inspire them.
- They have too much fun, too often.
- They spend hours with people who cannot stimulate them.
- They read every word of advertising circulars.
- They pause to explain why they did what they did, when they should be working on the next thing.
- They hurry to the movies when they should be going to night school.
- They daydream at work when they should be planning ahead for their job.
- They spend time and energy on things that don't count.

Someone once said, "Doers get to the top of the oak tree by climbing it. Dreamers sit on an acorn."

*Do you want to be a hero? Don't be the kind of person who watches others do great things or doesn't know what's happening. Go out and make things happen. The people who get things done have a burning desire to make things happen, get ahead, serve more people, become the best they can possibly be, and help improve the world around them.*

Remember: "Just ten minutes longer."

## VISUALIZE YOUR VISION

Author Irving Stone dedicated a lifetime to studying the lives of great people. He is renowned for having written novelized biographies of men such as Charles Darwin, Sigmund Freud, Vincent van Gogh, and Michelangelo.

Stone was once asked if any similarities or common characteristics were predominant in the lives of these successful people. He responded, "The people I write about sometime in their life have a vision or dream of something they believe should be accomplished and they commit themselves to it.

"These people are beaten over the head, knocked down, vilified, and for years they get nowhere. But every time they're knocked down, they stand back up. They cannot be destroyed. At the end of their lives, they've accomplished some modest part of what they set out to do."

Romana Banuelos was a person who could not be destroyed. When Romana was just sixteen years old, living in Mexico, her husband deserted her and her two children. She was poverty-stricken, untrained, and unable to speak English. Determined to improve her life, she boarded a bus with her two children and headed for Los Angeles.

Romana arrived in Los Angeles with only seven dollars. She gave the address of a distant relative to the cabdriver and spent her last dime on the cab ride.

Romana began her search for a life of meaning. Although beaten down, disappointed, and rejected, she held on to a vision of a better life. Her willingness to work and her commitment got her a job washing dishes and then making tacos from midnight to six-o'clock in the morning. Romana was able to save $500, which she invested in a taco machine. One thing led to another until finally Romana became the manager of the largest Mexican wholesale food business in the world.

That's not the end of this fabulous account. She was handpicked by the president of the United States to become the thirty-seventh United States Treasurer. Romana Banuelos had a dream. She believed that her dream could come true, and she committed herself to accomplishing more than anyone ever expected. Romana Banuelos exemplified this profound insight offered by Dwight D. Eisenhower: "We succeed only as we identify in life, or in war, or in anything else, a single overriding objective, and make all other considerations bend to that one objective."

## DON'T QUIT

Ignace Jan Paderewski, the famous composer-pianist, was scheduled to perform at a great concert hall in America. It was an evening to remember—black tuxedos and long evening dresses, a high-society extravaganza. Present in the audience that evening were a mother with her fidgety nine-year-old son. Weary of waiting, he squirmed constantly in his seat. His mother hoped her boy would be encouraged to practice the piano if he could just hear the immortal Paderewski at the keyboard. So—against his wishes—he had come.

As she turned to talk with friends, her son could stay seated no longer. He slipped away from her side, strangely drawn to the ebony concert grand Steinway and its leather tufted stool on the huge stage flooded with blinding lights. Without much notice from the sophisticated audience, the boy sat down at the stool, staring wide-eyed at the black-and-white keys. He placed his small, trembling fingers in the right location and began to play "Chopsticks." The roar of the crowd was hushed as hundreds of frowning faces turned in his direction. Irritated and embarrassed, they began to shout:

"Get that boy away from there!"

"Who'd bring a kid that young in here?"

"Where's his mother?"

"Somebody stop him!"

Backstage, the master overheard the sounds out front and quickly put together in his mind what was happening. Hurriedly, he grabbed his coat and rushed toward the stage. Without one word of announcement, he stooped over behind the boy, reached around both sides, and began to improvise a counter-melody to harmonize with and enhance "Chopsticks." As the two of them played together, Paderewski kept whispering in the boy's ear, "Keep going. Don't quit, son. Keep on playing. Don't stop. Don't quit."

And so it is with us. We hammer away on our project, which seems about as significant as "Chopsticks" in a concert hall. And about the time we are ready to give it up, along comes the master, who leans over and whispers, "Now keep going. Don't quit. Keep on. Don't stop. Don't quit" as He improvises on our behalf, providing just the right touch at just the right moment.

*Charles Swindoll*

# Action

*To know what has to be done, then do it, comprises the whole philosophy of practical life.*

**SIR WILLIAM OSLER**

4

I must lose myself in action, lest I wither in despair.

*Alfred, Lord Tennyson*

We learn by doing.

*Aristotle*

One of the big differences between the nonachiever and the achiever is that the latter has mastered the art of applying the obvious.

*Allan Cox*

A good follow-through is just as important in management as it is in bowling, tennis, or golf. Follow-through is the bridge between good planning and good results.

*Anonymous*

Don't be afraid to take a big step if one is indicated. You can't cross a chasm in two small jumps.

*David Lloyd George*

Our problem is not the lack of knowing; it is the lack of doing. Most Christians know far more than they think they do.

*Mark Hatfield*

The more extensive a man's knowledge of what has been done, the greater will be his power of knowing what to do.

*Benjamin Disraeli*

Never learn to do anything. If you don't learn, you'll always find someone else to do it.

*Mark Twain*

Even if you're on the right track, you'll get run over if you just sit there.

*Will Rogers*

A journey of a thousand leagues begins with a single step.

*Lao-tzu*

"I must do something" will always solve more problems than "Something must be done."

*Anonymous*

An active mind cannot exist in an inactive body.

*General George Patton*

Most people can stay motivated for two or three months. A few people can stay motivated for two or three years. But a winner can stay motivated for thirty years—or as long as it takes to win.

*Anonymous*

Somebody will always break your records. It's how you live that counts. The day you stop making any excuses is the day you start to the top.

*O. J. Simpson*

A lot of people have great ideas, but nothing in the world is cheaper than a good idea with no action.

*Anonymous*

Wisdom is knowing what to do next, skill is knowing how to do it, and virtue is doing it.

*David Starr Jordan*

The men who try to do something and fail are infinitely better than those who try to do nothing and succeed.

*Lloyd Jones*

All things come to him who goes after them.

*Anonymous*

The world belongs to the energetic.

*Ralph Waldo Emerson*

The longer I live, the more deeply I'm convinced that what makes the difference between one man and another, the great and the insignificant, is energy, that invincible determination, a purpose that once formed nothing can take away. The energetic quality will do anything that is meant by God to be done in this world, and no talent, training. opportunity, or circumstance will make any man without it.

*Sir Thomas Buxton*

No inspiration is worthy until someone takes action to make it work.

*Anonymous*

We need only in cold blood to act as if the thing in question were real, and it will infallibly end by growing into such a connection with our life that it will become real.

*William James*

AS-IF PRINCIPLE: If you want a quality, act as if you already had it.

*William James*

Action seems to follow feeling, but really action and feeling go together; and by regulating the action, which is under the more direct control of the will, we can indirectly regulate the feeling, which is not.

*William James*

Our grand business in life is not to see what lies dimly at a distance, but to do what clearly lies at hand.

*Thomas Carlyle*

Acting on a good idea is better than just having a good idea.

*Robert Half*

Whatever you can do or dream, you can begin it. Boldness has genius, power, and magic in it.

*Goethe*

Ideas not coupled with action never become bigger than the brain cells they occupied.

*Arnold H. Glasow*

You can't build a reputation on what you're going to do.

*Henry Ford*

Professionalism is knowing how to do it, when to do it, and doing it.

*Frank Tyger*

## ACTION SIGNS

In December 1931, Ted and Dorothy Hustead committed themselves to action. Ted, a pharmacist, and his wife Dorothy wanted to move to a town with a good school, a Catholic Church offering mass each day, a doctor, and an opportunity to make their business dream a reality.

They chose, of all places, Wall, South Dakota. Wall was in the middle of nowhere, geographically located between the Badlands and the Black Hills. It was here that they decided to open a drugstore.

It was a tough year. The dust was thick, the heat intense, and winds swirled through the land blackening the sky with earth's elements. Tired, throat-parched travelers rarely frequented the drugstore.

After a period of serious soul-searching, Ted and Dorothy Hustead decided to act on an idea that might lure weary travelers to their door. They constructed and placed many signs reading: FREE ICE WATER AT WALL DRUGSTORE. The signs soon became somewhat of a novelty. They eventually were placed farther and farther from their business location. Today, Wall Drugstore signs can be seen all over Europe, in Korea, in India, at the North Pole, and in Egypt.

Why were the Husteads successful? For years druggists had offered "free" ice water. However, no one had advertised the luxury like Wall Drugstore. Today, four to six thousand people a day stop at Wall Drugstore.

> *Ted and Dorothy Hustead had a dream. They took action, and when adversity stared them in the face, they took further action to overcome it. It should be clear to all of us that, without acting on our dreams, they may disappear as quickly as they first appeared.*

## HALF FINISHED

Winter in the Midwest provides ample opportunity for any youngster to benefit from the lack of motivation displayed by others. After a heavy snowfall, we would grab our shovels and go in search of adults discouraged by nature's actions. Youthful ingenuity led us to people whose driveways were half finished. In fact, hearing someone say, "Can't you see I'm already half finished?" tickled our hearts. These people lost interest in their activity and would usually turn over their driveway (and their money) to our ambitions and willingness to finish what they had started.

> *There is a lot of truth in Abraham Lincoln's statement that "All things come to those who wait but only what's left over by those who hustle." Stick-to-itiveness and a commitment to finish what we start will determine our satisfaction and success with projects we embark on.*

## LESSONS FROM THE ANIMAL KINGDOM

According to recent animal research, elephant seals spend almost all of their lives sleeping. *Science News* magazine reported, "Male elephant seals measure sixteen feet from trunklike nose to flipper, and they weigh about three tons. Occasionally, a seal will use a front flipper—incredibly tiny for such a massive body.'' Otherwise, these mammoth animals remain basically motionless. The article goes on to state that because they don't eat while on land during the breeding season, they sleep most of the time. Except for scratching, dirt-flipping, rolling over, or taking an infrequent short stroll, these ponderous animals seldom move.

Now consider the bee. It will make honey visits to 125 clover heads to make one gram of sugar. Using simple multiplication, that comes to 3.4 million trips for bees to make only one pound of honey. The undying action of the bee makes it an admirable specimen.

The ant is an admirable little creature as well. It seems tireless as it goes about the industrious work of storing up food for the colony. The little ant is not concerned about its physical stature. It depends on diligent, consistent action to make its efforts count.

So what do these three specimens in the animal kingdom teach us? The poignant lines in John Greenleaf Whittier's poem ''Maud Muller'' drive home the importance of taking action:

> Of all sad words of tongue or pen,
> The saddest are these: ''It might have been!''

# Adversity

*A man of character finds a special attractiveness in difficulty, since it is only by coming to grips with difficulty that he can realize his potentialities.*

CHARLES DE GAULLE

Nearly all men can stand adversity, but if you want to test a man's character, give him power.

*Abraham Lincoln*

Over every mountain there is a path, although it may not be seen from the valley.

*James D. Rogers*

Men stumble over pebbles, never over mountains.

*Anonymous*

An obstacle is something you see when you take your eyes off the goal.

*Anonymous*

You are a poor specimen if you can't stand the pressure or adversity.

*Proverbs 24:10*

Adversity is the springboard to great achievement.

*Anonymous*

Need and struggle are what excite and inspire us.

*William James*

'Tis easy enough to be pleasant, when life flows like a song. But the man worthwhile is the one who will smile when everything goes dead wrong.

*Ella Wheeler Wilcox*

What is the difference between an obstacle and an opportunity? Our attitude toward it. Every opportunity has a difficulty, and every difficulty has an opportunity.

*J. Sidlow Baxter*

Botanists say that trees need the powerful March winds to flex their trunks and main branches, so that the sap is drawn up to nourish the budding leaves. Perhaps we need the gales of life in the same way, though we dislike enduring them. A blustery period in our fortunes is often the prelude to a new spring of life and health, success and happiness, when we keep steadfast in faith and look to the good in spite of appearances.

*Jane Truax*

Consider the doomsday businessman who had a reason every single month as to why business was bad. His list of people-problems and business adversity is a comical reminder of our tendency to find excuses for our lack of success.

January: People spent all their cash for the holidays.

February: All the best customers have gone South.

March: Unseasonably cold and too rainy.

April: Everybody is preoccupied with income taxes.

May: Too much rain, farmers distressed.

June: Too little rain, farmers distressed.

July: Heat has everyone down.

August: Everybody away on vacation.

September: Everybody is back, broke.

October: Customers waiting to see how fall clearance sales turn out.

November: People upset over election results.

December: Customers need money for the holidays.

*Anonymous*

## IT CAME TO PASS

A vibrant old lady puzzled everyone with her consistent cheerfulness since she seemed to have an unusual amount of trouble and relatively few pleasures. When asked the secret of her cheery disposition, she replied, "Well, you see, it's like this. The Bible says often, 'And it came to pass,' never, 'It came to stay.'"

## THE STAR OF THE TEAM

One of the greatest stories ever told was shared by Bob Richards, the former pole-vault champion. A skinny little junior high school boy loved football with all his heart. He eagerly gave everything he had at practice, but being half the size of the other boys, he got absolutely nowhere. At all the games, this hopeful athlete sat on the bench and hardly ever played.

This teenager lived alone with his father, and the two of them had a very special relationship. Even though the boy sat on the bench game after game, his father was always in the stands cheering. He never missed a game.

When this young man entered high school, he was still the smallest of the class. His father encouraged him but also made it very clear that he did not have to play football if he didn't want to. But the young man loved football and decided to hang in there. He was determined to try his hardest at every practice, and perhaps he'd get to play when he became a senior. All through high school he never missed a practice nor a game but remained a bench-warmer all four years. His faithful father was always in the stands, always had words of encouragement for him.

It was time for the young man to go to college. When he got to the college campus, he decided to try out for the football team as a "walk-on." Everyone was sure he could never make the cut, but he did. The coach admitted that he kept him on the roster because he always seemed to put his heart and soul into every practice, and at the same time, provided the other team members with the spirit and hustle they badly needed.

The news that he survived the cut thrilled him so much that he rushed to the nearest phone and called his father. His father shared his excitement and was sent season tickets for all the college games.

This persistent young athlete never missed practice during his four years at college, but he never got to play in a game. It was the end of his senior football season, and as he trotted onto the practice field shortly before the big playoff game, the coach met him with a telegram. The young man read the telegram and became deathly silent. Swallowing hard, he mumbled to the coach, "My father died this morning. Is it all right if I miss practice today?" The coach put his arm gently around his shoulder and said, "Take the rest of the week off, son. And don't even plan to come back to the game on Saturday."

Saturday arrived, and the game was not going well. In the third quarter, when the team was ten points behind, a silent young man quietly slipped into the empty locker room and pulled on his football gear. As he ran onto the sidelines, the coach and his players were astounded to see their faithful teammate back so soon.

Approaching the coach, he said, "Coach, please let me play. I've just got to play today." The coach pretended not to hear him. There was no way he wanted his worst player in this close playoff game. But the young man badgered him constantly, and finally feeling sorry for the kid, the coach gave in. "All right," he said. "You can go in."

Before long, the coach, the players, and everyone in the stands could not believe their eyes. This little unknown, who had never played before, was doing everything right. The opposing team could not stop him. He ran, passed, blocked, and tackled like a star. His team began to triumph. The score was soon tied. In the closing seconds of the game, this kid intercepted a pass and ran all the way for the winning touchdown.

The fans broke loose. His teammates hoisted him onto their shoulders. Such cheering you never heard. Finally, after the stands had emptied and the team had showered and left the locker room, the coach noticed that his young hero was sitting quietly in the corner all alone. The coach came up to him and said, "Kid, I can't believe it. You were fantastic! Tell me, what got into you? How did you do it?"

He looked at the coach, tears in his eyes, and said, "Well, you knew my dad died, but did you know that my dad was blind?" The young lad swallowed hard and forced a smile, "Dad came to all my games, but today was the first time he could see me play, and I wanted to show him I could do it!"

## A TRAGEDY OR A BLESSING?

Years ago in Scotland, the Clark family had a dream. Clark and his wife worked and saved, making plans for their nine children and themselves to travel to the United States. It had taken years, but they had finally saved enough money and had gotten passports and reservations for the whole family on a new liner to the United States.

The entire family was filled with anticipation and excitement about their new life. However, seven days before their departure, the youngest son was bitten by a dog. The doctor sewed up the boy but hung a yellow sheet on the Clarks' front door. Because of the possibility of rabies, they were being quarantined for fourteen days.

The family's dreams were dashed. They would not be able to make the trip to America as they had planned. The father, filled with disappointment and anger, stomped to the dock to watch the ship leave—without the Clark family. The father shed tears of disappointment and cursed both his son and God for their misfortune.

Five days later, the tragic news spread throughout Scotland—the mighty *Titanic* had sunk. The unsinkable ship had sunk, taking hundreds of lives with it. The Clark family was to have been on that ship, but because the son had been bitten by a dog, they were left behind in Scotland.

When Mr. Clark heard the news, he hugged his son and thanked him for saving the family. He thanked God for saving their lives and turning what he had felt was a tragedy into a blessing.

## TENTH IN LINE

A young journalist, eager to begin his career, found what seemed like the perfect opportunity advertised in the newspaper. He called the newspaper and was informed that applicants would be interviewed at ten o'clock the next morning.

With résumé in hand, the young man arrived early the next morning. However, to his dismay he found nine other hopeful journalists in line ahead of him. He took his place in line, looked over his competition, and then after a moment's thought he wrote a note. He handed it to the secretary and told her that it was very important that her boss see it at once. When her boss read the note, he grinned and found himself eager to meet the young man who had written the note. The note read: "Dear Sir: I'm the young man who is tenth in line. Please don't make any decisions until you see me."

## THE MIRACLE BRIDGE

The Brooklyn Bridge that spans the river tying Manhattan Island to Brooklyn is truly a miracle bridge. In 1883, a creative engineer named John Roebling was inspired by an idea for this spectacular bridge. However, bridge-building experts throughout the world told him to forget it; it could not be done.

Roebling convinced his son, Washington, who was a young up-and-coming engineer, that the bridge could be built. The two of them developed the concepts of how it could be accomplished and how the obstacles could be overcome. With unharnessed excitement and inspiration, they hired their crew and began to build their dream bridge.

The project was only a few months under construction when a tragic accident on the site took the life of John Roebling and severely injured his son, Washington. Washington was left with permanent brain damage and was unable to talk or walk. Everyone felt that the project would have to be scrapped since the Roeblings were the only ones who knew how the bridge could be built.

Even though Washington was unable to move or talk, his mind was as sharp as ever, and he still had a burning desire to complete the bridge. An idea hit him as he lay in his hospital bed, and he developed a code for communication. All he could move was one finger, so he touched the arm of his wife with that finger, tapping out the code to communicate to her what to tell the engineers who were building the bridge. For thirteen years, Washington tapped out his instructions with his finger until the spectacular Brooklyn Bridge was finally completed.

## FROM CRUTCHES TO A WORLD-CLASS RUNNER

A number of years ago in Elkhart, Kansas, two brothers had a job at the local school. Early each morning their job was to start a fire in the potbellied stove in the classroom.

One cold morning, the brothers cleaned out the stove and loaded it with firewood. Grabbing a can of kerosene, one of them doused the wood and lit the fire. The explosion rocked the old building. The fire killed the older brother and badly burned the legs of the other boy. It was later discovered that the kerosene can had accidentally been filled with gasoline.

The doctor attending the injured boy recommended amputating the young boy's legs. The parents were devastated. They had already lost one son, and now their other son was to lose his legs. But they did not lose their faith. They asked the doctor for a postponement of the amputation. The doctor consented. Each day they asked the doctor for a delay, praying that their son's legs would somehow heal and that he would become well again. For two months, the parents and the doctor debated on whether to amputate. They used this time to instill in the boy the belief that he would walk again someday.

They never amputated the boy's legs, but when the bandages were finally removed, it was discovered that his right leg was almost three inches shorter than the other. The toes on his left foot were almost completely burned off. Yet the boy was fiercely determined. Though in excruciating pain, he forced himself to exercise daily and finally took a few painful steps. Slowly recovering, this young man finally threw away his crutches and began to walk almost normally. Soon he was running.

This determined young man kept running and running and running —and those legs that came so close to being amputated carried him to a world record in the mile run. His name? Glenn Cunningham, who was known as the "World's Fastest Human Being," and was named athlete of the century at Madison Square Garden.

*The Glenn Cunningham story is one of the best examples of courage and determination to overcome an overwhelming physical handicap and achieve an "impossible" goal. When we face our obstacles in our day-to-day living, our hurdles seem small in comparison to those Glenn Cunningham faced on his road to becoming a world-class runner. "Impossible" goals can be reached with determination and persistence.*

## THE MIND CAN MOVE MOUNTAINS

In James Neuman's book *Release Your Brakes,* he relates the story of a young U.S. Marine severely injured in the Korean War. For weeks this young man lay paralyzed in his hospital bed. He was unable to move a single muscle in his body, except his eyes and his jaw.

He feared he would lose his mind if he did not keep it active, so he devised a book rack over his bed, enabling him to read. After a while, this young man had another idea. He had always wanted to learn to type, so he asked for a typing textbook to be put into his rack over his bed. He quickly memorized the typewriter keyboard, and then in his imagination he visualized his fingers touching the proper keys with the words appearing on paper. Without moving a muscle, this bedridden American practiced typing for twenty to thirty minutes every day in his mind.

Months later, after extensive physical therapy, this persistent patient was finally able to move his arms and hands. Eager to try out his typing skills, he rushed to the hospital office and asked if he could use the typewriter. For the first time in his life, he fed a sheet of paper into the typewriter and placed his fingers on the keys—the same keyboard he had visualized in his daily practice sessions. His fingers flew, and in his very first attempt he typed fifty-five words per minute, with no errors.

*A miracle? Perhaps. But the mind can move mountains. When challenges face us, we must visualize where we are going or what we want. This motivation will help us move that mountain.*

## BLINDNESS MADE HER BETTER NOT BITTER

Fanny Crosby, the famous blind songwriter, was only six weeks old when she developed a minor eye inflammation. The doctor who treated her was careless, and his treatment caused her to become permanently blind. However, Fanny Crosby harbored no bitterness against the physician. She forgave him and turned her blindness into a gift rather than a handicap. In fact, she once said of him, "If I could meet that doctor now, I would thank him over and over for making me blind." She felt that her blindness helped her write the hymns that flowed so prolifically from her pen. Fanny Crosby wrote more than eight thousand songs.

*This talented blind woman was convinced that God had made her blind so that she could see more clearly in other ways and become a guide to men through her God-inspired music. Yes, Fanny Crosby allowed her tragedy to make her better instead of bitter.*

## WELCOME YOUR MOUNTAIN

When Marguerite Piazza, the well-known Metropolitan Opera star, was in her prime, it seemed as though everything was going her way. She was at the height of her career, was married to a loving and devoted husband, and had six healthy children.

Almost at the snap of a finger, Piazza's world was turned upside down. Her husband died suddenly, and almost at the same time, a spot on her cheek was diagnosed as melanoma, a deadly type of cancer. The beautiful singer was told that surgery was her only hope for survival, and doctors would have to remove her cheek, leaving her face disfigured.

What a mountain she had to climb! Losing her husband, being responsible for six children, and then receiving this devastating news about her melanoma—and on the same day she was to perform to a sellout crowd. She recalls, "What do you do at a time like that? You do what you are paid to do, and I was paid to lift people with my talent. So, as I stood in the wings of the opera house, I prayed. Then I hung my troubles on a hanger and left them in the closet." Piazza then went onstage and sang and danced her heart out. The audience loved her and loved her performance.

What a victory! She had her cheek removed but is still beautiful. She raised her family with the guidance of God. And she continued to share her God-given talent with music lovers all over the world. Marguerite Piazza climbed her mountain.

*Do you have a mountain in your life? Have faith, and welcome it!*

## "I WILL DECIDE!"

His life was torture. As a young man, William E. Henley endured operation after operation. He had one foot amputated because of tuberculosis of the bone and was later told he had only a short time to live. Yet he exemplified what it means to live productively in spite of limitations and adversity. William E. Henley went on to live for another thirty years. His reason for persevering was found inscribed on the side of his hospital bed:

It matters not how strait the gate,
How charged with punishments the scroll,
I am the master of my fate;
I am the captain of my soul!

## GRIND OR SHINE

Adversity is the grindstone of life. Intended to polish you up, adversity also has the ability to grind you down. The impact and ultimate result depend on what you do with the difficulties that come your way. Consider the phenomenal achievements of people experiencing adversity.

Beethoven composed his greatest works after becoming deaf. Sir Walter Raleigh wrote the *History of the World* during a thirteen year imprisonment. If Columbus had turned back, no one could have blamed him, considering the constant adversity he endured. Of course, no one would have remembered him either. Abraham Lincoln achieved greatness by his display of wisdom and character during the devastation of the Civil War. Luther translated the Bible while enduring confinement in the Castle of Wartburg. Under a sentence of death and during twenty years in exile, Dante wrote the *Divine Comedy*. John Bunyan wrote *Pilgrim's Progress* in a Bedford jail.

Finally, consider a more recent example. Mary Groda-Lewis endured sixteen years of illiteracy because of unrecognized dyslexia, was committed to a reformatory on two different occasions, and almost died of a stroke while bearing a child. Committed to going to college, she worked at a variety of odd jobs to save money, graduated with her high school equivalency at eighteen, was named Oregon's outstanding Upward Bound student, and finally entered college. Determined to become a doctor, she faced fifteen medical school rejections until Albany Medical College finally accepted her. In 1984, Dr. Mary Groda-Lewis, at thirty-five, graduated with honors to fulfill her dream.

*Adversity—the grindstone of life. Will it grind you down or polish you up?*

# Age

*Aging is a life-spanning process of growth and development from birth to death. Old age is an integral part of the whole, bringing fulfillment and self-actualization. I regard aging as a triumph, a result of strength and survivorship.*

MARGARET KUHN

"Wish not so much to live long as to live well." Eleven years later, Benjamin Franklin followed this comment with, "All would live long but none would be old."

Few envy the consideration enjoyed by the oldest inhabitant

*Ralph Waldo Emerson*

Our society automatically scraps people just like old automobiles. It's the Detroit syndrome, but the latest models are not always the best.

*Margaret Kuhn*

Youth longs and manhood strives, but age remembers.

*Oliver Wendell Holmes, Jr.*

One should never count the years—one should instead count one's interests. I have kept young trying never to lose my childhood sense of wonderment. I am glad I still have a vivid curiosity about the world I live in

*Helen Keller*

Measure life by its breadth not length

*Anonymous*

Nobody loves life like an old man.

*Sophocles*

It is said that most elephants have a longer life span than human beings. Mankind has been trying to determine the *why's* of this phenomenon. Maybe there is something to be said for working for peanuts. Then again, the elephant's long life may be the result of a thick skin.

*Anonymous*

44

We grow too soon old and too late smart.

*Pennsylvania Dutch saying*

I regard the aged as travelers who have gone on a journey on which we too may have to go, and of whom we ought to inquire whether the way is smooth and easy or rugged and difficult

*Socrates*

One day a woman approached a movie producer and expressed her desire to pursue acting. "How old are you?" asked the producer. "Approaching thirty," she responded. "From which end?" he asked.

*Anonymous*

You are as young as you feel after trying to prove it.

*Lou Erickson*

Age is a relative thing; you're young as long as you have a relative who is older

*Anonymous*

In the central place of every heart there is a recording chamber; so long as it receives messages of beauty, hope, cheer, and courage, so long are you young. When the wires are all down and your heart is covered with the snows of pessimism and the ice of cynicism, and then only, are you grown old.

*General Douglas MacArthur*

Old age: When actions creak louder than words.

*Dana Robbins*

What's important is not the years in your life but the life in your years.

*Anonymous*

It's no secret—the people who live long are those who long to live.

*Anonymous*

My only fear is that I may live too long.

*Thomas Jefferson*

Supreme Court justice, Oliver Wendell Holmes, Jr., was out for a stroll in the park with a friend when a pretty young girl happened by. Mr. Holmes, near ninety years of age, turned to his friend and said, "Oh, what I'd give to be seventy again!"

Old age is not a hindrance to men chasing women; they just have trouble remembering why.

*Anonymous*

You have, no doubt, heard about the little boy who asked his Sunday School teacher why dinosaurs and people in the Bible live so much longer than we do. The teacher's answer was perfect: "Because they didn't know they weren't supposed to."

*Anonymous*

A man is as old as he feels; a woman is as old as she looks.

*Anonymous*

To know how to grow old is the master work of wisdom, and one of the most difficult chapters in the great art of living.

*Henri Frederick Amiel*

If wrinkles must be written upon our brows, let them not be written upon the heart. The spirit should not grow old.

*James A. Garfield*

In youth the days are short and the years are long; in old age the years are short and the days are long.

*Panin*

The old believe everything; the middle-aged suspect everything; the young know everything.

*Oscar Wilde*

## YOU'RE NEVER TOO OLD

Grandma Moses painted over fifteen hundred popular paintings —mostly farm and country scenes. She did not begin to paint until she was eighty years old, and 25 percent of her paintings were painted after she was one hundred.

When Grandma Moses was a teenager, she worked as a hired girl on a New York farm. Anna Mary Robertson met and married a hired hand on that farm. His name was Tom Moses. They moved to a farm of their own in Cambridge Valley, Virginia, and raised ten children.

Anna loved to do needlework, but as she became older, her hands were stiffened with arthritis. Finally, at the age of eighty, she could no longer handle a large needle to embroider, so she decided to try painting. She found she could handle the paintbrush more easily and began painting pictures to show at the Cambridge Fair. She won prizes for her canned fruit and jam, but her paintings received no ribbons.

One day a New York City art collector passed through Cambridge and saw her pictures in a drugstore. That was the beginning of Grandma Moses' success as a painter who gained an international reputation.

Her popular works of art have appeared on greeting cards and in exhibitions at the Museum of Modern Art in New York City. Grandma Moses has been an inspiration to men and women of all ages.

## TIME FOR A YOUNGER MAN

The life of Henry Bailey Little is a fascinating one. In 1953, he celebrated fifty-five years as president of the Institution for Savings in Newburyport. Respected by his board of directors, Little was asked to serve another term. Surprisingly, he declined, stating it was time for a younger man to assume the leadership.

"So what's the big deal?" you may ask. Well, Henry Bailey Little was 102 years old and the "younger man" chosen to take his place was William Black. Oh, yes, the young replacement was eighty-three.

### I'm Fine

There is nothing whatever
the matter with me.
I'm just as healthy as
I can be.
I have arthritis in back
and knees
And when I talk, I talk
with a wheeze.
My pulse is weak, my
blood is thin.
But I'm awfully well
for the shape I'm in.

My teeth eventually
had to come out,
And my diet I hate
to think about.
I'm overweight and I
can't get thin.
My appetite is sure to win.
But I'm awfully well
for the shape I'm in.

The moral is this as the
tale we unfold,
That for all of those
who are growing old.
It's better to say, "I'm
fine" with a grin,
Than to let folks know
the shape you're in!

*Anonymous*

## WHO'S COUNTING?

Napoleon was involved in conversation with a colonel of a Hungarian battalion who had been taken prisoner in Italy. The colonel mentioned he had fought in the army of Maria Theresa.

"You must have a few years under your belt!" exclaimed Napoleon.

"I'm sure I've lived sixty or seventy years," replied the colonel.

"You mean to say," Napoleon continued, "you have not kept track of the years you have lived?"

The colonel promptly replied, "Sir, I always count my money, my shirts, and my horses—but as for my years, I know nobody who wants to steal them, and I shall surely never lose them."

## MAINTAINING DIGNITY

A certain professional photographer managed to build a faithful following of customers who used his services on a regular basis.

One such customer returned to him after six years, wanting a portrait sitting. The details were organized, the background set, several pictures taken, and the proofs returned. However, the woman was upset with the results.

"When you photographed me before, I looked more stunning," she complained.

"Well, I'm sorry," said the photographer, "but I was six years younger then."

## NEVER TOO YOUNG OR TOO OLD

Quality of living is not a chronological affair. Before deciding we are too young or too old to try a new adventure, or to make our mark in history, or to face new challenges, it might be wise to consider the lives of people who didn't let age interfere.

- George Burns won his first Oscar at eighty.
- Mickey Mantle hit twenty-three home runs his first full year in the major leagues. He was twenty years old.
- Golda Meir was seventy-one when she became prime minister of Israel.
- William Pitt was only twenty-four when Great Britain called on him to become prime minister.
- George Bernard Shaw was ninety-four when one of his plays was first produced. At ninety-six, he broke his leg when he fell out of a tree he was trimming in his backyard.
- Mozart published his first composition at seven years old.
- Ted Williams ended his baseball career with a home run in his last time at bat. Williams was forty-two.
- Grandma Moses didn't start painting until she was eighty years old. She completed over fifteen hundred paintings in the remainder of her life, with 25 percent of those produced after she was one hundred.
- Benjamin Franklin published his first newspaper column when he was sixteen and had the honor of framing the U.S. Constitution when he was eighty-one.
- Michelangelo was seventy-one when he painted the Sistine Chapel.
- Albert Schweitzer was still performing operations in his African hospital at eighty-nine.
- John D. Rockefeller was making $1 million a week when he died at ninety-three.
- Neither Henry Ford nor Abraham Lincoln realized any success until after they were forty years old.
- Doc Counsilman, at fifty-eight, became the oldest person ever to swim the English Channel.
- Gordie Howe remained a top competitor in the National Hockey League into his early fifties.
- S. I. Hayakawa retired as president of San Francisco State University at seventy, and was then elected to the U.S. Senate.
- Herbert Hoover, at eighty-four, served as U.S. representative to Belgium.

- Winston Churchill assumed the role of Great Britain's prime minister at sixty-five. At seventy, he addressed the crowds on V-E Day, standing on top of his car to speak.
- Charlie Chaplin, at seventy-six, was still directing movies.
- Casey Stengel didn't retire from the rigorous schedule of managing the New York Mets until he was seventy-five.

*There is no need to dread the future or the present. At whatever age, we can be creative, productive, and able to make the most of every day.*

## "IF I HAD MY LIFE TO LIVE OVER"

If I had my life to live over, I'd dare to make more mistakes next time. I'd relax, I'd limber up. I would be sillier than I've been this trip. I would take fewer things seriously, take more chances, take more trips. I'd climb more mountains, and swim more rivers. I would eat more ice cream and less beans. I would, perhaps, have more actual troubles, but I'd have fewer imaginary ones. You see, I'm one of those people who lived seriously, sanely, hour after hour, day after day. Oh, I've had my moments, and if I had it to do over again, I'd have more of them. I've been one of those persons who never goes anywhere without a thermometer, a hot-water bottle, a raincoat, and a parachute. If I had to do it again, I would travel lighter than this trip. If I had my life to live over, I would start going barefoot earlier in the spring, and stay that way later in the fall. I would go to more dances, I would ride more merry-go-rounds. I would pick more daisies.

*Anonymous*

## INACTIVE?—ARE YOU KIDDING?

In an issue of *New Horizons,* there appeared some heartwarming statistics. Elderly people are apparently not as inactive as we have been led to believe. Several years ago, the National Council on Aging hired pollster Lou Harris to interview fifteen hundred individuals under sixty-five and another twenty-five hundred who were over sixty-five. The younger ones thought that older people sleep and sit around a lot, that loneliness and poor health were their most serious problems, and that they didn't have enough to do. The response of the other group indicated, however, that only 31 percent of those over sixty-five are inactive, and only 12 percent complain of loneliness. Although 56 percent of the younger people thought that the elderly were disturbed by not feeling needed, this was true of only 7 percent of the older group. Most were active and functioning well.

As Amiel so beautifully said, "To know how to grow old is the master work of wisdom, and one of the most difficult chapters in the great art of living."

I wonder, how old would you be if you didn't know how old you were?

## Never Too Late

"It is too late!" Ah, nothing is too late—
Cato learned Greek at eighty; Sophocles
wrote his grand "Oedipus," and Simonides
Bore off the prize of verse from his compeers
When each had numbered more than fourscore years;
And Theophrastus, at fourscore and ten,
Had begun his "Characters of Men."
Chaucer, at Woodstock, with his nightingales,
At sixty wrote the "Canterbury Tales."
Goethe, at Weimar, toiling to the last,
Completed "Faust" when eighty years were past.
What then? Shall we sit idly down and say,
"The night has come; it is no longer day"?
For age is opportunity no less
Than youth itself, though in another dress.
And as the evening twilight fades away,
The sky is filled with stars, invisible by day.
It is never too late to start doing what is right.
Never.

*Henry Wadsworth Longfellow*

# Anger

*For every minute you remain angry,
you give up sixty seconds of peace of mind.*

RALPH WALDO EMERSON

7

Anyone who angers you conquers you.

*Sister Kenny's mother*

Swallowing angry words is much easier than having to eat them.

*Grit*

The greatest cure of anger is delay.

*Seneca*

It is better to choose what you say than say what you choose.

*Anonymous*

## WHAT HAVE YOU LEFT BEHIND?

It was a hot, humid day in the middle of Kansas City. The eight-hour shift seemed especially long for the veteran bus driver. Suddenly, a young woman, apparently upset about something, let loose with a string of unforgettable, not to mention, unrepeatable words. The bus driver, looking in his overhead mirror, could sense everyone around her was embarrassed by the string of profanity. Still mumbling, the angry passenger began to disembark a few blocks later. As she stepped down, the bus driver calmly said, "Madam, I believe you are leaving something behind."

She quickly turned and snapped, "Oh, and what is that?"

"A very bad impression," the bus driver responded.

## A SURE WAY TO SELF-DESTRUCT

A pointed fable is told about a young lion and a cougar. Both thirsty, the animals arrived at their usual water hole at the same time. They immediately began to argue about who should satisfy their thirst first. The argument became heated, and each decided he would rather die than give up the privilege of being first to quench his thirst. As they stubbornly confronted each other, their emotions turned to rage. Their cruel attacks on each other were suddenly interrupted. They both looked up. Circling overhead was a flock of vultures waiting for the loser to fall. Quietly, the two beasts turned and walked away. The thought of being devoured was all they needed to end their quarrel.

# Attitude

*It is our attitude at the beginning
of a difficult undertaking which,
more than anything else, will
determine its successful outcome.*

WILLIAM JAMES

8

An optimist is someone who goes after Moby Dick in a rowboat and takes the tartar sauce with him.

Zig Ziglar

There exist limitless opportunities in every industry. Where there is an open mind, there will always be a frontier.

Charles F. Kettering

Attitudes are more important than facts.

Dr. Karl Menninger

I don't sing because I'm happy; I'm happy because I sing.

William James

I complained because I had no shoes until I met a man who had no feet.

Arabic proverb

"You must be thrilled with your bumper crop of potatoes this year, Mr. Hibbe." "Aye, uh, they're plenty good, but we got no bad-uns to feed the pigs."

Anonymous

Our attitude toward the world around us depends upon what we are ourselves. If we are selfish, we will be suspicious of others. If we are of a generous nature, we will be likely to be more trustful. If we are quite honest with ourselves, we won't always be anticipating deceit in others. If we are inclined to be fair, we won't feel that we are being cheated. In a sense, looking at the people around you is like looking in a mirror. You see a reflection of yourself.

*Anonymous*

Attitude is the first quality that marks the successful man. If he has a positive attitude and is a positive thinker, who likes challenges and difficult situations, then he has half his success achieved. On the other hand, if he is a negative thinker who is narrow-minded and refuses to accept new ideas and has a defeatist attitude, he hasn't got a chance.

*Lowell Peacock*

Attitudes are much more important than aptitudes.

*Anonymous*

Instead of weeping when a tragedy occurs in a songbird's life, it sings away its grief. I believe we could well follow the pattern of our feathered friends.

*Robert S. Walker*

An easy task becomes difficult when you do it with reluctance.

*Terence*

There is a little difference in people, but that little difference makes a big difference. The little difference is attitude. The big difference is whether it is positive or negative.

*Clement Stone*

What good did it do to be grouchy today? Did your surliness drive any trouble away? Did you cover more ground than you usually do, because of the grouch you carried with you? If not, what's the use of a grouch or a frown, if it won't smooth a path, or a grim trouble drown? If it doesn't assist you, it isn't worthwhile. Your work may be hard, but just do it—and smile.

*Anonymous*

The greatest discovery of my generation is that human beings can alter their lives by altering their attitudes of mind.

*William James*

Believe that you possess significant reserves of health, energy, and endurance, and your belief will create the fact.

*Anonymous*

I am an optimist. It does not seem too much use being anything else.

*Sir Winston Churchill*

Sometimes only a change of viewpoint is needed to convert a tiresome duty into an interesting opportunity.

*Alberta Flanders*

The pessimist sees the difficulty in every opportunity; the optimist, the opportunity in every difficulty.

*L. P. Jacks*

## WITHIN—WITHOUT

We don't know much about this Greek poet except that he lived about four hundred years before Christ. His name was Hermesianax. He left with us four thought-provoking words. He said, "As within—so without." What you truly believe, want, perceive, and are atracted to will dictate the actions you take, the people you involve yourself with, and the activities you pursue.

### If You Think

If you think you are beaten, you are.
If you think you dare not, you don't!
If you want to win, but think you can't,
It's almost a cinch you won't.

If you think you'll lose, you're lost;
For out in the world we find
Success begins with a fellow's will;
It's all in the state of the mind.

Life's battles don't always go

To the stronger and faster man,
But sooner or later the man who wins
Is the man who thinks he can.

*Walter D. Wintle*


## THE SECURITY OF IMPRISONMENT

Charles Dickens wrote about a man who had been in prison for many years and longed for freedom from his dungeon of despair and hopelessness. Finally, the day of his liberation arrived. He was led from his gloomy cell into the bright and beautiful world. He momentarily gazed into the sunlight, then turned and walked back to his cell. He had become so comfortable with confinement, the thought of freedom was overwhelming. For him, the chains and darkness were secure.

*We have the opportunity to unleash the chains of negativism. However, not unlike the man in Charles Dickens' story, many of us have become secure in our negative thinking. The thought of change is frightening. Yet freedom comes only to those who are willing to surrender the security of imprisonment.*


## YOU CHOOSE

As a senior in high school, I was required to read Victor Frankl's *Man's Search for Meaning*. However, the message contained in that powerful work didn't make a lasting impression on me until a few years ago. *Man's Search for Meaning* is the written account of Dr. Frankl's experiences as a courageous Jew who became a prisoner during the Holocaust.

Imagine this for a moment: Your family has been taken away. You are stripped of all personal belongings—your home, possessions, watch, and even your wedding ring are gone. Head shaved and all clothes removed, you are marched into a Gestapo courtroom. Falsely accused and interrogated, the German high command finds you guilty. Years of indignity and humiliation follow in the concentration camp. No hope. No light at the end of the tunnel. You give up. Right? It need not be.

Dr. Frankl experienced devastating events. However, he realized he had the power to choose one thing—his attitude. No matter what the future had in store for him, he could choose his state of mind. Do I throw in the towel or persevere? Do I hate the Gestapo command or forgive them? Do I exist in a world of deprivation and self-pity or endure the hardships? Dr. Frankl *chose* to exist in a world he created in his mind. He survived and was finally liberated. His attitude toward those painful years sustained him.

> *You and I can also be liberated by unlocking the resources of our mind. Dr. Frankl lived the belief that life is 10 percent what happens to us and 90 percent how we respond to it.*
> *You choose!*

## YOUR FACE SAYS IT ALL

The great theologian, Charles H. Spurgeon, was teaching his class the finer points of public speaking. He emphasized the importance of making the facial expression harmonize with the speech.

"When you speak of heaven," he said, "let your face light up, let it be irradiated with a heavenly gleam, let your eyes shine with reflected glory. But when you speak of hell—well, then your ordinary face will do."

It is amazing how vividly we wear our attitude on our face, and we are responsible for the message it delivers.

During the days of Lincoln's presidency, a trusted adviser recommended a candidate for the Lincoln cabinet. Lincoln briefly considered the possibility before declining to make the appointment. When asked why, he said, "I don't like the man's face."

"But the poor man is not responsible for his face," Lincoln's adviser pleaded.

"Every man over forty is responsible for his face," Lincoln insisted, and the prospect was considered no further.

> *The outward expression on our face bears the hidden truths of our heart.*

## WHAT DO YOU SEE?

A small town chamber of commerce invited a speaker to address its annual dinner. The community's economy was bad, people were discouraged, and they wanted this motivational speaker to give them a boost.

During her presentation, the speaker took a large piece of white paper and made a black dot in the center of it with a marking pen. Then she held the paper up before the group and asked them what they saw. One person quickly replied, "I see a black dot."

"Okay, what else do you see?"

Others joined in agreement: "A black dot."

"Don't you see anything besides the dot?" she asked.

A resounding "No" came from the audience.

"The most important thing has been overlooked," replied the speaker. "No one noticed the sheet of paper! Listen carefully," she pleaded. "In our business, family, personal, and social lives, we are often distracted by small, dotlike failures and disappointments. There is a tendency to forget the wonderful things around us. Those blessings, successes, and joys are far more important than the little black dots that monopolize our attention and energies. Finally, this community will become strong and grow as you learn to focus your energies on what's right."

*This speaker's admonishment reminds me of a little saying I read some time ago: "As you travel down life's highway, may it ever be your goal; to keep your eye upon the doughnut, and not upon the hole!"*

## WHAT A HOT DOG

Some people allow the negativism of others to inhibit their own personal growth and success. It's like the man who lived by the side of the road and sold hot dogs for a living. He was hard of hearing, so he never listened to the radio. He couldn't see very well, so he never spent much time reading newspapers. But he sold great hot dogs. People who saw his advertising signs on the highway stopped to experience this businessman's hot dog delicacies. Day in and day out, he would stand on the side of the road and sincerely beckon, "Come buy the greatest hot dogs around." And buy they did. He had to increase his bun orders and purchase a larger cooker to keep up with sales.

He finally decided to ask his son to come home from college to help handle this expanding business. Being an educated fellow, the son asked, "Dad, haven't you been hearing on the radio about the recession we are in? The newspapers are full of failures in the European and domestic marketplace. Surely, this hot dog business can't last for long."

"How could I be so naive?" thought the father. "Why didn't I consult my educated son first? He's been reading the newspapers and keeping his ear to the news on the radio. He ought to know what is going on."

Heeding his son's warning, the man cut back on his meat and bun order, took down his signs along the highway, and quit standing by the side of the road asking people to buy his hot dogs. Soon his sales fell to an all-time low.

"Thanks for the warning," the father said to his son. "We certainly are in the middle of tough times. Our hot dog business can no longer exist."

## PAN-FACED

It was an exciting discovery! After many long days and short nights, four men panning for gold came across an unusual stone. Breaking it open, they saw to their delight a nugget of gold. Their hopes renewed and spirits lifted, the men worked eagerly to uncover an abundance of the precious metal. They began celebrating their newfound wealth and congratulated one another. "We finally did it! We found the gold! We're rich!"

They interrupted their ecstatic celebration to make a trip into a nearby village and stock up on the supplies they would need to continue their venture. The four men agreed not to breathe a word about their discovery. Each man kept his word. However, when they prepared their return to camp, several village people were packed and ready to travel with them. Angered and disappointed, each man wanted to know who had revealed the discovery. The following crowd replied, "No one said a word. We saw it on your faces."

*Our expressions and actions can reveal more than any words will ever tell. People will see on our faces the attitudes we hold within. We are all responsible for our own expressions.*

## COMPLAIN! COMPLAIN! COMPLAIN!

It takes a disciplined spirit to endure the monastery on Mount Serat in Spain. One of the fundamental requirements of this religious order is that the young men must maintain silence. Opportunities to speak are scheduled once every two years, at which time they are allowed to speak only two words.

One young initiate in this religious order, who had completed his first two years of training, was invited by his superior to make his first two-word presentation. "Food terrible," he said. Two years later the invitation was once again extended. The young man used this forum to exclaim, "Bed lumpy." Arriving at his superior's office two years later he proclaimed, "I quit." The superior looked at this young monk and said, "You know, it doesn't surprise me a bit. All you've done since you arrived is complain, complain, complain."

*Exaggerated? Maybe. What if you were asked to share two words that describe your life? Would your focus be the lumps, bumps, and unfairness, or are you committed to dwell on those things that are good, right, and lovely?*

## GET YOURSELF TOGETHER

The young mother was ready for a few minutes of relaxation after a long and demanding day. However, her young daughter had other plans for her mother's time.

"Read me a story, Mom," the little girl requested.

"Give Mommy a few minutes to relax and unwind. Then I'll be happy to read you a story," pleaded the mother.

The little girl was insistent that Mommy read to her now. With a stroke of genius, the mother tore off the back page of the magazine she was reading. It contained a full-page picture of the world. As she tore it into several pieces, Mom asked their daughter to put the picture together and then she would read her a story. Surely this would buy her considerable relaxing moments.

A short time later, the little girl announced the completion of her puzzle project. To her astonishment, she found the world picture completely assembled. When she asked her daughter how she managed to do it so quickly, the little girl explained that on the reverse side of the page was the picture of a little girl. "You see, Mommy, when I got the little girl together, the whole world came together."

*Each of us has the responsibility to put our world together. It starts by getting ourselves put together. We can become better parents, friends, spouses, employees, and employers. The first step is changing our attitude.*

## THE WHOLE WORLD STINKS

Wise men and philosophers throughout the ages have disagreed on many things, but many are in unanimous agreement on one point: "We become what we think about."

Ralph Waldo Emerson said, "A man is what he thinks about all day long."

The Roman emperor Marcus Aurelius put it this way: "A man's life is what his thoughts make of it."

In the Bible we find: "As a man thinks in his heart, so is he."

One Sunday afternoon, a cranky grandfather was visiting his family. As he lay down to take a nap, his grandson decided to have a little fun by putting Limburger cheese on Grandfather's mustache. Soon, grandpa awoke with a snort and charged out of the bedroom saying, "This room stinks." Through the house he went, finding every room smelling the same. Desperately he made his way outside only to find that "the whole world stinks!"

*So it is when we fill our minds with negativism. Everything we experience and everybody we encounter will carry the scent we hold in our mind.*

## HE CAN'T SWIM

The story is told of an avid duck hunter who was in the market for a new bird dog. His search ended when he found a dog who would walk on water to retrieve a duck. Shocked by his discovery, the man wondered how he would break this news to his hunting friends. No one would believe him.

So the hunter invited a buddy to go with him. They made their way to the blind and waited. When a flock of ducks flew nearby, they drew their guns and shot. The dog responded by running across the water and retrieving the bird. However, the friend remained silent. Not one word about this amazing dog.

Driving home, the hunter said to his friend, "Did you notice anything unusual about my dog?"

"I sure did," responded the friend. "He can't swim."

## I'M COMING HOME

You've probably heard about the shoe company who sent a salesman to Africa to check into the potential for marketing their products there. A few days later, the salesman reported back: "I'm coming home. There is no market here. Nobody wears shoes."

The company decided to send one of their more positive salesmen to check out the situation. Within a matter of hours, the salesman enthusiastically reported the findings to his company. "The market is ripe here. There are fantastic opportunities. Nobody owns shoes yet."

*These two different people have two different perspectives. Life is a matter of perspective. It all depends on how you choose to see it. What are you looking for?*

## EXCITEMENT FOR LEARNING IS CONTAGIOUS

John Erskine was one of the greatest teachers Columbia University ever had. He was one of the most versatile men of his era—an educator, a concert pianist, the author of sixty books, the head of Julliard School of Music, and a popular and witty lecturer. But all of his impressive credits were not what made him a great teacher. His students and his colleagues would be quick to tell you that John Erskine was a great teacher because of his excitement for learning. That excitement was contagious. His students hungered to learn and were eager to do the best they could do. Why? Because John Erskine convinced his students that the world was theirs. He told them, "The best books are yet to be written; the best paintings have not yet been painted; the best governments are yet to be formed; the best is yet to be done by you!" Is it any wonder John Erskine was called a man of "defiant optimism"?

## WHAT ARE YOU CULTIVATING?

One of the books considered a true classic today is titled *As a Man Thinketh* by James Allen. In that book, he writes, "A man's mind may be likened to a garden, which may be intelligently cultivated or allowed to run wild; but whether cultivated or neglected, it must, and will, bring forth . . .

"Just as a gardener cultivates his plot, keeping it free from weeds, and growing the flowers and fruits, which he requires, so may a man tend the garden of his mind, weeding out all the wrong, useless, and impure thoughts, and cultivating toward perfection the flowers and fruits of right, useful, and pure thoughts. By pursuing this process, a man sooner or later discovers that he is the master gardener of his soul, the director of his life. He also reveals, within himself, the laws of thought, and understands, with ever-increasing accuracy, how the thought-forces and mind-elements operate in the shaping of his character, circumstances, and destiny."

## IT CAN LICK YOU

In the novel *Gone With the Wind,* at the funeral of Gerald O'Hara, his prospective son-in-law gives the eulogy. He says: "There warn't nothin' that come to him from the outside that could lick him. He warn't scared of the English government when they wanted to hang him. He just lit out and left home. And when he come to this country and was pore, that didn't scare him a mite neither. He went to work and he made his money. And he warn't scared to tackle this section when it was part wild and the Injuns had just been run out of it. He made a big plantation out of a wilderness. And when the war come on and his money begun to go, he warn't scared to be pore again. And when the Yankees came through Tara and might of burnt him out or killed him, he warn't fazed a bit and he warn't licked neither. He just planted his front feet and stood his ground. That's why I say he had our good points. There ain't nuthin' from the outside can lick any of us. But he had our failin's too, 'cause he could be licked from the inside. I mean to say that what the whole world couldn't do, his own heart could. . . .

"All you all and me, too, are like him. We got the same weakness and failin'. There ain't nothin' that walks can lick us, any more than it could lick him, not Yankees nor Carpetbaggers nor hard times nor high taxes nor even downright starvation. But that weakness that's in our hearts can lick us in the time it takes to bat your eye."

## HANG IN THERE

Nicolo Paganini was a well-known and gifted nineteenth-century violinist. He was also well known as a great showman with a quick sense of humor. His most memorable concert was in Italy with a full orchestra. He was performing before a packed house and his technique was incredible, his tone was fantastic, and his audience dearly loved him. Toward the end of his concert, Paganini was astounding his audience with an unbelievable composition when suddenly one string on his violin snapped and hung limply from his instrument. Paganini frowned briefly, shook his head, and continued to play, improvising beautifully.

Then to everyone's surprise, a second string broke. And shortly thereafter, a third. Almost like a slapstick comedy, Paganini stood there with three strings dangling from his Stradivarius. But instead of leaving the stage, Paganini stood his ground and calmly completed the difficult number on the one remaining string.

## WHAT KIND OF PEOPLE LIVE IN YOUR TOWN?

Hattie Billings, a wrinkled old woman in her seventies, is the city hostess in a small town in Alabama. She volunteers her services because she genuinely loves welcoming newcomers to her town. Her speech is broken and her manner plain, but she has a sixth sense about people and what makes them tick.

When Hattie calls on the town's newcomers, they soon find themselves caught up in her homespun warmth.

"What kind of people live in this town?" many would ask her.

Hattie, squinting over her glasses, would quietly respond with
another question, "What kinda people ya all have where ya all come
from?"

If the newcomer says he had left a community where people were
bright and gay, friendly, and fun-loving, Hattie would answer confidently
that that's the kind of people who live in her community. But to the
newcomers who complain that they left a town where the people were
ugly, quarrelsome, and unfriendly, Hattie would sadly shake her little
gray head and say, "Ah'm afeared ya all 'ul find 'em much the same
here."

## ARE YOU AN OPTIMIST OR A PESSIMIST?

You may have heard the story of the little twin brothers Harry and
Larry. Harry is a pessimist and Larry is an optimist. The little pessimist
was always complaining and very negative, while the optimist viewed
everything through rose-colored glasses. It was their birthday, and their
father decided to test their attitudes. He bought every kind of beautiful
toy imaginable for the pessimist—a new bike, a basketball, a rifle, and
dozens of things that would make a little boy happy, but for the optimist, a
pile of horse manure was to be his only gift.

When Harry, the pessimist, saw all of his beautiful birthday gifts, he
immediately began to complain. "If I ride this bike on the street, I might
wreck it and hurt myself, and I know if I take this basketball outside
someone will probably steal it, and this rifle is dangerous. I'll probably
end up shooting somebody's window out." Harry went on and on in deep
negativism. He had turned his birthday into gloom and doom.

Then, it was the little optimist's turn for his birthday present. When
Larry saw the pile of horse manure with his name on it, he enthusiastically began to run throughout the house looking in all of the rooms, in the
garage, and in the backyard. When his father caught him by the arm and
asked, "Son, what are you looking for?" Larry replied, "Dad, with all of
the horse manure you gave me, I just know there's gotta be a pony
around here someplace!"

# Communication

*Why is it that those who have something to say can't say it, while those who have nothing to say keep saying it.*

ANONYMOUS

9

We can communicate an idea around the world in seventy seconds, but it sometimes takes years for an idea to get through ¼″ of human skull.

*Charles F. Kettering*

There is nothing so frustrating as a person who keeps right on talking while I'm trying to interrupt.

*Anonymous*

The word *communication* comes from the Latin *communico,* meaning *share.*

*Anonymous*

It is better to ask some of the questions than know all the answers.

*James Thurber*

Talk to a man about himself and he will listen for hours.

*Benjamin Disraeli*

If you don't say anything, you won't be called upon to repeat it.

*Calvin Coolidge*

It appears then that genuine friendship cannot exist where one of the parties is unwilling to hear the truth and the other is equally indisposed to speak it.

*Cicero*

It is wiser to choose what you say than say what you choose.

*Anonymous*

The tongue is the only tool that gets sharper with use.

*Washington Irving*

Nothing derails a train of thought more effectively than listening to a person with a one-track mind.

*Anonymous*

It is the province of knowledge to speak, and it is the privilege of wisdom to listen.

*Oliver Wendell Holmes, Jr.*

A good listener is not only popular everywhere, but after a while he knows something.

*Wilson Mizner*

If you can't get people to listen to you any other way, tell them it is confidential.

*Farmer's Digest*

The road to the heart is the ear.

*Voltaire*

Nature gave us one tongue and two ears so we could hear twice as much as we speak.

*Epictetus*

The first duty of love is to listen.

*Paul Tillich*

It takes two to speak the truth—one to speak and another to hear.

*Henry David Thoreau*

It's always wise to raise questions about the most obvious and simple assumptions.

*C. West Churchman*

White-collar workers, on the average, devote at least 40 percent of their workday to listening. Apparently, 40 percent of their salary is paid to them for listening.

*Ralph G. Nichols*

Listen to me for a day—an hour!—a moment. Lest I expire in my terrible wilderness, my lonely silence! O God, is there no one to listen?

*Seneca*

I know you believe you understand what you think I said, but I am not sure you realize that what you heard is not what I meant.

*Anonymous*

How wonderful it is to say the right thing at the right time. A good man thinks before he speaks; the evil man pours out his evil words without a thought.

*Proverbs 15:23, 28*

Dialogue takes place when two people communicate the full meaning of their lives to one another, when they participate in each other's lives in the most meaningful ways in which they are capable.

*Dwight Small*

Give every man thy ear, but few thy voice.

*William Shakespeare*

An open ear is the only believable sign of an open heart.

*David Augsburger*

## COMPLICATED COLLISIONS

The following quotes are taken from accident reports submitted to various insurance companies by hapless policyholders:

The accident happened when the right front door of a car came around the corner, without giving a signal.
Coming home, I drove into the wrong house and collided with a tree I don't have.

The other car collided with mine without giving warning of its intentions.

I thought my window was down, but found it was up when I put my hand through it

I collided with a stationary truck coming the other way.

The guy was all over the road; I had to swerve a number of times before I hit him.

I pulled away from the side of the road, glanced at my mother-in-law, and headed over the embankment.

In my attempt to kill a fly, I drove into a telephone pole.

I had been driving for forty years when I fell asleep at the wheel and had the accident.

To avoid hitting the bumper of the car in front, I struck the pedestrian.

My car was legally parked as it backed into the other vehicle.

An invisible car came out of nowhere, struck my vehicle, and vanished.

I told the police that I was not injured, but on removing my hat, I found that I had a fractured skull.

I was sure the old fellow would never make it to the other side of the road when I struck him.

The pedestrian had no idea which direction to run, so I ran over him.

The indirect cause of this accident was a little guy in a small car with a big mouth.

I was thrown from my car as it left the road. I was later found in a ditch by some stray cows.

The telephone pole was approaching. I was attempting to swerve out of its way when it struck my front end.

I was unable to stop in time and my car crashed into the other vehicle. The driver and passengers then left immediately for vacation with injuries.

I was on my way to the doctor with rear-end trouble when my universal joint gave way causing me to have an accident.

I had been shopping for plants and was on my way home. As I reached an intersection, a hedge sprang up, obscuring my vision.

*Anonymous*

## CRICKETS AND CHOIRS

Harry and Florence sat on their country home porch nearly every summer evening. This night the moon was shining full, and the stars had a brilliant sparkle. Not far from their home, a small creek flowed, and from the creek banks came a chorus of crickets. Harry listened to the crickets and said, "Crickets sure do sing." Florence agreed saying. "Yep, they sure know how to sing." Just then Florence heard the voices of the choir coming from the nearby country church and remarked, "Beautiful music, isn't it?" Harry responded, "Yeah, and to think they do it just by rubbing their legs together."

*What we hear depends on what we're listening to.*

## DON'T EXAGGERATE

Four-year-old Johnny ran into the house hollering, "Mommy, Mommy, there's a cat out in the yard as big as a lion."

"Now calm down," said his mother. "If I've told you once, I've told you a thousand times, don't exaggerate."

## TRAIN YOUR MIND

Statisticians tell us the average man speaks twenty-five thousand words a day and the average woman thirty thousand.

I don't have a problem with that except that when I get home each day, I've used my quota, and my wife hasn't started her thirty thousand. Considering that the average person listens at a 25 percent efficiency rate, it takes a special effort for me to really listen. Wanting our relationship to grow, I need to continually train my mind to absorb the messages my wife has been waiting all day to share.

*As Paul Tillich is quoted as saying, "The first duty of love is to listen".*

## AN UNCOMMON SKILL

The Bible says, "Let us speak the truth in love." Have you ever seriously considered how difficult a task that really is?

The great French statesman Richelieu built a reputation as a man capable of speaking in love. In fact, the story is told of a young man who applied to Richelieu for a job, knowing all along his request would be turned down. Richelieu exhibited a manner of speech that was warm and accepting. Those closest to him said it was worth having a request denied just to hear how graciously he expressed himself. Even when he gave out bad news, it was easy to accept.

> *Richelieu's sweet spirit proved it's not what we say but how we say it that really counts.*

According to some often-quoted statistics, the average person spends at least one-fifth of his or her life talking. Ordinarily, in a single day, enough words are spoken to fill a fifty-page book. Over the span of one year, the average person's words would fill 132 books, each containing at least 400 pages.

*Anonymous*

On the flip side, listening occupies an average of about 29.7 percent of the average waking day. Listening is used more than talking, three times as much as reading, and four times as much as writing.

*Paul T. Rank*

Communication does require both effective sending and receiving.

*Anonymous*

Precision of communication is important, more important than ever, in our era of hair-trigger balances, when a false or misunderstood word may create as much disaster as a sudden thoughtless act.

*James Thurber*

## SAINTLY BLOOPERS

Imagine sitting in church on Sunday morning waiting for the service to begin. Suddenly, you read an unclear, hilarious announcement like one of these tidbits gleaned from church bulletins:

1. This afternoon there will be a meeting in the north and south ends of the church, and children will be baptized at both ends.
2. Tuesday at 7:00 P.M., there will be an ice-cream social. All ladies giving milk please come early.
3. Wednesday the Ladies' Society will meet and Mrs. Tracy will sing, "Put Me in My Little Bed" accompanied by the reverend.

4. Thursday at 7:00 P.M. there will be a meeting of the Little Mothers' Club. All ladies wishing to become Little Mothers will please meet the minister in his office at 7:00 sharp!!!

5. This being Easter Sunday, we will ask Mrs. Daly to come forward and lay an egg on the altar.

6. The service will close with "Little Drops of Water," which Mrs. Nelson will start quietly. The rest of the congregation will join in.

7. On Sunday, a special collection will be taken to defray the expenses of the new carpet. Will those wishing to do something on the carpet, please come forward and get a piece of paper?

Yes, even churches have difficulty ensuring their intended messages are understood.

## SCRUMPTIOUS ASSUMPTION

Two brothers were so jealous of each other and constantly tried to outdo one another. One Christmas the older brother wanted to buy their mother the best gift she had ever received, so he bought her a new car.

When the second son found out that his older brother bought a new car for their mother, he searched all the stores for something even better than a car—something extra special. He finally found the perfect gift. A man had spent years training his pet parrot to speak seventeen different languages, but he was willing to sell the parrot. However, his price was $10,000.

The second son finally decided he just had to have the parrot for his mother. It would definitely outshine his brother's gift. He scraped together all his savings and paid the man $10,000, packaged the parrot, and sent it to his mother.

On Christmas morning, he called his mother and asked, "How did you like the bird, mother?"

"Oh, it was delicious, son. Thank you so much," she told him.

"Good grief, mother, you weren't supposed to eat it. That was a $10,000 bird," he explained hotly. "It spoke seventeen different languages!"

"You're kidding," his mother answered. "Why didn't the dumb bird say something then?"

*Bob Conklin*

# Compliments

*Speak ill of no man, but speak all the good you know of everybody.*

BENJAMIN FRANKLIN

10

I can live for two months on one good compliment.

*Mark Twain*

A drop of honey catches more flies than a gallon of gall.

*Abraham Lincoln*

Anything scarce is valuable; praise, for example.

*Anonymous*

Use what language you will, you can never say anything to others but what you are.

*Ralph Waldo Emerson*

Silent gratitude isn't very much use to anyone.

*Anonymous*

I always prefer to believe the best of everybody; it saves so much trouble.

*Rudyard Kipling*

What really flatters a man is that you think him worth flattering.

*George Bernard Shaw*

Sincere praise reassures individuals. It helps them neutralize doubts they have about themselves.

*Anonymous*

The rare individual who honestly satisfies this heart-hunger [praise] will hold people in the palm of his hand, and even the undertaker will be sorry when he dies.

*Dale Carnegie*

The sweetest of all sounds is praise.

*Xenophon*

Many men know how to flatter, few men know how to praise.

*Greek proverb*

The greatest humiliation in life is to work hard on something from which you expect great appreciation, and then fail to get it.

*Edgar Watson Howe*

If you want to get the best out of a man, you must look for the best that is in him.

*Bernard Haldane*

He who praises another enriches himself far more than he does the one praised. To praise is an investment in happiness. The poorest human being has something to give that the richest could not buy.

*George Matthew Adams*

Praise does wonders for our sense of hearing.

*Arnold H. Glasow*

Make the most of the best and the least of the worst.

*Robert Louis Stevenson*

All of us, in the flow of feeling we have pleased, want to do more to please.

*William James*

You do not have to be right to be generous. If he has the spirit of true generosity, a pauper can give like a prince.

*Corrine V. Wells*

## HOW THE MASTERS DID IT

Charles M. Schwab was one of the first men ever to earn a million dollars a year working for someone else. Schwab was paid such a handsome amount largely because of his ability to deal with people.

Here is the secret as described by Schwab himself: "I consider my ability to arouse enthusiasm among the men the greatest asset I possess, and the way to develop the best that is in a man is by appreciation and encouragement. There is nothing else that so kills the ambitions of man as criticism from his superiors. I never criticize anyone. I believe in giving a man incentive to work. So I am anxious to praise but loath to find fault. If I like anything, I am hearty in my approbation and lavish in my praise."

### Appreciation

I have often had occasion,
As the paths of life I tread,
Just to watch folks get some
little gift
And hear the things they said.

For some there are who take the gift
As though it was their due,
And never think of speaking
Of their gratefulness to you.

And some there are who gush until
You wish that they would cease.
The less the gratitude they feel,
The more their words increase.

But some there are who let
you know,
With words both deep and true,
How much they do appreciate
The little things you do.

Although I know we should not act
Just for the thanks we get,
Real gratitude, and well expressed,
Will bring us no regret.

It's easier far, to serve again
The one who lets you know

That he appreciates your help,
And gladly tells you so.

*Vera Beall Parker*

## CONFUSING COMPLIMENT

The story is told of the young mother putting moisturizer on her face when her little girl asked what she was doing. Trying to enlighten her daughter concerning beauty secrets, she told her that the cream was good for wrinkles. "It's sure doing a great job, Mommy," she replied. "You're getting lots of wrinkles."

## FLATNESS OF FLATTERY

I recently came across a definition of flattery that may be worth considering: "Flattery is telling the other person precisely what he thinks about himself."

### It Isn't Enough!

It isn't enough to say in our hearts
That we like a man for his ways,
It isn't enough that we fill our minds
With paeans of silent praise;
Nor is it enough that we honor a man
As our confidence upward mounts,
It's going right up to the man himself,
And telling him so that counts!

If a man does a work you really admire,
Don't leave a kind word unsaid,
In fear that to do so might make him vain
And cause him to "lose his head."
But reach out your hand and tell him,
"Well done," and see how his gratitude swells;
It isn't the flowers we strew on the grave,
It's the word to the living that tells.

*Anonymous*

# Conceit

*Conceit wouldn't be so terrible
if only the right people had it.*

ANONYMOUS

11

### Of Hens and Catfish

The catfish lays ten thousand eggs.
The lonely hen lays one.
The hen will proudly cackle,
To tell us what she's done.
We scorn the humble catfish,
While the lowly hen we prize;
Which only goes to show you—
It pays to advertise.

*Anonymous*

### ENOUGH ABOUT ME

The following story illustrates beautifully the absurdity of conceit. A young singer was on her first date with a handsome and charming man. She was eager to impress him, so all through dinner, she talked about herself. She told him about her career, bragged about the favorable comments she had received from several famous people, and spoke glowingly about her prospects for an upcoming gold record. When the dessert came, she finally said, "Enough about me. Now let's talk about you. What did you think of my last song that I recorded?"

### Proper Perspective

Sometime, when you're feeling important!
Sometime, when your ego's in bloom;
Sometime, when you take it for granted
You're the best qualified in the room;

Sometime, when you feel that your going
Would leave an unfillable hole,
Just follow these simple instructions,
And see how it humbles your soul.

Take a bucket and fill it with water,
Put your hand in it, up to the wrist;
Pull it out, and the hole that's remaining,
Is a measure of how you'll be missed.

You may splash all you please when you enter,
You can stir up the water galore,
But stop, and you'll find in a minute
That it looks quite the same as before.

The moral in this quaint example,
Is do just the best that you can;
And be proud of yourself, but remember
There's no indispensable man.

*Anonymous*

# Confidentiality

*I have often regretted my speech,
never my silence.*

PUBLILIUS SYRUS

12

## Zip the Lip

If your lips would keep from slips,
Five things observe with care:
To whom you speak; of whom you speak;
And how, and when, and where

*William Norris*

## "OH, NO!"

Frustrated with his life, his wife, and his strife, a young man decided to drink his troubles away. Inebriated, he came stumbling out of the bar and nearly knocked over the minister from his congregation, who just happened to be walking by

"Oh, pastor, I hate for you to see me like this," the young man lamented.

"Remember, Pete, God sees you this way," responded the minister.

"Yeah, I know," said the young man, "but he keeps things to himself."

## PICK 'EM UP!

Because she was jealous of the mayor's wisdom and power, a young lady spread malicious untruths about him throughout the town. The rumors and gossip brought the life of the community's leader under much scrutiny. Unable to maintain the respect of his voters, the mayor resigned.

Overcome with remorse, the young lady went to the ex-mayor begging his forgiveness. Fearful of his revenge, she pleaded, "Tell me, how can I make amends? I'll do anything you say."

The man softly responded, "Take the feathers of a mature goose, go to the town square, and throw the feathers into the air."

The young lady set out to do as asked and then returned to the man she had destroyed asking, "What do I do next?"

"Go back to the town square and pick up all the feathers," he said.

"What good could this possibly do?" she asked herself, scurrying about to locate all the feathers she had released.

When she returned with only a portion of the feathers, the wise mayor sensed her dismay.

"How did you do?" he asked.

"The feathers are spread throughout the community, and I am unable to retrieve all of them," she said.

"Let that be your lesson," the man replied. "Once spread, rumors and gossip are impossible to get back."

# Cooperation

*It is amazing how much people can get done if they do not worry about who gets the credit.*

SANDRA SWINNEY

13

No man can become rich without himself enriching others.

*Andrew Carnegie*

If you argue and rankle and contradict, you may achieve a victory sometimes; but it will be an empty victory because you will never get your opponent's good will.

*Benjamin Franklin*

Here lies the body of William Jay,
Who died maintaining his right of way.
He was right, dead right, as he sped along,
But he's just as dead as if he were wrong.

*Boston Transcript*

Better give your path to a dog than be bitten by him in contesting for the right. Even killing the dog would not cure the bite.

*Abraham Lincoln*

A man convinced against his will is of the same opinion still.

*Anonymous*

I have always felt sorry for people afraid of feeling, of sentimentality, who are unable to weep with their whole heart. Because those who do not know how to weep do not know how to laugh either.

*Golda Meir*

A little four-year-old boy had one of those trouble-filled days. After his father reprimanded him, his mother finally said to him, "Son, you go over to that chair and sit on it now!" The little lad went to the chair, sat down, and said, "Mommy, I'm sitting down on the outside, but I'm standing up on the inside."

*Anonymous*

If you come at me with your fists doubled, I think I can promise you that mine will double as fast as yours; but if you come to me and say, "Let us sit down and take counsel together, and, if we differ from one another, understand why it is that we differ from one another, just what the points at issue are," we will presently find that we are not so far apart after all, that the points on which we differ are few and the points on which we agree are many, and that if we only have the patience and the candor and the desire to get together, we will get together.

*Woodrow Wilson*

There is a story about four men named Everybody, Somebody, Anybody, and Nobody. There was an important job to be done, and Everybody was asked to do it. Everybody was sure that Somebody would do it. Anybody could have done it, but Nobody did it. Somebody got angry about that, because it was Everybody's job. Everybody thought that Anybody could do it, and Nobody realized that Everybody wouldn't do it. It ended up that Everybody blamed Somebody, when actually Nobody did what Anybody could have done.

*Anonymous*

Competition brings out the best in products and the worst in people.

*David Sarnoff*

## WHEN DID YOU QUIT HOLDING HANDS?

A troop of Boy Scouts gathered for their annual hike in the woods. Taking off at sunrise, they commenced a fifteen-mile trek through some of the most scenic grounds in the country. About midmorning, the Scouts came across an abandoned section of railroad track. Each, in turn, tried to walk the narrow rails, but after only a few unsteady steps, each lost his balance and tumbled off.

Two of the Scouts, after watching one after another fall off the iron rail, offered a bet to the rest of the troup. The two bet that they could both walk the entire length of the railroad track without falling off even once.

The other boys laughed and said, "No way!" Challenged to make good their boast, the two boys jumped up on opposite rails, simply reached out and held hands to balance each other, and steadily walked the entire section of track with no difficulty.

*How easy it was simply by working together as a team. When people help each other, freely and voluntarily, there is a spirit of teamwork that can conquer a multitude of problems. When we don't cooperate, the whole system can fall apart. Reach out to your teammates and never quit holding hands.*

## IN OR OUT?

On his way to work, a well-groomed businessman paused momentarily to watch a muscular professional mover struggling with a heavy box. The mover was trying to heave the huge box through an apartment entrance, but the box was almost as wide as the doorway.

"Would you like me to help you?" the onlooker asked.

"Sure thing," smiled the mover. "Grab hold of the other side of this box."

For two minutes the two men, on opposite sides of the box, lifted and pulled and perspired. However, the box did not move one inch. Finally, the young businessman straightened up and shook his head, "I don't think we're ever going to get it out!"

"Well, no wonder!" roared the mover. "I'm trying to get it in!"

## A LETTER FROM SCHOOL

The following is a letter written by a college freshman to her parents:

Dear Mom and Dad,

Just thought I'd drop you a note to clue you in on my plans. I've fallen in love with a guy named Buck. He quit high school between his sophomore and junior year to travel with his motorcycle gang. He was married at 18 and had two sons. About a year ago he got a divorce.

We've been going steady for two months now and plan to get married in the fall. (He thinks he should be able to find a job by then.) Until then, I've decided to move into his apartment. I think I might be pregnant.

At any rate, I dropped out of school last week. I was just bored with the whole thing. Maybe I'll finish college sometime in the future.

[On the next page she continued, hoping to soften the blow of her real problems: Low grades and no money.]

Mom and Dad, I just wanted you to know that everything I've written so far in this letter is false. NONE OF IT IS TRUE!

But Mom and Dad, it IS true that I got a C in French and flunked Math. And it IS true that I'm overdrawn and need more money for my tuition payments.

Your loving daughter,

Donna

## KINDNESS WINS MORE FANS

Do you remember Bob Beaman, world record holder in the long jump at the Olympic Games of 1968? Time blurs our memory of even the great athletes.

Beaman was contracted to make a television commercial during the 1984 Summer Olympic Games coverage. He consented and was featured in the commercial. During the commercial, he turned to the camera and said, "Back in the Olympic Games of 1968, I set a world record in the long jump. At the time, some people said no one would ever jump that far again. Well, over the years I've enjoyed watching them try, and I'm told who might have a chance of breaking my record. Well, there's just one thing I have to say about that—" At this point the television viewer was set up for some kind of self-centered comment. Instead, Beaman's face softened, and in a most sincere, caring way he said, "I hope you make it, kid!" Beaman won more goodwill with that one commercial than he had ever won with his incredible long-jump record of 29 feet, 2½ inches.

*Our Daily Bread*

## HOW DO WARS BEGIN?

"How do wars begin?" a little boy asked his father. The father pulled a long draw on his pipe and proceeded to answer his son's question. "Well, let's take the war of 1914 for example—that began because Germany invaded Belgium."

At this point, his wife interrupted him coldly, "Well, Frank, tell the boy the truth, for crying out loud. It began because somebody was murdered."

"Are you answering the question or am I?" retorted the husband angrily.

She stomped out of the room and slammed the door. A tense silence followed, with the husband doing a slow burn. The boy peered at his father and said meekly, "Daddy, you don't have to tell me how wars begin. I think I know!"

## FLYING FURTHER

Observe closely the beautiful Canada geese flying in their V formation. Have you ever wondered why one wing of the V is longer than the other wing of the V? (Answer: The longer wing has more geese.)

Seriously, these geese instinctively know the value of cooperation. Did you know that they regularly change leadership? Why? The leader fights the head wind, helping to create a partial vacuum for the geese on his right, as well as the geese on the left. When he becomes exhausted, another goose takes over.

Scientists have discovered in wind tunnel tests that a flock of geese can fly 72 percent farther and faster by cooperating in this manner. People can do the same thing. People must cooperate with, instead of fighting against, their fellow men.

*Zig Ziglar*

## NO SYMPHONY WITHOUT HARMONY

During a rehearsal at the Metropolitan Opera House in New York City, the great Italian conductor Arturo Toscanini offered a few words of constructive criticism to a featured soloist.

The soloist, too proud to accept help, expressed her anger by exploding, "I am the star of this performance!" Toscanini responded calmly but with firm conviction. "Madam," he said, "in this performance there are no stars!"

*All, from the greatest to the humblest, must work together in harmony and devotion. We can make no advances with only solo work. Unless the soloists and the members of the chorus are ready to work together in harmony, there can be no symphony.*

*Jackson Wilcox*

## IT TAKES TWO TO PERFORM

Many years ago a master organist performed a concert before a sellout crowd. In those days someone had to pump large bellows backstage to provide air for the organ pipes. At the conclusion of each popular selection, the musician received the thunderous applause of a delighted audience. Before his final number, he stood up and said, "I shall now play," and he announced the title of his final masterpiece. Taking his seat before the keyboard, he adjusted his music and checked the stops. With feet placed over the pedals and hands over the keys, he began with a mighty chord. But the organ remained silent. An uncomfortable silence fell over the audience. Just then a voice was heard from backstage: "Say 'We'!"

## MAINTAIN THEIR SELF-ESTEEM

A newly educated teacher named Mary went to teach at a Navajo Indian reservation. Mary couldn't figure it out. Nothing she had studied in her educational curriculum helped, and she certainly hadn't seen anything like it in her student-teaching days back in Phoenix, Arizona. What would happen, almost daily, went something like this: She would ask five of the young Navajo students to go to the chalkboard. She would ask them to complete a simple math problem from their homework. There they all stood, silently, without moving, unwilling to complete the task.

"What am I doing wrong? *Could I have chosen five students who can't do the problem?*" Mary thought. *"No, it couldn't be that."* And so she finally asked the students what was wrong. And in their answer, she got a surprising lesson about self-image and a sense of self-worth from her young Indian pupils.

It seemed that the students respected each other's individuality and knew that not all of them were capable of doing the problems. Even at their early age, they understood the senselessness of the win-lose approach in the classroom. They believed *no one* would win if any students were shown up or embarrassed at the chalkboard. So they refused to compete with each other in public. Once she understood, Mary had no problem. She changed the system so she could check each child's problems individually, but not at any child's expense in front of his classmates. They all wanted to learn—but not at someone else's expense.

*Anonymous*

# Creativity

*To break through creativity, we must defer judgment.
That is, learn to accept all ideas, without prejudice,
and examine them each in turn.*

**SCOTT ISAKSEN**

14

The creative person is willing to live with ambiguity. He doesn't need problems solved immediately and can afford to wait for the right idea.

*Abe Tannenbaum*

Imagination is more important than knowledge.

*Albert Einstein*

The human race is governed by its imagination.

*Napoleon*

Imagination disposes of everything; it creates beauty, justice, and happiness, which is everything in the world.

*Blaise Pascal*

Capital isn't so important in business. Experience isn't so important. You can get both of these things. What is important is ideas. If you have ideas, you have the main asset you need, and there isn't any limit to what you can do with your business and your life. They are any man's greatest asset—ideas.

*Harvey Firestone*

Creativity is essentially a lonely art. An even lonelier struggle. To some a blessing. To others a curse. It is in reality the ability to reach inside yourself and drag forth from your very soul an idea.

*Lou Dorfsman*

An idea, to be suggestive, must come to the individual with the force of a revelation.

*William James*

Inspiration and imagination go hand in hand.

*Anonymous*

Ideas not coupled with action never become bigger than the brain cells they occupied.

*Arnold H. Glasow*

Acting on a good idea is better than just having a good idea.

*Robert Half*

Every vital organization owes its birth and life to an exciting and daring idea.

*James B. Conant*

Creative people exhibit a continuous discontent with uniformity.

*Glenn Van Ekeren*

Basic research is what I am doing when I don't know what I am doing.

*Wernher von Braun*

## POST-IT NOTES

The 3M Company encourages creativity from its employees. The company allows its researchers to spend 15 percent of their time on any project that interests them. This attitude has brought fantastic benefits not only to the employees but to the 3M Company itself. Many times, a spark of an idea turned into a successful product has boosted 3M's profits tremendously.

A few years ago, a scientist in 3M's commercial office took advantage of this 15 percent creative time. This scientist, Art Fry, came up with an idea for one of 3M's best-selling products. It seems that Art Fry dealt with a small irritation every Sunday as he sang in the church choir. After marking his pages in the hymnal with small bits of paper, the small pieces would invariably fall out all over the floor.

Suddenly, an idea struck Fry. He remembered an adhesive developed by a colleague that everyone thought was a failure because it did not stick very well. "I coated the adhesive on a paper sample," Fry recalls, "and I found that it was not only a good bookmark, but it was great for writing notes. It will stay in place as long as you want it to, and then you can remove it without damage."

Yes, Art Fry hit the jackpot. The resulting product was called Post-it™ and has become one of 3M's most successful office products.

## SOAP THAT FLOATS

In 1879, Procter and Gamble's best seller was candles. But the company was in trouble. Thomas Edison had invented the light bulb, and it looked as if candles would become obsolete. Their fears became reality when the market for candles plummeted since they were now sold only for special occasions.

The outlook appeared to be bleak for Procter and Gamble. However, at this time, it seemed that destiny played a dramatic part in pulling the struggling company from the clutches of bankruptcy. A forgetful employee at a small factory in Cincinnati forgot to turn off his machine when he went to lunch. The result? A frothing mass of lather filled with air bubbles. He almost threw the stuff away but instead decided to make it into soap. The soap floated. Thus, Ivory soap was born and became the mainstay of the Procter and Gamble Company.

Why was soap that floats such a hot item at that time? In Cincinnati, during that period, some people bathed in the Ohio River. Floating soap would never sink and consequently never got lost. So, Ivory soap became a best seller in Ohio and eventually across the country also.

*Like Procter and Gamble, never give up when things go wrong or when seemingly unsurmountable problems arise. Creativity put to work can change a problem and turn it into a gold mine.*

## GETTING RID OF THE OLD TUBE

A New York City businessman decided to avoid a $20 service charge by replacing a seven-foot fluorescent lighting tube himself. He managed to smuggle a new tube into his office without being seen by the building staff. But then he had to face the problem of how to get rid of the old tube. He recalled that a construction site near his subway stop had a large dumpster. He decided to deposit the tube there.

The man got on the subway that night, holding the white tube vertically with one end resting on the floor. As the train became crowded, other passengers also took hold of the tube, assuming it was a stanchion.

By the time the man had reached his stop, he had come up with a better plan. He had decided there was no need to haul the lighting tube to the construction site dumpster. He simply removed his hand, leaving the other passengers to continue holding the tube. The businessman tipped his hat to those holding the tube, got off the subway, and walked away.

*Bits and Pieces*

## SERENDIPITY

What is serendipity? It is discovering something totally unrelated to the problem you are trying to solve. Call it an accident, dumb luck, or fate—serendipity has given our world great products, new hope, and better ways of doing things.

For example, Columbus discovered America while searching for a route to India. It is said that the American Indians, finding no water for cooking, tapped a maple tree and made the first maple syrup as the sap boiled down. Pioneers, traveling westward, stopped for water and found gold nuggets in a stream. These are all examples of serendipity.

However, the classic example of serendipity must go to George Ballas. As George Ballas drove his car through a car wash, he watched the strings of the brushes surround his car. His mind relaxed and turned to the chores he had to do before the day drew to a close. Finishing the tedious chore of trimming and edging his lawn was first on his list.

Suddenly an idea struck him. He studied the strings in the car wash again and watched them straighten out when revolving at high speed, and yet they were flexible enough to reach into every nook and cranny. Why not use a nylon cord, whirling at high speed to trim the grass and weeds around trees and the house? Bingo! The Weedeater was born!

Ballas's first Weedeater was homemade. He punched holes in a popcorn can and threaded the holes with cord. Then he took the blade off his edger and bolted the can in place. His crude invention tore up the turf and made a terrible noise, but it whipped off the weeds just as he knew it would.

When he decided to go commercial, Ballas found the way rough going. He was turned down by the first twenty distributors he approached. "You must be crazy!" they told him. "Cut grass with a nylon string? Impossible!"

Finally, in 1971, Ballas invested his own money in the first thirty-pound Weedeater. He and his son filmed their own commercials, and then Ballas bought $12,000 worth of local TV airtime. Immediately, he was swamped with orders from all across the nation. "There must have been a convention in town because I only advertised on our local TV channel," Ballas recalls.

Before long, Weedeater, Inc., grew into a multimillion-dollar international corporation. Yes, one idea can be worth a fortune. Weedeater, Inc., was born from a simple idea in a car wash.

## THE BIRTH OF SLACKS

J. M. Haggar, founder of the Haggar Company, became inspired by Henry Ford's idea of the production line and mass production. If automobiles can be mass-produced, why can't men's fine trousers be mass-produced and sold at popular prices?

Those in the clothing industry said he'd never make it. However, using the ends of suit fabrics instead of denim, Haggar made a new kind of dress pants he called "slacks," and in the process, J. M. Haggar revolutionized the clothing industry.

## TAKE A RISK

When young F. W. Woolworth was a store clerk, he tried to convince his boss to have a ten-cent sale to reduce inventory. The boss agreed, and the idea was a resounding success. This inspired Woolworth to open his own store and price items at a nickel and a dime. He needed capital for such a venture, so he asked his boss to supply the capital for part interest in the store. His boss turned him down flat. "The idea is too risky," he told Woolworth. "There are not enough items to sell for five and ten cents."

Woolworth went ahead without his boss's backing, and he not only was successful in his first store, but eventually he owned a chain of F. W. Woolworth stores across the nation. Later, his former boss was heard to remark, "As far as I can figure out, every word I used to turn Woolworth down cost me about a million dollars."

## CREATIVITY FROM THE BASICS

There are only three pure colors—red, blue, and yellow—but look at what Michelangelo did with those three colors. There are only seven notes, but look what Chopin, Beethoven, and Vivaldi did with those seven notes. Lincoln's Gettysburg Address contained only 262 words, and 202 of them had one syllable. Think of the impact those simple, direct words have had on our society.

## TURN A NEGATIVE INTO A POSITIVE

An irate banker demanded that Alexander Graham Bell remove "that toy" from his office. "That toy" was the telephone.

A Hollywood producer scrawled a curt rejection note on a manuscript that became *Gone With the Wind.*

Henry Ford's largest original investor sold all his stock in 1906.

Roebuck sold out to Sears for $25,000 in 1895. Today, Sears may sell $25,000 worth of goods in sixteen seconds.

The next time somebody offers you an idea that leaves you cold, put it on the back burner. It might warm up.

*Bits and Pieces*

## CREATIVITY SUSTAINS LIFE

Carson McCullers, one of America's most successful authors, wrote several distinguished novels. She was not only a creative writer but also a tenacious fighter and a persistent survivor.

Before she was twenty-nine, Carson McCullers had suffered three strokes. Crippled, partially paralyzed, and in constant pain, she was dealt yet another blow: Her husband committed suicide.

Others may have surrendered to such tragedies, but not McCullers. Driven by her creative inspiration and her love of writing, she put her own suffering behind her and began writing with true dedication. With her personal goal of writing no less than one page a day, she gave birth to novels such as *The Member of the Wedding, The Ballad of the Sad Café, Reflections in a Golden Eye,* and *The Heart Is a Lonely Hunter.*

Carson McCullers died in 1967 at the age of 50 and was eulogized by the *Saturday Review.* The article noted: "Carson was one of two or three best Southern writers. If bad luck restricted her work, that was just bad luck. She was a very great artist and human being."

## A BOLT OUT OF THE BLUE

Lightning has an impressive and terrifying power. Scientists have found that a single bolt can carry 100,000 volts of power. Worldwide, lightning strikes the earth 360,000 times every hour. July is the most dangerous month for lightning. When lightning descends, it follows the easiest path to earth: through a tree, a tall building, or an antenna. But it does not always follow a straight course. It can strike at an angle—even hitting where the sun is shining. Thus, there can literally be "a bolt out of the blue."

Creativity can also be like a bolt out of the blue. Unfortunately, many exciting ideas go undeveloped, resulting in a waste of powerful energy. Creative bolts must be followed by a sustained energy to make it work. That is how we capture the power of creativity.

## DOES YOUR CREATIVITY LEVEL DROP?

When individuals at various ages were tested for creativity, the results were as follows:

| Age | How Many Are Creative |
|---|---|
| 40 | 2% |
| 35 | 2% |
| 30 | 2% |
| 17 | 10% |
| 5 | 90% |

These statistics indicate that between the ages five and seventeen, there is an extreme drop in the creative level in both male and female students. During that young, vulnerable growing period, a "we-are-not-creative" attitude takes over, and we begin to deny that particular part of our God-given equipment.

## TIME TO THINK

Henry Ford hired an efficiency expert to go through his plant. He said, "Find the nonproductive people. Tell me who they are, and I will fire them!"

The expert made the rounds with his clipboard in hand and finally returned to Henry Ford's office with his report. "I've found a problem with one of your administrators," he said. "Every time I walked by, he was sitting with his feet propped up on the desk. The man never does a thing. I definitely think you should consider getting rid of him!"

When Henry Ford learned the name of the man the expert was referring to, Ford shook his head and said, "I can't fire him. I pay that man to do nothing but think—and that's what he's doing."

# Criticism

*If it is very painful for you to criticize your friends,*
*you are safe in doing it. But if you take the slightest*
*pleasure in it, that is the time to hold your tongue.*

ALICE MILLER

15

If we had no faults, we would not take so much pleasure in noting those of others.

*François de La Rochefoucauld*

It is much easier to be critical than correct.

*Benjamin Disraeli*

Judge not, that ye be not judged.

*Matthew 7:1*

It is often our own imperfection which makes us reprove the imperfection of others; a sharp-sighted self-love of others.

*François Fénelon*

Gladly we desire to make other men perfect, but we will not amend our own fault.

*Thomas À Kempis*

I will not judge my brother until I have walked two weeks in his moccasins.

*Sioux Indians*

There is something wrong with a man, as with a motor, when he knocks continually.

*Anonymous*

Criticizing others is a dangerous thing, not so much because you may make mistakes about them, but because you may be revealing the truth about yourself.

*Judge Harold Medina*

The moon could not go on shining if it paid any attention to the little dogs that bark at it.

*Anonymous*

Don't mind criticism. If it is untrue, disregard it. If it is unfair, keep from irritation. If it is ignorant, smile. If it is justified, learn from it.

*Anonymous*

The human race is divided into two classes—those who go ahead and do something and those who sit still and inquire, "Why wasn't it done the other way?"

*Oliver Wendell Holmes, Jr.*

Whatever you have to say to people, be sure to say it in words that will cause them to smile, and you will be on pretty safe ground. And when you do find it necessary to criticize someone, put your criticism in the form of a question which the other fellow is practically sure to have to answer in a manner that he becomes his own critic.

*John Wanamaker*

Placing the blame is a bad habit, but taking the blame is a sure builder of character.

*Dr. O. A. Battista*

Any fool can criticize, complain, condemn, and most fools do.

*Anonymous*

There is nothing as easy as denouncing. It don't take much to see that something is wrong, but it does take some eyesight to see what will put it right again.

*Will Rogers*

Don't find fault; find a remedy.

*Henry Ford*

Until we know all, we should not pass judgment at all.

*Watchman-Examiner*

Deal with the faults of others as gently as your own.

*Chinese proverb*

A true critic ought to dwell rather upon excellencies than imperfections.

*Joseph Addison*

The easiest faults to notice are those you don't have.

*Anonymous*

Most of us can live peacefully with our own faults, but the faults of others get on our nerves.

*Banking*

Think of your own faults the first part of the night when you are awake and of the faults of others the latter part of the night when you are asleep.

*Chinese proverb*

There is no character, howsoever good and fine, but it can be destroyed by ridicule, howsoever poor and witless.

*Mark Twain*

Why then do you criticize your brother's actions, why do you try to make him look small?

*Romans 14:10*

We all make mistakes, but everyone makes different mistakes.

*Ludwig van Beethoven*

One has only to grow older to become more tolerant. I see no fault that I might not have committed myself.

*Goethe*

God Himself, sir, does not propose to judge a man until his life is over. Why should you and I?

*Samuel Johnson*

Two taxidermists stopped before a window in which an owl was on display. They immediately began to criticize the way it was mounted. Its eyes were not natural; its wings were not in proportion with its head; its feathers were not neatly arranged; and its feet could be improved. When they had finished with their criticism, the old owl turned his head—and winked at them.

*Pulpit Helps*

The wife of a hard-to-please husband was determined to try her best to satisfy him for just one day. "Darling," she asked, "what would you like for breakfast this morning?" He growled, "Coffee and toast, grits and sausage, and two eggs—one scrambled and one fried." She soon had the food on the table and waited for a word of praise. After a quick glance, he exclaimed, "Well, if you didn't scramble the wrong egg!"

*Maranatha Magazine*

A good cure for a critical spirit is an honest look at ourselves—not at others.

*Anonymous*

Be patient with the faults of others; they have to be patient with yours.

*Anonymous*

When a man's fight begins with himself, he is worth something.

*Robert Browning*

A man takes contradiction and advice much more easily than people think, only he will not bear it when violently given, even if it is well-founded. Hearts are flowers; they remain open to the softly falling dew, but shut up in the violent downpour of rain.

*George Matthew Adams*

Rare is the person who can weigh the faults of others without putting his thumb on the scale.

*Anonymous*

### Criticism

If an impulse comes to say
Some unthoughtful word today
That may drive a friend away,
Don't say it!

If you've heard a word of blame
Cast upon your neighbor's name
That may injure his fair fame,
Don't tell it!

If malicious gossip's tongue
Some vile slander may have flung
On the head of old or young,
    Don't repeat it!

Thoughtful, kind, helpful speech,
'Tis a gift promised to each—
This the lesson we would teach:
    Don't abuse it!

*Anonymous*


## MEAN AND MISERABLE

When folks is mean, it ain't that they hate you personal. It's more likely because they are miserable about something in their inside. You got to remember how most of the time when they yell at you or get after you, it ain't you they are yelling at but something inside themselves you never even heard tell of, like some other person has been mean to them, or something they hoped for didn't come true, or they done something they are shamed even to think of, so they get mad at you just to keep their minds off it.

*Boy George*


### A Little Walk Around Yourself

When you're criticizing others and are
    finding here and there
A fault or two to speak of, or a weakness
    you can tear;
When you're blaming someone's meanness
    or accusing one of pelf—
It's time that you went out to take a
    walk around yourself.

There's lots of human failures in the
    average of us all,
And lots of grave shortcomings in the
    short ones and the tall;
But when we think of evils men should
    lay upon the shelves,

It's time we all went out to take a walk
around ourselves.

We need so often in this life
this balancing of scales,
This seeing how much in us wins and
how much in us fails;
Before you judge another—just to lay
him on the shelf—
It would be a splendid plan to take a
walk around yourself.

*Helen Welshimer*


## FROM SEED TO WEED

An article was shared with me from a church bulletin that teaches a good lesson about criticizing. It began with this poem:

A little seed lay in the ground
And soon began to sprout;
Now, which of all the flowers around,
Shall I, it mused, come out?

The seed could be heard saying, "I don't care to be a rose. It has thorns. I have no desire to be a lily. It's too colorless. And I certainly wouldn't want to be a violet. It's too small, and furthermore, it grows too close to the ground." The final verse explains the destiny of this fault-finding seed.

And so it criticized each flower,
That supercilious seed,
Until it woke one summer hour
And found itself a weed!


## A QUIET SCOLDING

The late John Wanamaker was the king of retail. One day while walking through his store in Philadelphia, he noticed a customer waiting for assistance. No one was paying the least bit of attention to her. Looking around, he saw his salespeople huddled together laughing and talking among themselves. Without a word, he quietly slipped behind the counter and waited on the customer himself. Then he quietly handed the purchase to the salespeople to be wrapped as he went on his way.

Later, Wanamaker was quoted as saying, "I learned thirty years ago that it is foolish to scold. I have enough trouble overcoming my own limitations without fretting over the fact that God has not seen fit to distribute evenly the gift of intelligence."

## LET IT DRY!

Did you know the German army won't allow a soldier to file a complaint or make a rebuttal immediately after a confrontation has occurred? He is required to sleep on his grudge first and cool off. Filing an immediate complaint results in punishment.

That's the same process Father Graham taught those who sought his advice. One day a young man came to him angered by the insults of a fellow worker. He explained the situation to Father Graham and let him know he was on his way to demand an apology. "Young man," Father Graham began, "sometimes it is difficult to understand the actions of others. As an old man who desires peace, consider this bit of advice. Criticism and insults are not unlike mud. It is removed much easier once dried. Wait a little, cool down, and then resolve your differences. If you go now, the matter may only get worse."

The young man heeded the wise advice, thought about the situation, and later resolved the issue.

*Let it dry—before you try!*

## BLURRED VISION

A businessman was highly critical of his competitors' storefront windows. "Why, they are the dirtiest windows in town," he claimed. Fellow businesspeople grew tired of the man's continual criticism and nitpicking comments about the windows. One day over coffee, the businessman carried the subject just too far. Before leaving, a fellow store owner suggested the man get his own windows washed. He followed the advice, and the next day at coffee, he exclaimed, "I can't believe it. As soon as I washed my windows, my competitor must have cleaned his too. You should see them shine."

*Confucius once declared, "Don't complain about the snow on your neighbor's roof when your own doorstep is unclean."*

## DO MORE THAN HONK

The story is told of a young woman driving to work during the morning rush hour. The light turned red as she approached an intersection, requiring her to make a screeching stop. As a result, her car stalled. As she desperately attempted to restart her car, the light turned back to green. A truck approached the rear of the car, and the driver began honking the horn. Through one light change, then two, the young lady nervously pumped the gas and turned the ignition. The truck driver continued to honk his horn. Frustrated by her inability to get the car going again, and the impatience of the truck driver behind her, the young woman calmly got out of her car and walked back to the truck. As he opened his window, she politely asserted, "If you will start my car for me, I would be happy to continue honking your horn for you."

*So it is with criticism. We can honk our critical horns as long as we want, but it won't change the situation or the people. All it does is make negative emotions surface or explode.*

## A "HEARTY" LESSON

Children have an amazing ability to teach adults practical lessons about living. Such an incident occurred with my son on one summer vacation. The first couple of days, Matt seemed to misbehave constantly, and I seemed to be constantly rebuking and correcting him. No son of mine was going to act that way, and I made that clear to him in no uncertain terms. One day later that week, Matt tried especially hard to live up to his dad's standards. In fact, he hadn't done a single thing that called for correcting. After he said his prayers and jumped into bed, Matt's bottom lip began to quiver. "What's the matter, buddy?" I asked. Barely able to speak, Matt looked at me with his glassy eyes and asked, "Daddy, haven't I been a good boy today?"

Those words cut through my parental arrogance like a knife. I had been quick to criticize and correct his misbehavior but failed to mention my pleasure with his attempts to be a good boy. My son taught me never to put my children to bed without a word of appreciation and encouragement.

*Criticism comes without thought, but smart people will think before they speak.*

*Glenn Van Ekeren*

# Decisions

*There is no more miserable human being than the one in whom nothing is habitual but indecision.*

WILLIAM JAMES

16

What's popular isn't always right, and what's right isn't always popular!

*Anonymous*

Once to every man and every nation comes the moment to decide.

*James Russell Lowell*

We are free up to the point of choice; then the choice controls the chooser.

*Mary Crowley*

An idealist is one who, on noticing that a rose smells better than a cabbage, concludes that it will also make better soup.

*H. L. Mencken*

## DON'T MAKE ONE-SIDED DECISIONS

Two women wanted to order drapes that they had seen hanging in the store the week before. The clerk asked them to describe the drapes.

"It was a beautiful shade of blue," replied one woman.

"No, you're wrong," the other woman fired back. "It was an olive green."

Soon they were fighting, each insisting she was right. When the clash finally subsided, they discovered to their chagrin that they were both right—and both wrong! The clerk retrieved the drapes from the back room; one side of the drapes was definitely blue, and the other side indeed was green.

*The message to this story is very clear: Don't make one-sided decisions.*

## HATE TO MAKE DECISIONS?

It is common knowledge that most people simply do not like to make decisions. They're somewhat like Clifford, a businessman who finally admitted that he had a problem when he was faced with a decision, and it was keeping him from advancement in his profession. Clifford finally decided to go to a psychiatrist to see if he could get help with his decision-making problem.

"I understand you have trouble making decisions. Is that true?" the psychiatrist asked him.

Clifford looked at the psychiatrist, somewhat puzzled for a moment, and then he finally replied, "Well, yes—and no!"

## CLEAR YOUR MIND

Henry Ford accomplished much in his lifetime. It wasn't by accident that he was able to record such monumental success. He believed time was something to be creatively managed if people were serious about success.

"A weakness of all human beings," Henry Ford said, "is trying to do too many things at once. That scatters effort and destroys direction. It makes for haste, and haste makes waste. So we do things all the wrong ways possible before we come to the right one. Then we think it is the best way because it works, and it was the only way left that we could see. Every now and then I wake up in the morning headed toward that finality, with a dozen things I want to do. I know I can't do them all at once."

When asked how he handled the pressures of decision making, Ford replied, "I go out and trot around the house. While I'm running off the excess energy that wants to do too much, my mind clears, and I see what can be done and should be done first."

## DECISIONS ARE HARD TO MAKE

Some people find it difficult to make a decision even after they have made it. This confusing action is evident in a letter received by the *Christian Science Monitor*, from one of its readers.

"Dear Sir: When I subscribed a year ago, you stated that if I was not satisfied at the end of the year I could have my money back. Well, I would like to have it back. On second thought, to save you the trouble, you may apply it on my next year's subscription."

## THE SIGNING OF THE EMANCIPATION PROCLAMATION

On January 1, 1863, Abraham Lincoln spent the entire morning meeting dignitaries, shaking their hands, and spreading goodwill. Exhausted by his nonstop morning, Lincoln finally returned to his office at noon.

With a deep sigh, he settled in his chair, only to be interrupted by William Seward, the secretary of state. Lincoln was presented with the final draft of the Emancipation Proclamation for his signature. Twice the president picked up his pen to sign it, but his hand shook so badly that he finally put his pen down.

He turned to Seward and said, "I've had an exhausting morning. In fact, I've been shaking hands since nine this morning, and my right arm almost feels paralyzed. I don't want to sign this document until my hand is more steady. If my name ever goes into history, it will be for this act, and I want you to know that my whole soul is in it. So you see, if my hand trembles when I sign the proclamation, all who examine it hereafter will say, 'He hesitated—look at his handwriting.'"

A short time afterward, the president took up his pen with a strong and steady hand and firmly wrote, "Abraham Lincoln." That historic act endeared Lincoln to the world as the Great Emancipator.

## LISTEN TO GOOD ADVICE

The folly of human nature is neatly summed up by the case of the middle-aged school teacher who invested her life savings in a business enterprise which had been elaborately explained to her by a swindler.

When her investment disappeared and the wonderful dream was shattered, she went to the office of the Better Business Bureau. "Why on earth," they asked, "didn't you come to us first? Didn't you know about the Better Business Bureau?"

"Oh yes," said the lady sadly. "I've always known about you. But I didn't come because I was afraid you'd tell me not to do it."

*Bits and Pieces*

## QUICK DECISIONS

A game warden noticed how a particular fellow named Sam consistently caught more fish than anyone else, whereas the other guys would only catch three or four a day. Sam would come in off the lake with a boat full. Stringer after stringer was always packed with freshly caught trout.

The warden, curious, asked Sam his secret. The successful fisherman invited the game warden to accompany him and observe. So the next morning the two met at the dock and took off in Sam's boat. When they got to the middle of the lake, Sam stopped the boat, and the warden sat back to see how it was done.

Sam's approach was simple. He took out a stick of dynamite, lit it, and threw it in the air. The explosion rocked the lake with such a force that dead fish immediately began to surface. Sam took out a net and started scooping them up.

Well, you can imagine the reaction of the game warden. When he recovered from the shock of it all, he began yelling at Sam. "You can't do this! I'll put you in jail, buddy! You will be paying every fine there is in the book!" Sam, meanwhile, set his net down and took out another stick of dynamite. He lit it and tossed it in the lap of the game warden with these words, "Are you going to sit there all day complaining, or are you going to fish?"

The poor warden was left with a fast decision to make. He was yanked, in one second, from an observer to a participant. A dynamite of a choice had to be made and be made quickly!

Life is like that. Few days go by without our coming face to face with an uninvited, unanticipated, yet unavoidable decision. Like a crashing snow bank, these decisions tumble upon us without warning. Quick. Immediate. Sudden. No council, no study, no advice. Pow!

*Max Lucado*

# Discouragement

*Discouragement is dissatisfaction with the past, distaste for the present, and distrust of the future. It is ingratitude for the blessings of yesterday, indifference to the opportunities of today, and insecurity regarding strength for tomorrow. It is unawareness of the presence of beauty, unconcern for the needs of our fellow man, and unbelief in the promises of old. It is impatience with time, immaturity of thought, and impoliteness to God.*

WILLIAM A. WARD

17

## PITFALLS OF DISCOURAGEMENT

A very real problem within all of us that can cause an attitude crash is the dread of discouragement.

The following are four pitfalls of discouragement:

1. Discouragement hurts our self-image.
2. Discouragement causes us to see ourselves as less than we really are.
3. Discouragement causes us to blame others for our predicament.
4. Discouragement causes us to blur the facts

## TO JUMP OR NOT TO JUMP

There is a story about a young man so desperate that he decided to commit suicide. He crawled out a top-story window in the tallest skyscraper in the city and worked his way onto a narrow ledge. A caring police officer was called to the scene to try to talk the young man out of jumping. Trained for this type of emergency, the officer slowly, methodically moved toward him, talking to him all the time.

When the officer got within inches of the man, he said, "Surely nothing could be so bad for you to take your life. Tell me about it. Talk to me!"

The would-be jumper cried out how he had nothing to live for. He told how his wife had left him, how he had lost his job, how his friends had deserted him, and how his only son had been killed in a drunken street fight. For thirty minutes, he told the officer his sad story.

Finally, the officer agreed with the desperate young man, life really had lost meaning. So they *both* jumped!

## NOT OUT OF IT YET

Discouragement comes when we feel that opportunity for success is gone. The test of your character is seeing what it takes to stop you. We need the spirit of the boy in Little League. A man stopped to watch a Little League baseball game. He asked one of the youngsters the score.

"We're behind 18 to nothing," was the answer.

"Well," said the man, "I must say you don't look discouraged."

"Discouraged?" the boy asked. "Why should we be discouraged? We haven't come to bat yet."

# Encouragement

*People have a way of becoming what you encourage them to be—not what you nag them to be.*

SCUDDER N. PARKER

18

Say only what is good and helpful to those you are talking to, and what will give them a blessing.

*Ephesians 4:29*

Acceptance recognizes persons as they now are. Encouragement celebrates what they may yet become with God's help.

*Anonymous*

An effective way to express appreciation: "If you don't like what I do, tell me. If you like what I do, tell my boss."

*Anonymous*

As we must account for every idle word, so we must for every idle silence.

*Benjamin Franklin*

Man lives more by affirmation than by bread.

*Victor Hugo*

Those who bring sunshine to the lives of others cannot keep it from themselves.

*Sir James Barrie*

Look for strength in people, not weakness; good, not evil. Most of us find what we search for.

*Anonymous*

Encouragers know there is a big difference between advice and help.

*Anonymous*

No one is useless in the world who lightens the burden of it for anyone else.

*Charles Dickens*

There are 750,000 people in mental hospitals in America. I'm convinced . . . that 80 percent of those people could be out if enough of us cared.

*Dr. William C. Menninger*

Dear Lord,
As in this world I toil and through this world I flit, I pray make me a drop
of oil and not a piece of grit.

*Anonymous*

As a neglected garden is soon invaded by weeds, so a love carelessly
guarded is quickly submerged by unkind feelings.

*André Maurois*

There are high spots in all of our lives, and most of them have come about
through encouragement from someone else. I don't care how great, how
famous, or successful a man or woman may be, each hungers for
applause.

*George Matthew Adams*

### A Short Course in Human Relations

The six most important words:
I admit that I was wrong.
The five most important words:
You did a great job.
The four most important words:
What do you think?
The three most important words:
Could you please . . .
The two most important words:
Thank you.
The most important word:
We.
The least important word:
I.

*Anonymous*

## HELP OTHERS LIKE THEMSELVES

Making others feel important and better about themselves should be
a driving force in our relationships.

Lord Chesterfield, in his famous letters to his son, said something
like this: "My son, here is the way to get people to like you. Make every

person like himself a little better, and I promise that he or she will like you very much."

## Which Am I?

I watched them tear a building down;
A gang of men in a busy town.
With a mighty heave and lusty yell,
They swung a beam and a side wall fell.

I said to the foreman, "Are these men as skilled
As the men you'd hire if you had to build?"
He gave a laugh and said, "No indeed!
Just a common laborer is all I need.
And I can wreck in a day or two
What it took the builder a year to do."

And I thought to myself as I went my way,
"Just which of these roles have I tried to play?
Am I a builder who works with care
Measuring life by the rule and square,
Or am I a wrecker as I walk the town
Content with the labor of tearing down?"

*Anonymous*

## BEYOND LIMITATIONS

Mahatma Gandhi inspired millions of people to go beyond their limitations to accomplish great things. It was said of Gandhi that he refused to see the bad in people. He inspired, even changed, human beings by regarding them not as what they were but as though they were what they wished to be, and as though the good in them was all of them.

*This uplifting and challenging way of working with people is what Ralph Waldo Emerson was encouraging when he said, "Our chief want in life is somebody who shall make us do what we can."*

## IT COULD HAVE BEEN DIFFERENT

He began his life with all the classic handicaps and disadvantages. His mother was a powerfully built, dominating woman who found it difficult to love anyone. She had been married three times, and her second husband divorced her because she beat him up regularly. The father of the child I'm describing was her third husband; he died of a heart attack a few months before the child's birth. As a consequence, the mother had to work long hours from his earliest childhood.

She gave him no affection, no love, no discipline, and no training during those early years. She even forbade him to call her at work. Other children had little to do with him, so he was alone most of the time. He was absolutely rejected from his earliest childhood. He was ugly and poor and untrained and unlovable. When he was thirteen years old, the school psychologist commented that he probably didn't even know the meaning of the word "love." During his adolescence, the girls would have nothing to do with him, and he fought with the boys.

Despite a high IQ, he failed academically and finally dropped out during his third year of high school. He thought he might find a new acceptance in the Marine Corps; they reportedly built men, and he wanted to be one. But his problems went with him. The other marines laughed at him and ridiculed him. He fought back, resisted authority, and was court-martialed and thrown out of the marines with an undesirable discharge.

So there he was—a young man in his early twenties—absolutely friendless and shipwrecked. He was small and scrawny in stature. He had an adolescent squeak in his voice. He was balding. He had no talent, no skill, no sense of worthiness. He didn't even have a driver's license. Once again he thought he could run from his problems, so he went to live in a foreign country. But he was rejected there, too. Nothing had changed. While there, he married a girl who herself had been an illegitimate child, and he brought her back to America with him. Soon, she began to develop the same contempt for him that everyone else displayed. She bore him two children, but he never enjoyed the status and respect that a father should have. His marriage continued to crumble. His wife demanded more and more things that he could not provide. Instead of being his ally against the bitter world, as he hoped, she became his most vicious opponent. She could outfight him, and she learned to bully him. On one occasion, she locked him in the bathroom as punishment. Finally, she forced him to leave.

He tried to make it on his own, but he was terribly lonely. After days of solitude, he went home and literally begged her to take him back. He surrendered all pride. He crawled. He accepted humiliation. He came on her terms. Despite his meager salary, he brought her seventy-eight dollars as a gift, asking her to take it and spend it any way she wished. But she laughed at him. She belittled his feeble attempts to support the family in front of a friend who was there. At one point, he fell on his knees and wept bitterly, as the great darkness of his private nightmare enveloped him.

Finally, in silence, he pleaded no more. No one wanted him. No one had ever wanted him. He was perhaps the most rejected man of our time. His ego lay shattered in fragmented dust! The next day, he was a strangely different man. He arose, went to the garage, and took down a rifle he had hidden there. He carried it with him to his newly acquired job at a book-storage building. And from a window on the third floor of that building, shortly after noon, November 22, 1963, he sent two shells crashing into the head of President John Fitzgerald Kennedy.

*James Dobson*

## YOU ARE WONDERFUL!

The following true story captured my heart. It happened several years ago in the Paris opera house. A famous singer had been contracted to sing, and ticket sales were booming. In fact, the night of the concert found the house packed and every ticket sold. The feeling of anticipation and excitement was in the air as the house manager took the stage and said, "Ladies and gentlemen, thank you for your enthusiastic support. I am afraid that due to illness, the man whom you've all come to hear will not be performing tonight. However, we have found a suitable substitute we hope will provide you with comparable entertainment." The crowd groaned in disappointment and failed to hear the announcer mention the stand-in's name. The environment turned from excitement to frustration. The stand-in performer gave the performance everything he had. When he had finished, there was nothing but an uncomfortable silence. No one applauded. Suddenly, from the balcony, a little boy stood up and shouted, "Daddy, I think you are wonderful!" The crowd broke into thunderous applause.

*We all need people in our lives who are willing to stand up once in a while and say, "I think you are wonderful."*

### Two Kinds of People

There are only two kinds of people on earth today
Two kinds of people, no more I say.
Not the rich and the poor, for to know a man's wealth
You must first know the state of his conscience and health,
Not the happy and sad, for in life's passing years,
Each has his laughter and each has his tears.
No, the two kinds of people on earth I mean
Are the people who lift and the people who lean.
In which class are you? Are you lifting the load
Of some overtaxed lifter who's going down the road,
Or are you a leaner who lets others share
Your portion of toil and labor and care?

*Ella Wheeler Wilcox*


## YOU'RE A WINNER

Daniel Webster left his country home and went to Boston to study law. He entered, without invitation, the office of Christopher Gore, then head of the Massachusetts bar. There he was looked upon as an intruder, and nobody paid any attention to him. One day Rufus King saw the lonely, solitary student. He warmly shook his hand and said, "I know your father well. Be studious and you will win. If you need any assistance or advice, come to me." Years later, after he had achieved greatness, Webster said: "I can still feel the warm pressure of that hand and hear those challenging words of encouragement."

*God's Revivalist*


## WINNING TOGETHER

Paul "Bear" Bryant, the football coaching legend, understood the value of encouragement. Several years ago, he was quoted as saying this about his ability to build quality teams and win football games: "I'm just a plowhand from Arkansas, but I have learned how to hold a team together. How to lift some men up, how to calm down others, until finally they've got one heartbeat together, a team. There's just three things I'd ever say:

If anything goes bad, I did it.
If anything goes semi-good, then we did it.
If anything goes real good, then you did it.

That's all it takes to get people to win football games for you."

## EXPRESS YOUR FAITH

Tell a child, a husband, or an employee that he is stupid or dumb at a certain thing, that he has no gift for it, and that he is doing it all wrong and you have destroyed almost every incentive to try to improve. But use the opposite technique; be liberal with encouragement; make the thing seem easy to do; let the other person know that you have faith in his ability to do it, that he has an undeveloped flair for it—and he will practice until the dawn comes in at the window in order to excel.

*Dale Carnegie*

## HARD TO HANDLE

You may have heard about the man who attended a workshop on encouragement. He left convinced about his need to show his wife more appreciation. So, on the way home, he stopped at the drugstore to pick up a delicious box of chocolates. Across the street, he purchased a dozen long-stemmed roses and proudly made his way toward home. This was the day he would begin showing his wife how much he appreciated her. Thinking he would make this an extra special occasion, he proudly grasped his presents and rang the front doorbell. His wife opened the door, took one look at him, and began sobbing. "What's wrong, Sweetheart?" he asked. Through her tears she replied, "It's been a horrible day! First, the television went on the blink; then Susie hurt herself playing on the swing set; the cat tore our living room curtains; and now, my husband comes home drunk."

*If expressing our appreciation has not been a frequent activity in our lives, others may be confused with our first attempt.*

## JUST BE THERE

Sometimes our physical presence is enough to comfort or encourage others. I am reminded of the little girl who went to comfort the mother of a playmate who had recently died. When she returned home, the little girl's mother asked her what she had done to comfort her friend's mother. The little girl softly replied, "I just sat on her lap and cried with her."

## WRANGLERS AND STRANGLERS

Years ago there was a group of brilliant young men at the University of Wisconsin, who seemed to have amazing creative literary talent. They were would-be poets, novelists, and essayists. They were extraordinary in their ability to put the English language to its best use. These promising young men met regularly to read and critique each other's work. And critique it they did!

These men were merciless with one another. They dissected the most minute literary expression into a hundred pieces. They were heartless, tough, even mean in their criticism. The sessions became such arenas of literary criticism that the members of this exclusive club called themselves the "Stranglers."

Not to be outdone, the women of literary talent in the university were determined to start a club of their own, one comparable to the Stranglers. They called themselves the "Wranglers." They, too, read their works to one another. But there was one great difference. The criticism was much softer, more positive, more encouraging. Sometimes, there was almost no criticism at all. Every effort, even the most feeble one, was encouraged.

Twenty years later an alumnus of the university was doing an exhaustive study of his classmates' careers when he noticed a vast difference in the literary accomplishments of the Stranglers as opposed to the Wranglers. Of all the bright young men in the Stranglers, not one had made a significant literary accomplishment of any kind. From the Wranglers had come six or more successful writers, some of national renown such as Marjorie Kinnan Rawlings, who wrote *The Yearling*.

Talent between the two? Probably the same. Level of education? Not much difference. But the Stranglers strangled, while the Wranglers were determined to give each other a lift. The Stranglers promoted an atmosphere of contention and self-doubt. The Wranglers highlighted the best, not the worst.

*Ted Engstrom*

### Little Things

It's the little things we do or say
That make or break the beauty of the average passing day.
Hearts, like doors, will open with ease
To very, very little keys,
And don't forget that two of these
Are "I thank you," and "If you please."

*Anonymous*

## THINKING ISN'T GOOD ENOUGH

Some people think about encouraging others but fail to take action. They are like the man who says to his wife, "Sometimes, Sue, when I think about how much you mean to me, I can hardly keep from telling you so." Encouragement is activated through expression. Depending on others to read our minds will never encourage anyone.

It has occurred to me, on more than one occasion, that most of us are unmindful of the tremendous power available through encouragement. Suppose, for example, that I encouraged two individuals one day and that each of them was motivated to encourage two others the next day. If this process continued, 120 people would be encouraged by the seventh day. And, if people would continue, sixteen thousand people would experience encouragement by the end of fourteen days, and at the end of three weeks, two million persons would be encouraged.

*What a powerful tool! We can positively impact the lives of other people.*

## WATCH YOUR LANGUAGE

I read recently about a little boy who had been naughty. During family devotions one night, the father prayed for his son, and he specifically mentioned a number of bad things the boy had done. Later that evening, the mother heard the six-year-old sobbing. When she asked what was wrong, the heartbroken boy cried out, "Daddy always tells God the bad things about me. He never tells Him the good things I do!"

## FROM PUNISHMENT TO FAME

The teacher was frustrated. Her class of primary school boys insisted on being the noisiest group in school. In desperation, she punished them by assigning each boy the problem of adding together all the numbers from one to one-hundred. Surely that would calm their unruly spirits, she thought.

However, one little boy scratched briefly on his slate, then turned the assignment in. His turned out to be the only right answer.

The astonished teacher asked how he did it. "Quite simply," the boy replied. "I thought there must be a shortcut and sure enough, I found it. You see, 100 plus 1 is 101; 99 plus 2 is 101; 98 plus 3 is 101; and if I continue like that all the way to 50 plus 51, I have 101 fifty times, which of course is 5,050.''

This young man then experienced ongoing encouragement and tutoring to refine his mathematical talents. This young man, Karl Friedrich Gauss, became the great mathematician of the nineteenth century.

*Punishment revealed his talents; however, success came through the encouraging follow-up efforts.*

## WARM FUZZIES

Somewhere there is a beautiful place called the Land of Warm Fuzzies. The Land of Warm Fuzzies has in the middle of it the most beautiful garden you have ever seen. Flowers of every color, shape, and variety bloom in full beauty. A crystal-clear stream of water flows through the middle of the Land of Warm Fuzzies, and every kind of tree that you can imagine grows there—towering fir trees, stalwart oaks, beautiful maples, and fruit trees in abundance. The Land of Warm Fuzzies is a paradise.

The people who live in the Land of Warm Fuzzies are happy and healthy. Life excites them. They have no drug or alcohol problems. There are no divorces, child abuse, or emotional illness. When one person has a need, the others respond and take care of it. A close observation of the citizens in the Land of Warm Fuzzies shows that they practice the Golden Rule principle by treating others as they want to be treated. They are always giving others a smile, a warm hug, or a kind word. You might say they are high on love. It seems that they are always giving love away, and as a consequence they are always happy.

Each person who lives in the Land of Warm Fuzzies, whether adult or child, has a well-worn sack over his shoulder. These sacks, which the people carry with them everywhere, are filled with warm fuzzies. And wherever they go, whomever they meet, they give that person a warm fuzzy. That warm fuzzy melts all over the person and makes him feel warm and good from the inside out.

On the other side of the mountain from the Land of Warm Fuzzies lives a wicked old witch. She lives in the Land of the Cold Pricklies. There no one gets along with another person. People stick their tongues out at each other. And they keep their distance from one another.

One day the old witch ventures over the mountain into the Land of Warm Fuzzies, and the warmth and love that she sees there enrage her with jealousy. She decides right there and then she's got to do something to destroy all of this love and happiness. She gives quite a bit of thought to this and comes up with a shameful scheme. She waits under a tree, and soon a young man comes along who, sure enough, has his bag of warm fuzzies over his shoulder. Just as the young man greets her with a smile and reaches in his bag to get a warm fuzzy to give to her, she says, "Stop! You keep giving those warm fuzzies away to everyone you meet, and you're going to run out of warm fuzzies. You had better hold back your warm fuzzies and give them only on special occasions, when someone really needs one."

Deceived by the wicked witch, the young man starts spreading the rumor that if people keep giving their warm fuzzies away, they will soon run out.

Soon the happy land becomes a sad land. The warmth turns to coldness. The love turns to rejection and loneliness. Instead of passing out warm fuzzies, people now give each other cold pricklies. A cold prickly is something like an SOS pad. It gives you a scratchy, cold feeling. A cold prickly is a frown, a rejection, an accusation. A cold prickly comes out in words such as, "Do it yourself, idiot," or, "Leave me alone." In a marriage, a cold prickly comes out: "You're sleeping on the couch," or, "No warmth for you tonight."

*Dale Galloway*

### Never Mind!

Sometimes when nothing goes just right
And worry reigns supreme,
When heartache fills the eyes with mist
And all things useless seem,
There's just one thing can drive away
The tears that scald and blind—
Someone to slip a strong arm 'round
And whisper, "Never mind."

No one has ever told just why
Those words such comfort bring;
Nor why that whisper makes our cares
Depart on hurried wing.
Yet troubles say a quick "Good-day,"
We leave them far behind
When someone slips an arm around,
And whispers, "Never mind."

But love must prompt that soft caress—
That love must, aye, be true

Or at that tender, clinging touch
No heart ease come to you,
But if the arm be moved by love,
Sweet comfort you will find
When someone slips an arm around,
And whispers, "Never mind!"

*Evangelical Visitor*

## Say It Now

If you have a tender message,
Or a loving word to say,
Don't wait 'til you forget it,
But whisper it today!

The tender words unspoken,
The letter never sent,
The long-forgotten messages,
The wealth of love unspent

For these some hearts are breaking,
For these some loved ones wait,
Then give them what they're needing,
Before it is too late!

*Anonymous*

## SMALL EFFORTS MAKE A BIG DIFFERENCE

As the old man walked down a Spanish beach at dawn, he saw ahead of him what he thought to be a dancer. A young man was running across the sand rhythmically, bending down to pick up a stranded starfish and throw it far into the sea. The old man gazed in wonder as the young man again and again threw the small starfish from the sand to the water. The old man approached him and asked why he spent so much energy doing what seemed a waste of time. The young man explained that the stranded starfish would die if left until the morning sun.

"But there must be thousands of miles of beach and millions of starfish. How can your efforts make any difference?"

The young man looked down at the small starfish in his hand and as he threw it to safety in the sea, said, "It makes a difference to this one."

*Anonymous*

# Enthusiasm

*People who are unable to motivate themselves must be content with mediocrity, no matter how impressive their other talents.*

**ANDREW CARNEGIE**

19

A person can succeed at anything for which there is enthusiasm.

*Charles M. Schwab*

Apathy can only be overcome by enthusiasm.

*Arnold Toynbee*

Enthusiasm reflects confidence, spreads good cheer, raises morale, inspires associates, arouses loyalty, and laughs at adversity . . . it is beyond price.

*Allan Cox*

Confidence and enthusiasm are the greatest sales producers in any kind of economy.

*O. B. Smith*

Great accomplishments have resulted from the transmission of ideas and enthusiasm.

*Thomas J. Watson*

Every great and commanding movement in the annals of the world is a triumph of enthusiasm.

*Ralph Waldo Emerson*

Genius is intensity. The salesman who surges with enthusiasm, though it is excessive, is superior to the one who has no passion. I would prefer to calm down a geyser than start with a mudhole.

*Former sales manager*

Enthusiasm is a kind of faith that has been set afire.

*George Matthew Adams*

Henry David Thoreau used to lie in a bed for a while in the morning telling himself all the good news he could think of: that he had a healthy body, that his mind was alert, that his work was interesting, that the future looked bright, that a lot of people trusted him. He then arose to meet the day in a world filled for him with good things, good people, and good opportunities. He activated enthusiasm before beginning his day. In that way, Thoreau took responsibility for his own level of enthusiasm throughout the day.

Enthusiasm is the greatest asset in the world. It beats money and power and influence.

*Henry Chester*

Nothing great or new can be done without enthusiasm. Enthusiasm is the fly-wheel which carries your saw through the knots in the log. A certain excessiveness seems a necessary element in all greatness.

*Dr. Harvey Cushing*

The secret of genius is to carry the spirit of the child into old age, which means never losing your enthusiasm.

*Aldous Huxley*

Assume a virtue, if you have it not.

*William Shakespeare*

The worst bankrupt is the man who has lost his enthusiasm. Let a man lose everything in the world but his enthusiasm and he will come through again to success.

*H. W. Arnold*

Enthusiasm, like measles, mumps, and the common cold, is highly contagious.

*Emory Ward*

Every production of genius must be the production of enthusiasm.

*Benjamin Disraeli*

You can do anything if you have enthusiasm. Enthusiasm is the yeast that makes your hopes rise to the stars. Enthusiasm is the spark in your eye, the swing in your gait, the grip of your hand, the irresistible surge of your will and your energy to execute your ideas. Enthusiasts are fighters, they have fortitude, they have staying qualities. Enthusiasm is at the bottom of all progress! With it, there is accomplishment. Without it, there are only alibis.

*Henry Ford*

You can't sweep people off their feet if you can't be swept off your own.

*Clarence Day*

No one keeps up his enthusiasm automatically. Enthusiasm must be nourished with new action, new aspirations, new efforts, new vision. It is one's own fault if enthusiasm is gone.

*Papyrus*

William James, the Harvard psychologist, suggested that you feel the way you act. Therefore, enthusiasm works like this: If you are going to feel enthusiastic, you must be enthusiastic.

Let your enthusiasm radiate in your voice, your actions, your facial expressions, your personality, the words you use, and the thoughts you think! Nothing great was ever achieved without enthusiasm.

*Ralph Waldo Emerson*

## A NINETY-FOUR-YEAR-OLD FAN OF LIFE

The heart of living life to its fullest is exemplified by a ninety-four-year-old woman from Arizona. Her friends described her as charming, delightful, and always positive. When asked her secret of living, she responded, "It is my enthusiasm for life. Because I think positive, I am positive." Pausing for a moment, she continued, "Even at ninety-four, I have four boyfriends. I begin each day with Will Power, then go for a walk with Arthur Ritis. I usually return home with Charlie Horse and spend the evening with Ben Gay. Need I say anymore?"

The Greek biographer Plutarch observed, "For the wise man, every day is a festival."

## ENTHUSIASTIC EDISON

The events of December 9, 1914, exemplify Thomas Alva Edison's undefeatable spirit.

On that evening, the well-known Edison Industries was destroyed by fire. The total loss in that disaster exceeded $2 million, along with Edison's life's work. He was insured for only $238 because the buildings were constructed of concrete, at that time thought to be fireproof. At sixty-seven years old, Edison watched his life go up in flames.

Edison stood in the winter wind as firefighters tried to control the fiery blaze. The thoughts that permeated his mind that evening must have been confused and ringing with disappointment.

The next morning, Edison surveyed his charred dreams and crushed hopes. As he stood amid the disaster, Edison was quoted as saying, "There is great value in disaster. All our mistakes are burned up. Thank God we can start anew."

Edison sincerely believed that. Three weeks after the fire, Edison Industries delivered the first phonograph. That is the result of a leader who had incredible vision, was capable of sustaining enthusiasm, and undoubtedly possessed a great deal of flexibility. Edison's positive, consistent example inspired others.

# Failure

*The man who does things makes many mistakes, but he never makes the biggest mistake of all —doing nothing.*

BENJAMIN FRANKLIN

20

Only those who dare to fail greatly can ever achieve greatly.

*Robert F. Kennedy*


The difference between failure and success is doing a thing nearly right and doing a thing exactly right.

*Edward Simmons*


Experience is the name everyone gives to their mistakes.

*Oscar Wilde*


The men who try to do something and fail are infinitely better than those who try to do nothing and succeed.

*Lloyd Jones*


Show me a thoroughly satisfied man and I will show you a failure.

*Thomas Alva Edison*


Nothing is ever always wrong. Even a clock that stops is right twice a day.

*Anonymous*


More people would learn from their mistakes if they weren't so busy denying them.

*J. Harold Smith*


The man who makes no mistakes does not usually make anything.

*Bishop W. C. Magee*


Failures can be divided into those who thought and never did, and those who did and never thought.

*W. A. Nance*

Man swims in the sea of self-satisfaction, nibbles at the bait of procrastination, swallows the hook of mediocrity, and ends up in the net of failure.

*William A. Ward*

From failure can come valuable experience; from experience—wisdom; from wisdom—mutual trust; from mutual trust—cooperation; from cooperation—united effort; from united effort—success.

*William A. Ward*

The only people who never fail are those who never try.

*Ilka Chase*

The greatest right in the world is the right to be wrong.

*Harry Weinberger*

Ninety-nine percent of the failures come from people who have the habit of making excuses.

*George Washington Carver*

I would sooner fail than not be among the greatest.

*John Keats*

I cannot give you a formula for success, but I can give you the formula for failure—which is: Try to please everybody.

*Herbert Bayard Swope*

In great attempts it is glorious even to fail.

*Cassius Longinus*

Fear of failure: We hide it. We deny it. We fear it. We ignore it, and we hate it.

*Anonymous*

If at first you don't succeed, destroy all the evidence that you have tried.

*Anonymous*

A man can fail many times, but he isn't a failure until he gives up.

*Anonymous*

Failure is not failure to meet your goal. Real failure is failure to reach as high as you possibly can. No man will ever truly know that he has succeeded until he experiences an apparent failure.

*Robert Schuller*

We have forty million reasons for failure, but not a single excuse.

*Rudyard Kipling*

He who has never failed has never tried.

*Emmett LeCompte*

The greatest failure is the failure to try

*William A. Ward*

No man ever fails until he fails on the inside.

*Anonymous*

More men fail through lack of purpose than lack of talent.

*Billy Sunday*

People do not inadvertently stumble into failure. They think their way into it.

*John B. Johnson*

Failure is the line of least persistence.

*W. A. Clarke*

Finish every day and be done with it. You have done what you could. Some blunders and absurdities no doubt crept in; forget them as soon as you can. Tomorrow is a new day; begin it well and serenely and with too high a spirit to be cumbered with your old nonsense. This day is all that is good

and fair. It is too dear, with its hopes and invitations, to waste a moment
on yesterdays.

*Ralph Waldo Emerson*


I don't know what success is, but I know what failure is. Failure is trying
to please everybody.

*Sammy Davis, Jr.*

## If You Think


If you think you are beaten, you are.
If you think you dare not, you don't!
If you want to win, but think you can't,
It's almost a cinch you won't.

If you think you'll lose, you're lost;
For out in the world we find
Success begins with a fellow's will;
It's all in the state of the mind.

Life's battles don't always go
To the stronger and faster man,
But sooner or later the man who wins
Is the man who thinks he can.

*Walter D. Wintle*


## THE THRILL OF VICTORY AND THE AGONY OF DEFEAT

In his classic work *The Book of Failures,* Stephen Pile shares an
unforgettable story. In 1978, during the firefighters' strike in England,
the British army had taken over emergency firefighting. This made
possible one of the greatest animal rescue attempts of all time. On
January 14, the army was called to assist an elderly woman in south
London retrieve her cat. Responding immediately to the call, they cleverly
and carefully rescued the cat, and celebrated their triumphant victory. As
they started to drive away, the lady insisted that this battalion of heroes
stay for tea. Driving away later with warm farewells and festive spirits, they
ran over the cat and killed it.

## FOOD FOR FAILURE

Charles Swindoll, in his book *Growing Strong in the Seasons of Life,* says the prize for the most useless weapon of all time goes to the Russians. They invented the dog mine. The plan was to train the dogs to associate food with the undersides of tanks in the hope that they would run hungrily beneath advancing Panzer divisions. Bombs were then strapped to the dogs' backs, which endangered the dogs to the point where no insurance company would insure them.

Unfortunately, the dogs associated food solely with Russian tanks. The plan was begun the first day of the Russian involvement in World War II and abandoned on the second day. The dogs with bombs on their backs forced an entire Soviet tank division to retreat.

## PANACEA OF FAILURE

Some failures of the past provided direction for the future. For instance:

- Thomas Alva Edison spent $2 million on an invention that never materialized. However, his lifelong track record isn't bad.

- Henry Ford forgot to put reverse gear in the first car he manufactured. Then in 1957, he bragged about the car of the decade. It was the Edsel, renowned for doors that wouldn't close, a hood that wouldn't open, paint that peeled, a horn that stuck, and a reputation that made it impossible to resell. However, Ford's future track record contains more glowing productions.

- How would you like to be credited with designing the Leaning Tower of Pisa? (It wasn't meant to be built twenty feet from the perpendicular.) However, the designer provided a foundation only 10 feet deep for a building that would stand 179 feet tall. That's no small mistake, but I'm sure architects learned from this practical flop.

- Members of the English Parliament hissed Benjamin Disraeli as he stood, for the first time, to address them. They laughed when he said, "Though I sit down now, the time will come when you will hear of me." And hear of him they did. Benjamin Disraeli went on to become a noted British statesman.

- Struggling a little in his early years, a Munich schoolmaster told ten-year-old Albert Einstein, "You will never amount to much." Guess who got the last laugh?

- A newspaper owner told this young artist to pursue another line of work, saying, "You don't have any creative, original ideas." However, Walt Disney went on to build the Disney empire beginning with the creative, original Mickey Mouse.

- "Your voice sounds like wind whistling through a window." Those were the words of Enrico Caruso's first voice teacher. Enrico Caruso later became famous as the great Italian tenor.

- In 1962 the Decca Recording Company turned down the opportunity to work with the Beatles. Their rationale? "We don't like their sound. Groups of guitars are on their way out." Of course, the Beatles turned that imminent failure into prominent success.

- I wonder what Simon Newcomb would say today? Living from 1835 to 1909, Newcomb was quoted as saying, "Flight by machines heavier than air is unpractical and insignificant . . . utterly impossible." Thank goodness Orville and Wilbur Wright didn't take him seriously.

Of course, there have been failures that yielded no benefit to mankind. For instance:

- A thought materialized in the mind of one man to irrigate the deserts of the world via giant peashooters sending snowballs from the polar region.

- Then there was the possibility of designing a golf ball that could be hit and steered in flight by the owner.

- How about the bicycle? No, not your run-of-the-mill bicycle, but a model with amphibious capability.

- Don't forget the contraption designed to allow people to drive their car from the backseat. Commercial manufacturers decided we had had enough backseat drivers without this new invention.

Credit for these fumbling attempts goes to Arthur Pedrick, the one-man think tank Basic Research Laboratories of Sussex, England. Between 1962 and 1977, he patented 162 inventions that never materialized on the commercial market. He must empathize with Wendell Phillips' classic comment: "What is defeat? Nothing but education; nothing but the first step to something better."

## A FRESH START

Remember the story of the woman whose name was accidentally printed in the obituary column of the local newspaper. Needless to say, she was upset. Stomping her way into the newspaper office, she demanded to see the editor.

"What kind of paper is this anyway? Your mistake will ruin my career, not to mention the embarrassment I will have to endure. How could you make such an error?" she asked. The editor responded with diplomatic apologies, but the lady continued in her anger, eventually proving herself unreasonable. "Look, lady," the editor said with disgust. "Tomorrow I'll put your name in the birth announcements and give you a fresh start."

## THE LINCOLN LEGACY

When failure continually knocks at your door, welcome it in. Once experienced and learned from, failure becomes the steppingstone to success.

Consider a man whose life was engulfed with failure, setbacks, and letdowns. He once wrote, "I am the most miserable man living. Whether I shall be better, I cannot tell."

He experienced a difficult childhood. When he was only seven years old, his family was forced out of their home on a legal technicality. He went to work to support his family, and at nine, his mother died. He completed less than one year of formal schooling.

At twenty-two, he lost his job as a store clerk. His desire was to go to law school, but his lack of education restricted him from being admitted.

He borrowed money to become a partner in a small business. A few years later, his partner died, leaving him swamped in debt that took seventeen years to repay.

In 1832, he was defeated for the legislature; this was followed by another business failure one year later.

In 1835, the young woman he loved refused to marry him, and a woman he had loved earlier died, leaving him rejected, confused, and heartbroken.

He was defeated for speaker in 1838 and defeated for the elector in 1840. Two years later he married into a burdensome life and an ultimately unhappy relationship.

He was defeated for Congress in 1843, but finally, after his third try, was elected in 1846. Two years later, at thirty-nine, he ran again and failed to be reelected.

His personal life was also in shambles. His four-year-old son died. (In fact, only one of his four sons lived past eighteen). At this point, he experienced a nervous breakdown. The next year, he failed to get an appointment to the U.S. Land Office.

At forty-five, he ran and was badly defeated for the U.S. Senate. Two years later, in 1856, he became candidate for the vice presidency and again experienced defeat.

Failure stood at his door in 1858 when he was again badly defeated for the U.S. Senate.

Amazingly enough, this man withstood a lifetime of crisis, criticism, public denial, personal defeat, deep depression, and loneliness to become a U.S. president in 1860. At fifty-one years old, he experienced the success he so badly desired. However, his second term of office was cut short by a final earthly defeat—his assassination.

As Abraham Lincoln lay dying, Edwin M. Stanton spoke of this man as most of us remember him: "There lies the most perfect ruler of men the world has ever seen . . . [and] now he belongs to the ages."

Because of his accomplishments, his foresight, his insight, and his wisdom, Abraham Lincoln was an example of how failure can produce achievement.

Lincoln would surely have agreed with Charles F. Kettering, who believed, "It is not a disgrace to fail. Failing is one of the greatest arts in the world."

## MURPHY'S LAWS

Everyone has heard of Murphy's first law: "If anything can go wrong, invariably it will." But hardly anybody has even a foggy idea of who Murphy was.

The search for Murphy's notebooks led to a garage in Toledo, Ohio; an inventor's junk loft in Aliquippa, Pennsylvania; and the home of a retired female blackmailer in Sarasota, Florida. It was learned that Murphy had no first name, that he never could hold a job, and that his writings were returned by the post office for insufficient postage.

It seems everything Murphy wrote about had some explanation for why things go wrong. Consider a few more Murphy classics:

- Nothing is ever as simple as it first seems.
- Everything you decide to do costs more than first estimated.
- Every activity takes more time than you have.
- It's easier to make a commitment or to get involved in something than to get out of it.
- Whatever you set out to do, something else must be done first.
- If you improve or tinker with something long enough, eventually it will break.

- By making something absolutely clear, somebody will be confused.
- You can fool some of the people all of the time and all of the people some of the time, and that's sufficient.

*Anonymous*

## REMEMBER TO LIVE

Some people become so obsessed with the fear of failure that they forget to live. When those day-to-day problems, mistakes, and failures become discouraging, encourage yourself by thinking of the many successful people who overcome personal handicaps.

"I thank God for my handicaps," declared Helen Keller. Blind and deaf from birth, she became a prolific writer.

Winston Churchill refused to allow a serious speech impediment to inhibit his desire to become a dynamic leader and distinguished orator.

Gene Littler overcame cancer to make an incredible comeback in golf. Before him, Ben Hogan amazed the golf world. He won the Masters, the PGA, and the National Open golf championships after a severe auto accident. Doctors thought Hogan would have a lifetime of difficulty walking and thought he would never play golf again.

They called him "Straw Legs." As a young boy, his skinny legs were crippled by rickets. However, O. J. Simpson overcame his handicap to become one of the great running backs in the history of professional football.

Napoleon responded to his extremely short stature to become a giant in military conquests

They teased and tormented him, called him the "ninety-seven pound runt" as a boy. He worked endlessly to build his muscular physique. Charles Atlas created a physique that has been used as a model for numerous famous statues in America.

David Sarnoff, head of Radio Corporation of America, once declared, "Nothing worthwhile has been attained except by overcoming obstacles."

Beethoven knew that. He composed his greatest symphonies after becoming totally deaf.

Norman Vincent Peale also knew obstacles had to be overcome. Shy, tongue-tied, and suffering from feelings of inferiority, he became one of America's great preachers and religious leaders. He responded to his weakness, faced the challenge, and took control of his life.

The masterpiece *Messiah* was written when Handel was debt-ridden, spiritless, and failing in health. His creditors were threatening to throw him in jail.

Physical deformity, baldness, and "hefty physique" didn't stop Socrates from becoming a philosopher whose impact is still felt today.

Franklin D. Roosevelt served the United States as its president from the confines of a wheelchair.

## PAY YOUR DUES

Failure and mistakes are the dues we pay to understand the value of our successes. Those who persevere will be revered. People throughout history have shared their convictions concerning the necessity of failure and mistakes.

Seneca: "If thou art a man, admire those who attempt great things, even though they fail."

Jack Lemmon: "It's the fear of failure that kills you, that kills artists. You've got to go down that alley and take those chances."

Theodore Roosevelt: "The only man who never makes a mistake is the man who never does anything."

Richard J. Needham: "Strong people make as many and as ghastly mistakes as weak people. The difference is that strong people admit them, laugh at them, learn from them. That is how they become strong."

Charles Knight, chief executive officer of Emerson Electric, shared these thoughts concerning the existence of failure in management: "You need the ability to fail. I'm amazed at the number of organizations that set up an environment where they do not permit their people to be wrong. You cannot innovate unless you are willing to accept some mistakes."

Stanley E. Jones: "When life kicks you, let it kick you forward!"

## THE NEXT SHOT COUNTS

The great sports columnist Grantland Rice offered this advice in his autobiography *The Tumult and the Shouting*: "Because golf exposes the flaws of the human swing—a basically simple maneuver—it causes more self-torture than any game short of Russian roulette. The quicker the average golfer can forget the shot he had dubbed or knocked off line—and concentrate on the next shot—the sooner he begins to improve and enjoy golf. Like life, golf can be humbling. However, little good comes from brooding about mistakes we've made. The next shot in golf, or life, is the big one."

### When It Looks Like I Have Failed

Lord, are you trying to tell me something?
For
Failure does not mean I'm a failure;
It does mean I have not yet succeeded.
Failure does not mean I have accomplished nothing;
It does mean I have learned something.
Failure does not mean I have been a fool;
It does mean I had enough faith to experiment.
Failure does not mean I've been disgraced;
It does mean I dared to try.
Failure does not mean I don't have it;
It does mean I have to do something in a different way.
Failure does not mean that I am inferior;
It does mean that I am not perfect.
Failure does not mean that I have wasted my life;
It does mean that I have an excuse to start over.
Failure does not mean that I should give up;
It does mean that I must try harder.
Failure does not mean that I will never make it;
It does mean that I need more patience.
Failure does not mean you have abandoned me;
It does mean you must have a better idea. Amen.

*Anonymous*

## CONCENTRATE ON WINNING

I've admired the basketball coaching of Ray Meyer for many years. Meyer has inspired crowds with forty-two consecutive years of winning seasons at DePaul University. I was curious how Ray Meyer would respond to losing after having won twenty-nine straight home-court victories. His reported comment is a classic: "Great! Now we can start concentrating on winning, not on not losing."

No excuses for losing. No blaming, rationalizing, or spilling tears. Ray Meyer focuses on positive goals, putting all his energies into the task at hand.

Charles F. Kettering, the great inventive genius, once remarked, "I'm not interested in the past. I am interested only in the future, for that is where I expect to spend the rest of my life."

That attitude also exemplifies the winning attitude of the basketball coach legend Ray Meyer.

## TEMPORARY SETBACK—NOT PERMANENT DEFEAT

Someone once challenged Thomas Alva Edison by reminding him that he failed twenty-five thousand times while experimenting with the storage battery. "No, I didn't fail," the brilliant inventor replied. "I discovered 24,999 ways that the storage battery does not work." In his lifetime Edison received 1,093 patents for inventing devices such as the phonograph, motion pictures, the electric pen, waxed paper, and, of course, the incandescent lamp.

Failure was no stranger to Edison. Yet he refused to accept it as a permanent defeat. His long, remarkable career was inspired by the desire to make things work. At the time of his death, Edison left some 2,900 notebooks crammed with notes of his work and ideas.

## JUST ONE STEP CLOSER

The great inventor Charles F. Kettering suggested that we must learn to fail intelligently. He said, "Once you've failed, analyze the problem and find out why, because each failure is one more step leading up to the cathedral of success. The only time you don't want to fail is the last time you try."

## ARE YOU A TY COBB OR A MAX CAREY?

Every baseball fan knows that Ty Cobb was one of baseball's greatest players. His record for stealing bases stood for years. Cobb stole 96 bases the year he set the record.

Ask baseball fans if they know Max Carey, and most of them will shake their heads and ask, "Who was Max Carey?" Carey, too, had baseball talent. In fact, one season he attempted 53 stolen bases and succeeded 51 times—an unbelievable 96 percent. Ty Cobb stole 96 bases the year he set the record, but he tried 134 times. That is only 71 percent. Cobb was willing to chance failure, and because of it, he became legendary in the baseball Hall of Fame. Max Carey, who played it safe time after time, is not remembered today.

*Like Ty Cobb, you're going to make mistakes. But keep trying. If you win often enough, people will forget the times you failed. To succeed, you need to take risks. Don't always play it safe.*

# Forgiveness

*I can forgive, but I cannot forget is only another way of saying, I cannot forgive.*

HENRY WARD BEECHER

21

Write the wrongs that are done to you in sand, but write the good things that happen to you on a piece of marble. Let go of all emotions such as resentment and retaliation, which diminish you, and hold onto the emotions, such as gratitude and joy, which increase you.

*Arabic proverb*

A true apology is more than just acknowledgement of a mistake. It is recognition that something you have said or done has damaged a relationship and that you care enough about the relationship to want it repaired and restored.

*Norman Vincent Peale*

When I refuse to forgive, I am burning a bridge that someday I will need to pass over.

*Josh McDowell*

For me to fail to forgive myself or anyone else who has offended me is to imply that I have a higher standard of forgiveness than God, because whatever it is that has so hurt me that I can't forgive it, God already has.

*Hal Lindsay*

Forgiveness is our command. Judgment is not.

*C. Neil Strait*

Never does a man stand so tall as when he foregoes revenge, and dares to forgive an injury.

*J. Harold Smith*

## THIS DOESN'T COUNT

Old Bill was dying. With time running out, he wanted to make things right with his friend Harry. Once best friends, Bill knew their relationship was presently at odds. Bill had often challenged Harry on trivial matters, and in recent months, they hadn't spoken at all. Sincerely wanting to resolve the problem, Bill sent for Harry.

When Harry arrived at Bill's hospital bed, Bill apologized for his role in hurting their relationship. Bill said he was afraid of entering eternity with bad feelings between them, and he wanted to make things right before he died. Then he reached out for Harry's hand and said, "I forgive you. Will you please forgive me?" What joy that brought to Harry, and he agreed forgiveness was in order.

Just as Harry was leaving, however, old Bill shouted after him, "But remember, if I don't die and somehow get better, this doesn't count!"

## WILL YOU FORGIVE ME?

Many years ago, a professor at the University of Edinburgh was listening to his students as they presented oral readings. One young man rose to begin his recitation but was abruptly stopped by the professor. "You are holding the book in the wrong hand," criticized the educator. "Take your book in the right hand and be seated."

Responding to this strong rebuke, the young man held up his right arm. He didn't have a right hand! The other students were deathly quiet and began to shift in their seats. For a moment the professor sat in dumbfounded silence. Then he slowly made his way to the student, put his arm around him and with a tear in his eye, said, "I am so sorry. I never knew. Please, will you forgive me?"

This willingness made a strong impact on the young man and later inspired him to pursue the Christian ministry.

*Our Daily Bread*

*We never really know the far-reaching effect asking forgiveness can have on the people we wrong.*

## HISTORICAL

While visiting with a friend over coffee one morning, a young woman complained, "Every time my husband and I get into an argument, he gets historical!"

The friend interrupted, "Don't you mean hysterical?"

"No, I mean historical," the lady replied. "He always brings up the past."

*Forgiving requires people not to keep score.*

## AMAZING FORGIVENESS

*Moody Monthly* ran a story several years ago about a man who was arrested by the Communists during the Korean War and ordered to be shot. Moments before the death sentence was carried out, the Communist commander learned that his prisoner ran an orphanage that cared for small children. He decided to spare the man's life and kill his son instead. The young boy was murdered in the presence of his father.

Later in the war, the Communist leader was captured and condemned to death. Before the sentence was carried out, the father whose boy had been killed pleaded for the life of the killer. "Allow me to take him," he pleaded. "I want an opportunity to train him." His request was granted, and the father immediately expressed his forgiveness for the man's actions. He took the man to his home and treated him with love and cared for his wounds and physical needs.

That same leader requested forgiveness from the father and from God for his murderous deeds. He later went on to become a Christian pastor.

## SWEETER THAN REVENGE

Election campaigns can produce emotional confrontations. In 1755, a twenty-three-year-old colonel was in the midst of a campaign for a seat in the Virginia assembly. Exercising limited judgment, young George Washington made an insulting comment to a hot-tempered young man named Payne. He did not take kindly to the insult and responded by knocking Washington down with a hickory stick. Soldiers rushed to Washington's assistance, but he called them off, got to his feet, and exited from the scene.

Early the next morning, Washington wrote Payne a letter requesting that they meet at a tavern. Payne obliged, wondering what motives and demands Washington would have. He was sure an apology or even a duel might be requested. However, Washington met Payne with an apology for his derogatory remarks, requested forgiveness, and offered his hand in peace.

That may be called politically expedient, but Washington considered it personally necessary to ensure internal peace.

## HE BELONGS TO THE AGES!

As a young, struggling attorney, Abraham Lincoln felt honored to be employed on an important case. The other attorneys chosen to represent the case were well known for their legal and persuasive expertise. However, one attorney, upon seeing Lincoln, remarked, "What is that gawky ape doing here? I refuse to work with him. Get rid of him." Lincoln remained calm and pretended not to hear the deliberate insult.

As the trial proceeded, Lincoln was ostracized by the other lawyers. In fact, he was never recognized as one of the representing attorneys. He listened carefully to the court proceedings and observed his insulter's masterful handling of the case. He won the case hands-down. The next day, Lincoln was quoted as saying, "His brilliant argument was a revelation to me. He was expertly prepared, fluent in his presentation, and undoubtedly the most professional questioning I have ever witnessed. I can't hold a candle to his abilities. I am going home to study law all over again."

Years later, Abraham Lincoln became president of the United States. That same attorney who had rudely insulted Lincoln became his most outspoken critic. However, Lincoln never forgot the brilliance of this man. When an appointment was needed for secretary of war, Lincoln chose Edwin M. Stanton, the very man who had wounded and insulted him. Lincoln proved his character by offering a forgiving spirit rather than a lifetime grudge.

Shortly thereafter, an assassin's bullet pierced Lincoln's body. Stanton, filled with sorrow and inconsolable grief, sobbed, "Now he belongs to the ages!"

# Friendship

*We take care of our health, we lay up money, we make our room tight, and our clothing sufficient; but who provides wisely that he shall not be wanting in the best property of all—friends?*

RALPH WALDO EMERSON

22

At the death of his friend, A. H. Hallam, Lord Tennyson declared, "Tis better to have loved and lost than never to have loved at all."

*Anonymous*

People with trusting, quality friendships may be introverts, enthusiastic, dull, extroverts, young, old, homely, good-looking; but the two characteristics they always have in common are openness and sincerity.

*Glenn Van Ekeren*

A man, sir, must keep his friendships in constant repair. If a man does not make new acquaintances as he advances through life, he will soon find himself left alone.

*Samuel Johnson*

A friend is one who walks in when others walk out.

*Walter Winchell*

Friendship is like money, easier made than kept.

*Samuel Butler*

The New York Telephone Company made a detailed study of telephone conversations to find out which word is the most frequently used. You have guessed it: It is the personal pronoun *I, I, I.* It was used 3,990 times in 500 telephone conversations. *I. I. I. I.* Friendships result from the ability to transform "self-concern" into "other concern."

*Anonymous*

It is the individual who is not interested in his fellow men who has the greatest difficulties in life and provides the greatest injury to others. It is from among such individuals that all human failures spring.

*Alfred Adler*

With the death of every friend I love . . . a part of me has been buried . . . but their contribution to my being of happiness, strength, and understanding remains to sustain me in an altered world.

*Helen Keller*

One learns people through the heart, not the eyes or the intellect.

*Mark Twain*

In the words of William Shakespeare, it's nice to be among friends . . . even if they are somebody else's.

*Anonymous*

It's difficult to improve on George Eliot's definition of friendship: "Friendship is the inexpressible comfort of feeling safe with a person, having neither to weigh thoughts nor measure words."

*Anonymous*

"A true friend," a sage once said, "is the person who steps in when the whole world steps out."

*Anonymous*

A good friend is like toothpaste. He comes through in a tight squeeze.

*Anonymous*

A friend is one who knows you as you are, understands where you've been, accepts who you have become, and still gently invites you to grow.

*Anonymous*

Friendships are enriched when we experience the sweetness of this old Swedish proverb, "Shared sorrow is half a sorrow."

*Anonymous*

The only way to have a friend is to be a friend.

*Ralph Waldo Emerson*

I find as I grow older that I love those most whom I loved first.

*Thomas Jefferson*

I have room for one more friend and he is everyman.

*Woody Guthrie*

Friendship exists only when men harmonize in their views of things human and divine.

*Cicero*

We need the whole world as a friend.

*Herbert Hoover*

I am wealthy in my friends.

*William Shakespeare*

True friendship is a plant of slow growth.

*George Washington*

If I don't have friends, then I ain't got nothin'.

*Billie Holiday*

Friendship demands the ability to do without it.

*Ralph Waldo Emerson*

Friendship needs care.

*Richard M. Nixon*

Radiate friendship and it will be returned tenfold.

*Henry P. Davidson*

People are lonely because they build walls instead of bridges.

*Joseph Newton*

Friendship bridges the gap between what things are and what they could be.

*Roger Holmes*

Quarrel with a friend—and you are both wrong.

*Lao-tzu*

True friendship brings sunshine to the shade, and shade to the sunshine.

*Thomas Burke*

Friendship is a horizon—which expands whenever we approach it.

*E. R. Hazlip*

If you want to win a man to your cause, you must first convince him you are his friend.

*Abraham Lincoln*

I recreate in a friend my own world—or take to me his new one—and we two look at one mirror from different sides.

*Friedrich Emerson*

There is always something about your success that displeases even your best friends.

*Mark Twain*

Recipe for having friends: Be one.

*Elbert Hubbard*

Laughter is not a bad beginning for friendship, and it is the best ending for one.

*Oscar Wilde*

He who gives up a friendship for ambition burns a picture to obtain the ashes.

*Arabic proverb*

He is my friend, and he is me.

*Abraham Lincoln*

Love without friendship is like a shadow without the sun.

*Japanese proverb*

What is a friend? A single soul which dwells in two bodies.

*Aristotle*

Never trust a friend who deserts you in a pinch.

*Aesop*

The most I can do for my friend is simply to be his friend. I have no wealth to bestow on him. If he knows that I am happy in loving him, he will want no other reward. Is not friendship divine in this?

*Henry David Thoreau*

My friends are few, but altogether sufficient.

*Sir Winston Churchill*

Friendship? Yes, please.

*Charles Dickens*

An enemy should be hated only as much as one may be hated who could one day be a friend.

*Sophocles*

The antidote for fifty enemies is one friend.

*Aristotle*

It is better to have your friends learn of your faults than your enemies.

*Persius*

Imitating Christ is opening the door to friendship.

*Billy Graham*

Friendship has so much of sovereignty and of religion, too, that no prescription can be written against it.

*John Donne*

We have lost our sense of values: When your fence falls, you mend it; when your friendship fails, you run.

*Nathaniel Hawthorne*

One close friend is worth more than a thousand acquaintances.

*Anonymous*

Friendship is a pleasing game of interchanging praise

*Oliver Wendell Holmes, Jr*

When others are happy, be happy with them. If they are sad, share in their sorrow.

*Anonymous*

Friendship is a union of spirits.

*William Penn*

Friendship is constant in all other things, save in the office of affairs and love.

*William Shakespeare*

Life is to be fortified by many friendships. To love, and be loved, is the greatest happiness of existence.

*Sydney Smith*

You cannot be friends upon any other terms than upon the terms of equality.

*Woodrow Wilson*

A friend in need is a friend indeed.

*Anonymous*

The ornament of a house is the friends who frequent it.

*Ralph Waldo Emerson*

Friendship makes prosperity more shining and lessens adversity by dividing and sharing it

*Cicero*

A man cannot be said to succeed in this life who does not satisfy one friend

*Henry David Thoreau*

Be slow in choosing a friend, slower in changing.

*Benjamin Franklin*

A true friend unbosoms freely, advises justly, assists readily, adventures boldly, takes all patiently, defends courageously, and continues a friend unchangeably.

*William Penn*

A good friend can tell you what is the matter with you in a minute. He may not seem such a good friend after telling.

*Arthur Brisbane*

It is not good for a man to be alone.

*Genesis*

A friend in need is a friend to be avoided.

*Sunday Telegraph*

Reprove a friend in secret, but praise him before others.

*Leonardo Da Vinci*

Life is nothing without friendship.

*Cicero*

Friendship is a sheltering tree.

*Samuel Taylor Coleridge*

I desire so to conduct the affairs of this administration that if at the end, when I come to lay down the reins of power, I have lost every other friend on earth, I shall at least have one friend left, and that friend shall be down inside of me.

*Abraham Lincoln*

I have lost friends, some by death—others through sheer inability to cross the street.

*Virginia Woolf*

He who has a good friend needs no mirror.

*Joseph Addison*

A woman is, for man, the best of true friends, if man will let her be one.

*Olgivanna Wright*

The truth is friendship is to me every bit as sacred and eternal as marriage.

*Katherine Mansfield*

Every man needs one essential friend.

*Dr. William Glasser*

A friend is a present you give yourself.

*Robert Louis Stevenson*

One's friends are that part of the human race with which one can be human.

*George Santayana*

## Be My Friend

You told me you wanted to be my friend
but every time I try to tell you
what is on my heart
you interrupt and tell me
what you think
about what I haven't told you yet.
I am looking for a friend
who can listen sometimes.
Not always
but sometimes.

*Mary Dell Miles*

## IT'S ONLY NATURAL

The foundation for quality friendships lies in the belief, "When I meet the needs of other people, my needs will be met." Friendship, therefore, is an extension of the natural laws of life.

What you give—you get.
What you send out—comes back.
What you sow—you reap.

*Simply put, when you make a commitment to do everything in your power to help others fulfill the desires of their hearts, your desires will also be met. It's a natural law!*

## HOW TO MAKE FRIENDS

Dale Carnegie said, "You can make more friends in two months by becoming interested in other people than you can in two years by trying to get other people interested in you." To drive home his point, Carnegie tells how dogs have learned the fine art of making friends. When you get within ten feet of a friendly dog, he will begin to wag his tail, a visible sign he enjoys your presence. If you take time to pet him, he will become excited and lick and jump all over you to show how much he appreciates you. The dog became man's best friend by being genuinely interested in people.

*Friendship is the result of our efforts to be interested in what's going on in people's lives.*

### What Is a Friend?

A friend is someone who is concerned with
everything you do
A friend is someone to call upon during good
and bad times.
A friend is someone who understands
whatever you do.
A friend is someone who tells you the truth
about yourself.
A friend is someone who knows what you are
going through at all times.

A friend is someone who does not compete
with you.
A friend is someone who is genuinely happy
for you when things go well.
A friend is someone who tries to cheer you up
when things don't go well.
A friend is an extension of yourself without
which you are not complete.
Thank you for being my friend.

*Susan Polis Schultz*

## A TRUE FAN

Babe Ruth was one of the all-time greats in baseball. His powerful bat boomed ball after ball out of the park, and Babe's record of 714 home runs remained unbroken for years. Sports fans loved the Babe, and year after year he thrilled them with his talent on the diamond. As the Babe grew older, age took its toll, and finally the Yankees traded him to the Braves. Babe's life as a pro baseball player was winding down, and during one of his last games, Babe had a nightmare of a game. He struck out several times, made numerous errors, and in one inning he bobbled every ball hit to him, allowing five runs to score.

The fans viciously turned on him, screaming, "Hang it up!" "Go home, Babe!" "Boo! You're a has-been!" Some actually stood and shook their fists at him. Babe Ruth hung his head, fighting back tears as he made his way toward the dugout.

Just then a wonderful thing happened! A young boy jumped over the railing, and with tears streaming down his cheeks, he ran out to the great athlete. He flung his arms around the big Babe and held him tight. Babe smiled at his small fan, hugged him, and then scooped him up in his arms. Instantly, the crowd hushed, and in deafening silence everyone watched in awe as Babe Ruth and the young fan walked hand in hand to the dugout.

## A MEMORABLE FRIENDSHIP

Gayle Sayers was one of the best running backs the Chicago Bears ever had. He was black. In 1967, Sayers' sidekick in the backfield was another great running back by the name of Brian Piccolo. Piccolo was white. Blacks and whites often played on the same professional teams, but these two athletes were different. They were roommates on the road, which was a first for race relations in professional football. Sayers had never had a close relationship with any white man before, except with George Halas, the head coach of the Bears. And Piccolo admitted that he had never really known a black person during his lifetime.

These two athletes became friends immediately and grew exceptionally close. Their relationship deepened into one of the most memorable friendships in the history of sports. As the movie *Brian's Song* poignantly depicts, the men truly loved each other. During the 1969 season, Brian Piccolo was diagnosed as having cancer. Although he fought to play out the season, Piccolo was in the hospital more than he was on the playing field. It was during this time when Piccolo was battling his terminal illness and fighting the daily depths of depression, that these two athletes shared a very special relationship. Frequently, Sayers flew to be at the bedside of his friend, as the cancer gripped Piccolo's weakened body tighter and tighter. The smell of death became increasingly obvious, but both men, winners through and through, refused to surrender.

Sayers and Piccolo, and their wives, had made plans to sit together at the annual Professional Football Writers' Banquet in New York, where Gayle Sayers was to receive the coveted George S. Halas award as "the most courageous player in professional football." By the time of the banquet, Piccolo was too sick to attend.

At the banquet, Sayers stood to receive his award, and amid the resounding applause, unrestrained tears began to flow throughout the room. Sayers struggled to speak; choking through his tears, he said, "You flatter me by giving me this award, but I tell you here and now that I accept this award not for me, but for Brian Piccolo. However, Brian cannot be here tonight. He is too ill. But Brian is a man who has more courage than any of us here tonight. I love Brian Piccolo, and I'd like you to love him, too. When you hit your knees tonight, please ask God to love him, too."

Shortly after that memorable night, Brian Piccolo died. His memory will forever be etched in the heart of Gayle Sayers. Piccolo and Sayers had cultivated more than a superficial, tough-guy relationship. Although rugged and competitive men to the core, a true and caring love had developed between these two strong athletes.

*Anonymous*

## Worthy of My Friends

It is my joy in life to find
At every turning of the road

The strong arm of a comrade kind
To help me onward with my load.

And since I have no gold to give,
And love alone must make amends,
My only prayer is, while I live—
God make me worthy of my friends.

*Frank Dempster Sherman*

# Goals and Dreams

*What lies behind us and
what lies before us are
small matters compared
to what lies within us.*

RALPH WALDO EMERSON

23

In order for a goal to be effective, it must effect change.

*Anonymous*

Goals are not only absolutely necessary to motivate us. They are essential to really keep us alive.

*Robert Schuller*

If you're not sure where you are going, you're liable to end up someplace else

*Robert F. Mager*

Many people have the right aims in life. They just never get around to pulling the trigger.

*Sunshine Magazine*

For of sad words of tongue or pen, the saddest of these; it might have been.

*John Greenleaf Whittier*

Realistic goals: Beyond your grasp—but within your reach.

*Anonymous*

Goals determine your thoughts—thoughts determine your life.

*Anonymous*

Winding river concept: Move from bend to bend and enjoy each step of the way. Face the problems, but keep moving forward.

*Anonymous*

Some men see things as they are and say "Why?" I dream things that never were and say "Why not?"

*George Bernard Shaw*

Hitch your wagon to a star.

*Ralph Waldo Emerson*

Not failure, but low aim, is a crime.

*James Russell Lowell*

Far away there in the sunshine are my highest aspirations. I may not reach them, but I can look up and see their beauty, believe in them, and try to follow where they lead.

*Louisa May Alcott*

It may be those who do most, dream most.

*Stephen Leacock*

Efforts and courage are not enough without purpose and direction.

*John F. Kennedy*

Hold fast to your dreams, for if dreams die, then life is like a broken winged bird that cannot fly.

*Langston Hughes*

Ever notice how your goal to lose weight always runs into a snack?

*Anonymous*

We grow by dreams. All big men are dreamers. Some of us let dreams die, but others nourish and protect them, nurse them through bad days . . . to the sunshine and light which always come.

*Woodrow Wilson*

Goals serve as a stimulus to life. They tend to tap the deeper resources and draw out of life its best. Where there are no goals, neither will there be significant accomplishments. There will only be existence.

*Anonymous*

The task ahead of us is never as great as the power behind us.

*Ralph Waldo Emerson*


Vision is the art of seeing the invisible.

*Jonathan Swift*


You must know for which harbor you are headed if you are to catch the right wind to take you there.

*Seneca*


The most pathetic person in the world is someone who has sight but has no vision.

*Helen Keller*


## PERSISTENCE PAYS OFF

Once upon a time, there was a Louisville University quarterback, who had a dream, an obsession. His dream was to play pro football. However, upon graduation, this young quarterback was not drafted by the pros.

He did not give up. He wrote to several teams and finally got a tryout with the Steelers. He gave it his best shot but did not make even the third string.

"You got a raw deal." "It wasn't meant to be." "I guess it's time to hang it up," his friends told him. But the young athlete did not hang it up. Continuing to knock on doors and write letters, he finally received another invitation. Again, he did not make the team.

Most people would have given up long before this, but not this determined young man. He was fanatically committed to his personal dream. From his early days of playing sandlot football, through his success in high school and college football, he had hung tight to his goal.

Patiently and persistently, he continued to pursue tryouts with pro teams. He finally went to Baltimore and made the team. Training and working long hours on fitness and skill, he worked his way from third string to becoming known as the greatest quarterback in the NFL.

Who was this persistent goal-seeker? You guessed it—the dreamer was Johnny Unitas!

## LIFE'S JAMS

It's so frustrating to get caught in slow-moving traffic, especially when you want to get somewhere in a hurry. Even worse is the helpless feeling of a traffic jam. Being hemmed in between a solid line of cars in parallel lines, and a huge semi hovering over your front bumper, with another snuggled against the trunk is annoying to say the least.

Some people exist in a world not unlike a traffic jam. They get hemmed in by life's circumstances. The absence of clear-cut direction and ability to move thwarts their motivation. Goal-directed people work according to their plans and realize that "traffic jams" are only momentary. Sustaining movement requires something specific to move toward.

## NO WALL TOO BIG

Goal-setting is not new to this generation. I am fascinated by the biblical documentation of Nehemiah's quest to rebuild the wall of Jerusalem. Nehemiah believed in his heart that he had been called to quiet the moans and desperation of the people of Israel. The once-glorious city of David was surrounded by ruins of the wall for some 160 years since its destruction by the Babylonians. Enter Nehemiah, with little material, but with a specific plan for rebuilding. In just fifty-two days, Nehemiah and his recruits erected a perfect wall around the city, where only rubble lay before. This biblical account is an inspiration to those who believe their goals are impossible.

Nehemiah saw the wall in his mind, shared his dream with those who could help, and then activated his plan. That's what realistic goal-setting is all about.

## SPEAKING FROM EXPERIENCE

Paul Meyer of Success Motivation Institute says, "What you ardently desire, sincerely believe in, vividly imagine, enthusiastically act on, must inevitably come to pass."

Decide what you want, see it in your mind, speak positively about it to yourself, then remember the conviction of Abraham Lincoln: "Things may come to those who wait . . . but only the things left over from those who hustle."

Act! That's where the fun is.

When Sir Francis Chichester sailed around the world alone in a fifty-six-foot yawl, he did so at an age when most people are seriously considering retirement. When asked about the attainment of his goal, Sir Francis replied, "The thrill is in the journey, the hardship, not in tying up at the dock."

*Enjoy the adventure of pursuing what you ardently desire in life.*

## INVENTIVE SUCCESS

Thomas Alva Edison's life was filled with purpose. When he spoke about his success, he said, "The most important factors of invention can be described in a few words. (1) They must consist of definite knowledge as to what one wishes to achieve. (2) One must fix his mind on that purpose with persistence and begin searching for that which he seeks, making use of all of the accumulated knowledge of the subject which he has or can acquire from others. (3) He must keep on searching, no matter how many times he may meet with disappointment. (4) He must refuse to be influenced by the fact that somebody else may have tried the same idea without success. (5) He must keep himself sold on the idea that the solution of his problem exists somewhere and that he will find it."

## SHORT-TERM GOALS

It has been a bad day for Charlie Brown. He has struck out for the third straight time. In disgust, he says, "Rats!" Back in the dugout, he buries his face in his hands and laments to Lucy, "I'll never be a big-league ballplayer. All my life, I've dreamed of playing in the big leagues, but I just know I'll never make it."

Lucy responds, "You're thinking way too far ahead, Charlie Brown. What you need are more immediate goals."

"Immediate goals?" asks Charlie.

"Yes," says Lucy. "Start right now with this next inning. When you go out to pitch, see if you can walk out to the mound without falling down."

## LOCKING OUT SUCCESS

An article appeared in a major U.S. newspaper, reporting the plight of a thief who failed to work out all the details for his getaway. The fumbling thief approached an occupied car, threw open the door, and proceeded in his attempts at robbing the driver. When the victim resisted, the thief fled. He ran to the other end of the parking lot where his car was located. But when the robber tried to get into his car, a major problem surfaced. He had locked his keys in the car. A few minutes later the man was captured.

*Successful goal-setters plan their work and work their plan.*

## DECIDE WHAT YOU WANT

Henry J. Kaiser summarized his philosophy of success this way: "Decide what you want most of all out of life; then write down your goals and plan to reach them."

That seems simple enough. Yet many people are like the elderly woman standing on a street corner, scared to cross because there was no traffic signal to control the flow of vehicles. A man joined her on the street corner and asked if he could walk across with her. "Oh, yes," she replied, grabbing his strong arm for direction and support. They proceeded across the street in a haphazard fashion. Cars were honking, people screaming, and the screech of tires filled their ears. Finally reaching the other side, the elderly lady exclaimed in anger, "You almost got us killed. You walk as if you can't see the nose on your face."

"I can't," the man replied. "I'm blind. That's why I asked if I could walk with you."

*People without goals are blindly pursuing life. They have no clear direction except to dodge life's obstacles.*

## AN EXEMPLARY GOAL-SETTER

In 1972, *Life* magazine published a story depicting the adventures of John Goddard. His story was one of undying determination filled with personal purpose. When he was fifteen, he heard his grandmother say, "If only I had done this when I was young." Determined not to spend his life playing the "if only" game, John Goddard sat down and decided what he wanted to do with his life. When he finished writing, 127 goals existed. John Goddard decided there were ten rivers he wanted to explore, along with seventeen mountains he wanted to climb. He decided to become an Eagle Scout, visit every country in the world, learn to fly an airplane, and dive in a submarine. He wanted to retrace the travels of Marco Polo and ride a horse in the Rose Bowl parade. This was just the beginning. John Goddard committed himself to reading the Bible from cover to cover, reading the entire works of Shakespeare, Plato, Dickens, Aristotle, Socrates, and several other classic authors. He planned to read the entire

*Encyclopedia Britannica* and yet have time to learn to play the flute and violin. Marriage, children (he had five), and a stint with church missions were also in his plans, along with a desire for a career in medicine.

In 1972, John Goddard, at forty-seven, had accomplished 103 of his 127 goals. Goddard exemplifies the excitement of determining a purpose in life, setting goals, and pursuing them with determination.

## TAKE AIM

The famous cartoon character Charlie Brown just doesn't understand the value of established goals and clear aim. One day he was in his backyard, involved in target practice with his bow and arrows. Charlie would pull the string back as far as his muscles would allow and let the arrow fly into the fence. Then he would run over to the fence and draw a target around the arrow. Several arrows and targets later, Lucy showed up. "That's no way to have target practice!" Lucy screamed at Charlie Brown. "You are supposed to draw the target and then shoot at it," she said. Charlie's response is a classic. "I know that, Lucy, but if you do it my way, you never miss!"

*Sadly, many people approach life like Charlie Brown. They never set goals for fear they'll miss. A clear aim at established goals provides motivation for continuing performance. In life, decision making and applied effort become easier after you clarify where you are going.*

*Otherwise, we are like the pilot who comes over the intercom and announces to his passengers, "Ladies and gentlemen, I have some good news and some bad news. The bad news is we have lost one engine and our direction finder. The good news is we have a tail wind, and wherever we are going, we are getting there at the rate of two-hundred miles per hour."*

### Goals

I've dreamed many dreams that never came true,
I've seen them vanish at dawn;
But I've realized enough of my dreams, thank God,
To make me want to dream on.
I've prayed many prayers when no answer came,
I've waited patient and long;
But answers have come to enough of my prayers
To make me keep praying on.
I've trusted many a friend who failed

And left me to weep alone;
But I've found enough of my friends true-blue
To make me keep trusting on.
I've sown many seeds that fell by the way
For the birds to feed upon;
But I've held enough golden sheaves in my hand,
To make me keep sowing on.
I've drained the cup of disappointment and pain,
I've gone many days without song,
But I've sipped enough nectar from the rose of life
To make me want to live on.

*Anonymous*

## BELIEVE THE IMPOSSIBLE

Every great achievement was once impossible until someone set a goal to make it a reality.

Lewis Carroll's famous masterpiece *Through the Looking Glass* contains a story that exemplifies the need to dream the impossible dream. There is a conversation between Alice and the queen, which goes like this:

"I can't believe that!" said Alice.

"Can't you?" the queen said in a pitying tone. "Try again, draw a long breath, and shut your eyes."

Alice laughed. "There's no use trying," she said. "One can't believe impossible things."

"I daresay you haven't had much practice," said the queen. "When I was your age, I always did it for half an hour a day. Why, sometimes I've believed as many as six impossible things before breakfast."

*When we dare to dream, many marvels can be accomplished. The trouble is, most people never start dreaming their impossible dream.*

## VISUALIZE YOUR DREAM

When asked how he accounted for his amazing inventive genius, Thomas Alva Edison replied, "It is because I never think in words; I think in pictures." Edison was a master at picturing in his mind the objects he desired to invent.

Phenomenal achievements have been accomplished by people who were able to visualize what they wanted. Edison was told no light could exist in a vacuum, but he saw it and believed it could be done. The experts scoffed at Louis Pasteur's theories of germ life. William Harvey's far-out notion that blood flowed through the body was rejected, and Samuel Langley's vision for a flying machine was ridiculed.

However, each of these men was able to visualize his dream into reality.

Conrad Hilton said, "Man, with God's help and personal dedication, is capable of anything he can dream."

*Visualize your dream!*

## NEVER LOSE SIGHT OF YOUR GOALS

The California coast was blanketed in fog the Fourth of July morning in 1952. Twenty-one miles to the west, on Catalina Island, Florence Chadwick, a thirty-four-year-old long-distance swimmer, waded into the water and began swimming toward California. She had already conquered the English Channel, swimming both directions. Now she was determined to be the first woman to swim the Catalina Channel.

Millions of people were watching on national television. As the hours ticked off, Chadwick fought bone-chilling cold, dense fog, and sharks. Several times, sharks had to be driven away with rifles. Fatigue never set in, but the icy waters numbed Chadwick to the point of desperation. Straining to make out the shore through her swimmer's goggles, she could see only dense fog. She knew she could not go on. Although not a quitter, Chadwick shouted to her trainer and her mother in the boat and asked to be taken out of the water. They urged her not to give up, but when she looked toward the California coast, all she could see was thick fog.

So, after fifteen hours and fifty-five minutes of fighting the elements, she was hauled out of the water into the boat. Frozen to the bone and her spirit defeated, Chadwick was devastated when she discovered she was only a half mile from the California coast! She felt the shock of failure. The fog had done it. "Look, I'm not excusing myself," she told a reporter, "but if I could have seen land, I know I could have made it." She had been licked, not by fatigue or even by the cold. The fog alone had defeated her because it had obscured her goal. It had blinded her reason, her eyes, and most of all, her heart.

Two months, later, Chadwick swam that same channel, and again fog clouded her view, but this time she swam with her faith intact —somewhere behind that fog was land. This time she succeeded. Not only was she the first woman to swim the Catalina Channel, but she beat the men's record by two hours.

# Growth

*It may be all right to be content with what you have; never with what you are.*

**B. C. FORBES**

## 24

People are always blaming their circumstances for what they are. I don't believe in circumstances. The people who get on in this world are the people who get up and look for the circumstances they want and if they can't find them—make them!

*George Bernard Shaw*

That tree is very old, but I never saw prettier blossoms on it than it now bears. That tree grows new wood each year. Like that apple tree, I try to grow a little new wood each year.

*Henry Wadsworth Longfellow*

Consider how hard it is to change yourself and you'll understand what little chance you have of trying to change others.

*Jacob Braude*

It might be just as offensive to be around a man who never changed his mind as one who never changed his clothes.

*Country Parson*

Character is determined by what you accomplish when the excitement is gone.

*Anonymous*

Just for today I will exercise my soul in three ways: I will do somebody a good turn and not get found out. I will do at least two things I don't want to do.

*William James*

I cannot teach anybody anything, I can only make them think."

*Socrates*

Life is like riding a bicycle  You don't fall off unless you stop pedaling.

*Anonymous*

The largest room in the world is the room for improvement.

*Anonymous*

My life is like one long obstacle course with me being the chief obstacle

*Jack Paar*

A rose only becomes beautiful and blesses others when it opens up and blooms. Its greatest tragedy is to stay in a tight-closed bud, never fulfilling its potential.

*Anonymous*

It's not where you are today that counts  It's where you are headed

*Arthur F. Lenehan*

You must learn day by day, year by year, to broaden your horizons. The more things you love, the more you are interested in, the more you enjoy, the more you are indignant about—the more you have left when anything happens.

*Ethel Barrymore*

How often events, by chance and unexpectedly, come to pass, which you had not dared even to hope for.

*Terence*

Education is the ability to listen to almost anything without losing your temper or your self-confidence.

*Robert Frost*

Discovery consists of looking at the same thing as everyone else and thinking something different.

*Albert Szent-Gyorgyi*

You grow up the day you have your first real laugh—at yourself.

*Ethel Barrymore*


The best of all things is to learn. Money can be lost or stolen, health and strength may fail, but what you have committed to your mind is yours forever.

*Louis L'Amour*


O God, give us serenity to accept what cannot be changed, and courage to change what should be changed, and wisdom to distinguish the one from the other.

*Dr Reinhold Niebuhr*


Man is not a being who stands still, he is a being in the process of becoming. The more he enables himself to become, the more he fulfills his true mission.

*Rudolph Steiner*


Man is the only animal that laughs and weeps; for he is the only animal that is struck with the difference between what things are, and what they ought to be.

*William Hazlitt*


Most people want to improve themselves, but not too many are willing to work at it.

*Anonymous*

The nearest way to glory is to strive to be what you wish to be thought to be.

*Socrates*

Of all our human resources, the most precious is the desire to improve.

*Anonymous*

To be conscious that you are ignorant is a great step to knowledge.

*Benjamin Disraeli*

When you're through changing, you're through.

*Bruce Barton*

The man who does not read good books has no advantage over the man who can't read them.

*Mark Twain*

The intelligent man is always open to new ideas. In fact, he looks for them.

*Proverbs 18:15*

When I am wrong, dear Lord, make me easy to change, and when I am right, make me easy to live with.

*Peter Marshall*

"If you teach a man anything, he will never learn." Shaw was right. Learning is an active process. We learn by doing.

*George Bernard Shaw*

Our achievements of today are but the sum total of our thoughts of yesterday. You are today where the thoughts of yesterday have brought you and you will be tomorrow where the thoughts of today take you.

*Blaise Pascal*

It is not possible to step twice into the same river.

*Greek philosopher*

Life is now in session. Are you present?

*B. Copeland*

You will never stub your toe standing still. The faster you go, the more chance there is of stubbing your toe, but the more chance you have of getting somewhere.

*Charles F. Kettering*

To improve is to change. To be perfect is to have changed a lot.

*Sir Winston Churchill*

The important thing is this: to be able to give up in any given moment all that we are for what we can become.

*DeSeaux*

Potential: It's all in there. You've just got to work it out.

*Glenn Van Ekeren*

Life is a lively process of becoming.

*General Douglas MacArthur*

Don't be afraid to go out on a limb. That's where the fruit is.

*Arthur F. Lenehan*

I will go anywhere, as long as it is forward.

*David Livingstone*

**I Don't Ever Want To Be**

I don't ever want to be
what I want to be.
Because there's always something out there yet for me.
Oh, I enjoy living in the here and now.
But

I never want to feel I've learned the best way how.
There's always one hill higher
with a better view.
Something waiting to be learned
I never knew.
So till my days are over,
never fully fill my cup.
Let me go on growing
up.

*Anonymous*

## HOW TO ACQUIRE KNOWLEDGE

A young, devoted follower of Socrates pleaded with him to share the secret of acquired knowledge. Socrates willingly consented and led the young man to a river. "This is how," Socrates stated as he pushed the young man into the river, and then jumping in himself, he held the young man's head underwater. The young man struggled frantically to free himself, but Socrates held him tight and kept his head submerged.

Finally, after the young man scratched, clawed, and fought with every ounce of his being, he was able to break loose and emerge from the water. Socrates then asked him, "When you thought you were drowning, what one thing did you want most of all?"

Still gasping for breath, the young man exclaimed, "I wanted air!" Socrates smiled and then wisely commented, "When you want knowledge as much as you wanted air, then you will get it!"

## CAUGHT IN THE DOLDRUMS

In the days when ocean vessels were driven by wind and sail, seamen feared encountering doldrums. Doldrums are a part of the ocean near the equator, abounding in calls, squalls, and light, baffling winds. The weather is hot, and sailors became restless and uninspired. Caught in the doldrums, sailing vessels would lie helpless, waiting for the wind to blow.

*People get caught in the doldrums every day. They are waiting for winds to come and force them into action. In the meantime, they become dispirited and uninspired. Unlike the old sea vessels, people need not wait for prevailing winds. Change and growth will come when we take a conscious step forward out of the doldrums and into activity.*

## WHAT DO YOU SEE?

See yourself as you want to be and you will pave the way for becoming all you can be.

Michelangelo salvaged a piece of marble that had been discarded by other sculptors because it was too long and narrow. "Of what value is that strange piece of marble?" people asked. "What will you ever be able to produce from it?"

"I see David," Michelangelo responded. Then he put his imagination to work, chiseling and carving. When he was finished, there stood David.

The person you see yourself becoming is the person you will ultimately be.

## BECOME YOUR BEST

The poet Robert Browning said, "My business is not to remake myself, but to make the absolute best of what God made."

Art Linkletter has an excellent philosophy for making your best better:

Do a little more than you're paid to;
Give a little more than you have to;
Try a little harder than you want to;
Aim a little higher than you think possible;
And give a lot of thanks to God for health, family, and friends.

## FISH FOR YOURSELF

Some years ago in the West Coast town of Monterey, a crisis arose in the world of pelicans. Monterey had become a paradise for pelicans, because after cleaning their fish, the California fishermen would throw the entrails to the pelicans. The birds became content, fat, and lazy. They had become dependent on the cast-off fish remains from the fishermen. Eventually, new ways were discovered to use the entrails commercially. The poor pelicans were suddenly out of free meals.

The pelicans made no effort to fish for themselves. They would not struggle for food; they just waited around and became thin and weak. Many starved to death. They had forgotten how to fish for themselves.

Some people become like those pelicans. Growth requires that we be responsible and that we be independent. We are not children who are tended by loving parents forever, but mature adults who are in charge of ourselves.

## IT'S IN YOUR HANDS, SON

High on a hilltop overlooking the beautiful city of Venice, Italy, there lived a wise old man whom people called a genius. Legend had it that he could answer any question posed him.

Two local boys decided they could fool the old man. Figuring they had a plan that was perfectly foolproof, the boys caught a small bird and headed for the hilltop. As they approached the wise old man, one of the boys held the little bird in his hands.

"Wise old man," he said. "Could you tell me if this bird in my hands is dead or alive?"

The old man sized up the two boys, and without hesitation, he answered, "Son, if I tell you that the bird is alive, you will close your hands and crush the bird to death. If I say the bird is dead, you will open your hands and he will fly away. You see, son, in your hands you hold the power of life and death."

The boys looked at one another in total amazement. This old man truly is very wise, they thought. They had not fooled him for one minute. The old man then stroked his long white beard and smiled gently. "This I say to both of you without qualification," he explained with a sincere, caring voice. "In your hands you hold the seeds of failure—or the potential for success. Your hands are very capable, but they must be used for the right things. They must be used to reap rewards that you are capable of attaining."

As the boys descended from the wise old man's hill, a new attitude overtook them, and they eagerly freed their captive bird. As they both watched the bird flap his wings and fly to freedom, the boys realized how very precious the old man's advice really was.

## IS THERE A BETTER WAY?

Young Robert had wonderful, loving grandparents. He didn't always understand them, but he loved and respected them. One lazy summer day, Robert and his grandfather went fishing at a nearby lake. While sitting on the dock, Robert was fascinated by watching his grandfather fish. The old man caught many fish, but he would always throw away the larger fish and keep the smaller ones. Robert could not understand that.

He had always thought the object of fishing was to catch big fish. Finally, he could stand it no longer and asked his grandfather why he was throwing away the big fish and keeping the small ones. The old man smiled and answered, "Well, Bobby, our frying pan is only seven inches wide. The big fish won't fit!"

When Robert returned home with his string of fish, he laughed as he told his mother about Grandpa throwing the big fish away. "That's Grandpa for you," his mother chuckled as she began to clean the fish for the freezer. "I'll just freeze these fish for later, Bobby. We're having ham for dinner tonight."

Robert noticed that his mother had cut off both ends of the ham, a strange habit his mother had done for years. When Robert questioned her about it, she answered unhesitently, "That's the way my mother did it." Not totally satisfied with his mother's reasoning, Robert quizzed his grandmother during his next visit there.

"Why do you cut off the ends of a ham before you bake it, Grandma?" he asked. "I'm just curious."

She looked at him suspiciously and replied in a matter-of-fact tone, "Because my baking dish is too small!"

Robert only smiled. Both of his grandparents seemed to have very valid reasons for what they had done for years—never questioning, "Is there a better way?"

## HOW WRONG YOU WERE, MR. WRIGHT

In 1870, a shortsighted bishop expressed to the president of a small denominational college his firm biblical conviction that nothing new could be invented. The educator responded in disagreement and believed there was much yet to be discovered.

"Why, I believe it may even be possible for men in the future to fly through the air like birds," the college president said.

The bishop was taken aback. "Flying is reserved for the angels," he insisted. "I beg you not to mention that again lest you be guilty of blasphemy!"

That mistaken bishop was none other than Milton Wright, the father of Orville and Wilbur. Only thirty-three years later, his two sons made their first flight in a heavier-than-air machine, which was the forerunner of the airplane. How wrong you were, Mr. Wright!

## GROWTH BRINGS CHANGE

Little Jessica is an excellent example of how growth brings change. When Jessica was asked by her Sunday school teacher, "Who made you?"

she replied, "Well, God made a part of me."

"What do you mean, God made a part of you?" asked the surprised teacher.

"Well, God made me real little, and I just growed the rest myself."

*Like Jessica, we all grow the rest ourselves. We have a number of opportunities in our hands. Life is like a game of cards. The players must accept the cards dealt to them, but once those cards are in their hands, they alone decide how to play them to win the game. We must decide whether to take a risk and act on them. Nothing in life provides more opportunity for growth than new experiences, and our lives have the power to touch other lives in either positive ways or negative ways.*

## HOW HIGH CAN YOU JUMP?

Flea trainers have observed a predictable and strange habit of fleas while training them. Fleas are trained by putting them in a cardboard box with a top on it. The fleas will jump up and hit the top of the cardboard box over and over and over again. As you watch them jump and hit the lid, something very interesting becomes obvious. The fleas continue to jump, but they are no longer jumping high enough to hit the top. Apparently, Excedrin headache 1738 forces them to limit the height of their jump.

When you take off the lid, the fleas continue to jump, but they will not jump out of the box. They won't jump out because they can't jump out. Why? The reason is simple. They have conditioned themselves to jump just so high. Once they have conditioned themselves to jump just so high, that's all they can do!

*Many times, people do the same thing. They restrict themselves and never reach their potential. Just like the fleas, they fail to jump higher, thinking they are doing all they can do.*

## GET OUT OF THAT RUT

We should all follow the advice of Mark Twain, who said, "Take your mind out every now and then and dance on it. It is getting all caked up." It was his way of saying, "Get out of that rut." Too many times, we settle into a set way of thinking and accept limitations that need not be placed on us.

*It is too bad that most people are more comfortable with old problems than with new solutions. The Duke of Cambridge once said, "Any change, at any time, for any reason is to be deplored." How sad! People who believe that nothing should ever be done for the first time never see anything done.*

## DON'T BE AFRAID TO BECOME YOU

Elie Wiesel, author of *Souls on Fire,* makes a powerful statement that may be just the tonic for you. He reflects that when we die and go to meet our Maker, we're not going to be asked why we didn't become a Messiah or didn't find a cure for cancer. Instead, we will be asked, "Why didn't you become you?"

*"Becoming you" includes both the joy and the privilege of learning to recognize the marvelous differences that exist in those around you. "Becoming you" also frees you to reach your potential, using the talents God has given you.*

## DON'T FORGET TO LOOK UP

A small boy, walking along one bright summer day, spotted a copper penny glistening at his feet. He picked it up and clutched it protectively. He felt a glow of pride and excitement. It was his, and it cost him nothing!

From that day on, wherever he went, he walked with his head down, eyes surveying the ground for more treasure. During his lifetime, he found 302 pennies, 24 nickels, 41 dimes, 8 quarters, 3 half dollars, and one worn out paper dollar—a total of $12.82.

The money had cost him nothing—except that he missed the breathless beauty of 35,127 sunsets, the colorful splendor of 327 rainbows, the brilliance of hundreds of maples nipped by the autumn frost, babies growing, white clouds floating across the crystal blue sky, birds flying, animals running, sun shining, and the smiles of passing people.

*Too many people go through life so trapped in the same routine trivia that the magnificent adventure of living passes them by.*

## NATURE'S WAY

Nature has a beautiful way of illustrating the growth process. Take the Chinese bamboo tree, for instance. The seed is planted, watered, and fertilized, and for the first four years, there is no visible growth. However, during the fifth year, the Chinese bamboo grows ninety feet in six weeks. Now, did the tree really take five years to begin growing? Not at all. Although growth was not visible, the root system experienced tremendous development during those first four years, thereby making it possible for the Chinese bamboo to stand sturdy and secure.

*Personal growth may not suddenly manifest itself. That's just nature's way of preparing us for what's to come.*

## WELL ESTABLISHED

"I may not be making much progress in my life," proclaimed a man one day, "but I certainly am well established."

Benjamin Franklin was never satisfied with being well established. As ambassador to France, he was undoubtedly the most sought-after man in Paris. However, he had not always enjoyed such popularity. In fact, in his autobiography, Franklin describes himself as a blundering young man —uncouth and unattractive.

So what happened?

An old Quaker friend pulled young Franklin aside in a Philadelphia meeting and admonished him. "Ben," he said, "you are impossible. You have no tact, and your opinions demean others who don't agree with you. In fact, your friends find they enjoy themselves better when you're not around."

Many people would respond to such a smarting rebuke with anger or revenge. Not Ben Franklin. He accepted the painful criticism and set out to change. And change he did. Franklin became one of the most popular, respected, and sought-after men in history.

*Growth, not being well established, makes life fascinating and full of opportunity.*

## DEAD MEN DO BLEED

Sometimes it is impossible to convince people to change and grow.

Have you heard, for example, about the man who was convinced he was dead?

He visited his doctor several times. The doctor tried to change the man's mind but with no success. Finally, the doctor lost his patience. "If I can prove you're alive," the doctor said vehemently, "will you believe me?"

"Of course," replied the man.

"Well," said the doctor, "dead men don't bleed, right?"

"Right."

"Then give me your hand," said the doctor.

The man extended his hand, and the doctor jabbed it quickly with a needle until blood spurted out.

"There!" he said. "See the blood."

The man looked dumbfounded. "Gosh," he said, "dead men do bleed."

## ON BECOMING REAL

The Skin Horse had lived his lifetime in the nursery. He was older and more mature than the other toys. He was so old that his furry coat had bald spots, the seams showed underneath, and most of his tail was missing. He was wise and knew that mechanical toys would soon wear out and never grow into anything else. The nursery is a magical and wonderful place, and only those playthings that are old and wise and experienced like the Skin Horse understand all about it.

"What is real?" asked the rabbit one day.

"Real isn't how you are made or how you look," said the Skin Horse. "It's something that happens to you. When a child loves you for a long, long time, not just to play with, but really loves you, then you become real."

"How does it feel?" asked the rabbit.

"Sometimes it hurts," said the Skin Horse, for he was always truthful. "However, when you are real, you don't mind being hurt."

"I want to become real today," said the rabbit excitedly.

"It doesn't happen that quickly," said the Skin Horse. "It takes a long time. That's why it doesn't often happen to people who break easily, or have sharp edges, or need too much tender loving care. Generally, by the time you are real, most of your hair has been loved off, and your eyes droop, and your joints get loose. But do you know what? These things don't matter at all, because once you are real, you can't be ugly, except to people who don't understand."

*Margery Williams*

## DON'T LOSE YOUR LIFE

A boy was rowing a wise old-timer across a wide river. The old-timer picked a floating leaf from the water, studied it for a moment, and then handed it to the boy. "Son, do you know anything about biology?" he asked. "No, I don't," the boy replied. The wise old man said, "Son, if you don't learn biology, you will miss out on 25 percent of the beauty in life."

As they rowed on, the old-timer observed a rock formation on a nearby bank. He pointed it out to the boy and asked, "Son, do you know anything about geology?" The boy sheepishly replied, "No, I don't, sir." The old-timer said, "Son, you're missing 50 percent of life's enjoyment."

Soon twilight was approaching, and the old-timer gazed raptly at the Little Dipper that had begun to twinkle. He asked the boy, "Son, do you know anything about astronomy?" The boy, head bowed, responded sheepishly, "No, I don't, sir." The old-timer scolded, "Son, you're missing 75 percent of your life. How can you live such a shallow life?"

Just then, the boy heard a loud roar. Suddenly, their small canoe was thrown about by a swift current. The roaring water grew louder until finally their little canoe began to crumble. Quickly, the boy turned to the old-timer and shouted, "Sir, do you know how to swim?"

The old-timer grasped the sides of the rocking boat and screamed, "No, I don't!"

The boy dove into the water and as he began to swim to safety, he shouted back, "Sorry, you just lost your life."

*Moral of the story? Make sure what you learn does more than reveal your intellectual abilities. First, are you studying what you need to survive so that you can pursue your potential?*

## IT'S YOUR CHOICE

The Japanese bonsai tree is a beautiful and perfectly formed plant specimen. Its stature is small and remains that way no matter how old the tree gets. In fact, the bonsai only grows fifteen to eighteen inches tall.

When the bonsai peeks its head above the ground, the young sapling is pulled from the soil. The Japanese then tie off its taproot and some of the feeder roots; thus the growth of the bonsai is deliberately stunted. The result is a miniature tree. It's beautiful but small.

There is another tree that fascinates me  It grows on the other side of the continent. California possesses a forest of giant sequoias. In fact, one of these giants, the General Sherman, stands 272 feet high and measures 79 feet in circumference. This giant tree is so large that if someone were to cut it down, there would be enough lumber in that one tree to build thirty-five five-room homes. That is phenomenal!

A major difference exists between the growing patterns of the sequoia and the bonsai. The bonsai's growth is purposely stunted, while the sequoia was started as a small seed in the rich California soil. It was nourished by the minerals, rain, and pleasant sunshine. This little seed became a giant.

Neither the bonsai nor the General Sherman had a choice in determining how large it would become. You and I do.

## OUT OF THE POTHOLES

While shuffling down the road one day, a turtle fell into a large pothole in the center of a country road. Spinning his little legs to free himself proved futile, to say the least. Soon a rabbit friend came hopping by and offered his assistance. But no matter what they tried, the turtle remained stuck in the muddy hole. "It's no use," the turtle said. "Nothing will ever free me." Other friends passed his way, but the turtle refused their help, for he believed his destiny included death in the muddy mire. Therefore, he withdrew his head inside the safeness of his shell.

"It's hopeless," he lamented, but suddenly he heard a loud noise. Peeking from his internal home, the turtle spotted a tractor approaching the pothole where he sat. Without another thought, the four-legged creature jumped from the pothole to safety.

Later that day, his animal friends crossed his path. "How did you get free?" they asked. "We thought you couldn't get out."

"Oh, I couldn't," responded the turtle, "but then I saw a farmer on his tractor approaching, and I had to get out."

*According to psychologist Rollo May, we choose not to change—or get out of life's potholes—until we hurt intensely enough. Maybe there is a lesson to be learned from this fictional account. Why, even a turtle must stick its neck out if he wants to get anywhere. Don't avoid life's potholes, but do make the necessary changes to get out of them.*

# Happiness

*Most people are about as happy as they make up their mind to be.*

ABRAHAM LINCOLN

25

Much happiness is overlooked simply because it doesn't cost anything.

*Prism*

We would be happier with what we have if we weren't so unhappy about what we don't have.

*Frank A. Clark*

Action may not always bring happiness, but there is no happiness without action.

*Benjamin Disraeli*

Recipe for happiness: Take equal parts of faith and courage, mix well with a sense of humor, sprinkle with a few tears, and add a helping of kindness for others. Bake in a good-natured oven, and dust with laughter. Scrape away any self-indulgence that is apparent, and serve with generous helpings.

*Ohio State Grange Monthly*

Happiness is in the here and now not in the *somedays*. Not, I'll be happy when the camper is paid off, Mary's braces come off, the kids have made it through college, my husband gets that promotion, or we can buy that new car. Decide to be happy now. Only when you make a deposit into life will you reap the reward of life. You will reap the quality of life in proportion to the quality in which you plant.

*Anonymous*

The pursuit of happiness is mankind's favorite sport.

*Anonymous*

A wise man is he who does not grieve for the things which he has not, but rejoices for those which he has.

*Epictetus*

There are eight requisites for contented living: health enough to make work a pleasure; wealth enough to support your needs; strength to battle with difficulties and overcome them; grace enough to confess your sins and forsake them; patience enough to toil until some good is accomplished; charity enough to see some good in your neighbor; faith enough to make real the things of God; hope enough to remove all anxious fear concerning the future.

*Goethe*

The most wasted of all days is that during which one has not laughed.

*Sébastien Chamfort*

We have no right to ask when a sorrow comes, "Why did this happen to me?" unless we ask the same question for every joy that comes our way.

*Philip F. Bernstein*

I learned from experience that if there was something lacking, it might turn up if I went after it, saved up for it, worked for it, but never if I just waited for it. Of course, you had to be lucky, too, although I discovered that the more I hustled, the luckier I seemed to get. Besides, most of the happiness seemed to be in the pursuit. As my Uncle Benny used to say, "It's not the sugar that makes the tea sweet, but the stirring."

*Sam Levenson*

## LOOK INSIDE FOR HAPPINESS

There was an ancient Indian legend about a little-known tribe that was constantly at war with other Indian tribes. They abused their religion and their families, had no morals or feelings for others, laughed at wisdom or any kind of order. Murder, rape, theft, and plundering were a daily occurrence. This violent Indian tribe seemed doomed to wipe themselves off the face of the earth.

Finally, an old chief gathered together a few of the least violent of the braves and held a council to discuss how they could save their tribe from themselves. The wise old chief decided the only thing to do was to take the secret of happiness and success away from those who abused it. They would take this secret and hide it where no one would ever find it again. The big question was—where should they hide it?

One Indian brave suggested they bury the secret of happiness and success deep in the earth. But the chief said, "No, that will never do, for man will dig deep down into the earth and find it."

Another brave said to sink the secret into the dark depths of the deepest ocean. But again the chief replied, "No, not there, for man will learn to dive into the dark depths of the ocean and will find it."

A third brave thought they should take it to the top of the highest mountain and hide it there. But again, the chief said, "No, for man will eventually climb even the highest of mountains and find it, and again take it up for himself."

Finally, the old chief had the answer. "Here is what we will do with the secret of happiness and success," he stated. "We will hide it deep inside of man himself, for he will never think to look for it there."

To this day, according to that old Indian legend, man has been running to and fro all over the earth—digging, diving, and climbing—searching for something that he already possesses within himself.

## HELP OTHERS BE HAPPY

Happiness is not a celestial body to pursue and catch. In fact, happiness often comes on you unawares while you are helping others.

An old Hindu proverb pointedly and beautifully expresses this philosophy of happiness: "Help thy brother's boat across, and lo! Thine own has reached the shore."

## ACT HAPPY

Psychologist William James said, "I don't sing because I'm happy, I'm happy because I sing."

Some people wait for happiness to take residence on their doorstep, not realizing that if they act as if they are happy, they will tend to make others happy.

William James put it this way: "Action seems to follow feeling, but really action and feeling go together and by regulating the action, which is under the more direct control of the will, we can indirectly regulate the feeling, which is not."

That is powerful advice. Now, here's the final step to William James's philosophy: "Thus the sovereign voluntary path to cheerfulness, if our cheerfulness be lost, is to sit up cheerfully and to act and speak as if cheerfulness were already there."

## THE SECRET OF HAPPINESS

There is a wonderful fable about a young orphan girl who had no family and no one to love her. One day, feeling exceptionally sad and lonely, she was walking through a meadow when she noticed a small butterfly caught unmercifully in a thornbush. The more the butterfly struggled to free itself, the deeper the thorns cut into its fragile body. The young orphan girl carefully released the butterfly from its captivity. Instead of flying away, the little butterfly changed into a beautiful good fairy. The young girl rubbed her eyes in disbelief.

"For your wonderful kindness," the good fairy said to the girl, "I will grant you any wish you would like." The little girl thought for a moment and then replied, "I want to be happy!" The fairy said, "Very well," and leaned toward her and whispered in her ear. Then the good fairy vanished.

As the little girl grew up, there was no one in the land as happy as she. Everyone asked her the secret of her happiness. She would only smile and answer, "The secret of my happiness is that I listened to a good fairy when I was a little girl."

When she was very old, and on her deathbed, the neighbors all rallied around her and were afraid that her fabulous secret of happiness would die with her. "Tell us, please," they begged. "Tell us what the good fairy said."

The lovely old woman simply smiled and said, "She told me that everyone, no matter how secure they seemed, no matter how old or young, how rich or poor, had need of me."

## "I THANK THEE, LORD"

A legend tells about a servant whose master died—leaving the servant a bag of blessings—full to its brim. "The bag will always be full," said the master, "so long as you remember the four magic words." As the servant started off on his merry way, he partook of the blessings in the bag until finally the bag was almost empty. He then sought desperately to remember the words. Asking a wise man nearby what the four words were, he was told, "Perhaps the words are 'I wish I had.'" So, with his nearly empty bag, he ran down the road shouting: "I wish I had! I wish I had as much as all my neighbors have of health and wealth and such!"

But still the bag held no more. Some distance farther along the way, he asked another person, "Can you please tell me what the magic words are that will restore blessings to the bag?" This person said, "Perhaps the words are 'Give me some more.'" So once again he started on his way, shouting to the skies: "Give me some more! Give me some more! Oh, fill my bag of blessings up as full as it was before!"

Still the bag remained empty. Lonely and dejected, he sat down along a roadway to take the last piece of bread from his bag. As he started to eat it, a small waif of a child came up and out of hunger begged for the bread. He gave it—forgetting his own hunger. The little one placed the bread down, folded his hands, and said, "I thank Thee, Lord."

The servant jumped up with excitement to say, "Those are the words!" He took his empty bag and literally ran down the road shouting: "I thank Thee, Lord! I thank Thee, Lord! I thank Thee, Lord, once more for all the blessings in my bag. O Lord, how great a store!"

And the bag of blessings was full once more.

This is a legend, but its truth is deeply significant.

*Reynolds W. Greene, Jr.*

# Humor

*Laughter can relieve tension, soothe the pain of disappointment, and strengthen the spirit for the formidable tasks that always lie ahead.*

DWIGHT D. EISENHOWER

26

With the fearful strain that is on me night and day, if I did not laugh, I should die.

*Abraham Lincoln*

Medical experts tell us laughter is healthy. In fact, it is bad to suppress laughter. It goes back down and spreads your hips. Imagine how painful it would be if it settled in your colon.

*Anonymous*

A sense of humor is the one thing no one will admit not having.

*Mark Twain*

A man with a sense of humor doesn't make jokes out of life, he merely recognizes the ones that are there.

*Nuggets*

Anatomically considered, laughing is a sensation of feeling good all over and showing it principally in one spot. If a man cannot laugh, there was a mistake made in putting him together. Genuine laughing is a vent of the soul, the nostrils of the heart, and it is just as necessary for health and happiness as spring water is for a trout.

*Josh Billings*

Life does not cease to be funny when people die, any more than it ceases to be serious when people laugh.

*George Bernard Shaw*

A joyful heart is good medicine, but a broken spirit dries up the bones.

*Proverbs, 17:22*

If you can't take a joke, then you'll have to take the medicine.

*Anonymous*

Happy are the hard-boiled, for they never let life hurt them.

*J. B. Phillips*

Much may be known of a man's character by what excites his laughter.

*Goethe*

# Honesty

*Men occasionally stumble over the truth, but most of them pick themselves up and hurry off as if nothing had happened.*

SIR WINSTON CHURCHILL

27

## BEWARE OF HALF-TRUTHS

A sailor, caught up in the celebration of his ship leave, got drunk. The captain entered in the log: "Mate drunk tonight." The mate begged the captain, "I've never been drunk on board before. You know I have always been sober, and unless you add that truth, I'll be relieved of my naval duties." The captain refused to modify his entry. A few days later, the sailor was making his entries in the log. Among other notations, he made this one: "Captain was sober today." The captain was outraged when he read the entry. "You have created a false impression in the minds of those who read this entry. They'll believe it is unusual for me to be sober!" The sailor replied: "My statement is true, and it shall remain in the log."

*Although both men were accurate, they misrepresented each other. Overstatements as well as understatements may create a false inference. Simply stated, one half-truth plus another half-truth does not equal the truth.*

## GET YOUR STORY STRAIGHT

Three high school senior boys, possessed by spring fever, played hooky from their morning classes. After lunch, the boys reported to the teacher that they had experienced a flat tire. The teacher smiled and said, "Boys, you missed a test this morning. Take a seat apart from one another and get out a blank sheet of paper."

"Here is your first question," she said calmly. "Which tire was flat?"

*Needless to say, dishonesty will ultimately haunt us.*

## WHAT'S RIGHT?

A story is told about Abraham Lincoln, who, after listening to the case of a possible client, responded, "You have a pretty good case technically. But it just isn't right in justice and equity. So you'll have to find another lawyer to handle it for you, because all the time I'd be standing there talking to the jury I'd be thinking, 'Lincoln, you're a liar!' and I'm afraid I'd forget myself and say it out loud!"

## HONESTY IS CRUCIAL

Honesty in relationships is crucial. As a father said to his son in Shakespeare's *Hamlet:* "This above all; to thine ownself be true, and it must follow, as the night the day, though canst not then be false to any man."

## WHAT ARE YOU HIDING?

An executive was telling a new secretary what was expected of her. "I want you to be neat, organized, and courteous to all clients," he said. "Above all, I expect you not to gossip about me."

"Oh, yes, sir," replied the secretary. "I won't tell anybody anything. You have my total confidence." Then she leaned over the desk and whispered, "Just what is it you've done, sir, that you don't want others to know about?"

## OOPS!

Several years ago, a baker suspected that the farmer who was supplying his butter was giving him short weight. For several days he carefully checked the weight, and his suspicions were confirmed. This so angered him that he had the farmer arrested.

"I assume you have weights," said the judge at the farmer's hearing. "No, sir, I don't," replied the farmer.

"How then do you weigh the butter you sell?"

"Well," said the farmer, "when the baker began buying butter from me, I decided to get my bread from him. I just use the one-pound loaf he sells me as a weight for the butter I sell. If the weight of the butter is wrong, he has only himself to blame."

## FAMOUS FIBS

The following are well-used fibs from the business world:

- The check is in the mail.
- We service what we sell.
- Money is cheerfully refunded.
- This offer is limited to the first one hundred people.
- One size fits all.
- Your table will be ready in a minute.

Here are some excuses used by people caught speeding:

- I was hurrying to get to a restroom.
- I didn't know a policeman was in the area.
- I had no idea I was speeding.
- My accelerator was stuck.
- My wife is having a baby.
- The kids were driving me crazy, so I was in a hurry to get home.

These are some reasons for incomplete homework:

- The dog ate it.
- My mother threw it away by mistake.
- It blew away on the way to school.
- My little sister used it for toilet paper.
- I completed it while visiting my grandfather, and his house burned down.

And here are other fibs to consider:

- Open your mouth wide: I promise it won't hurt a bit.
- I'll start my diet tomorrow.
- This hurts me more than it hurts you.
- I just need a few minutes of your time.

# Humility

*Humility will save you from self-consciousness. It will take away from you the shadow of yourself and the constant sense of your own importance. It will save you from self-assertion and from thrusting your own personality upon the thoughts and attention of others. It will save you from the desire for display, from being prominent, from occupying the center of the stage, from being the object of observation and attention, and from having the eyes of the world turned upon you.*

DR. A. B. SIMPSON

28

## ACTIONS SPEAK LOUDER THAN COMMANDS

A rider on horseback, many years ago, came across a squad of soldiers who were trying to move a heavy piece of timber. The rider noticed a well-dressed corporal standing by, giving lordly commands to "heave." But the piece of timber was a trifle too heavy for the squad.

"Why don't you help them?" asked the quiet man on the horse, addressing the important corporal.

"Me? Why, I'm a corporal, sir!"

Dismounting, the stranger carefully took his place with the soldiers. He smiled at them and said, "Now, all together, boys—heave!" The big piece of timber slid into place. The stranger silently mounted his horse and then addressed the corporal.

"The next time you have a piece of timber for your men to handle, corporal, send for the commander-in-chief."

It was then that the corporal and his men first realized that the helpful stranger was none other than George Washington.

*Watchman-Examiner*

## DICKENS' SECRET: HE NEVER SPOKE OF HIMSELF

It is said of Charles Dickens that people who met him for the first time often would never have suspected that he was the most distinguished literary man of his time. He never spoke of himself. He always took a most modest interest in the affairs of others, and they learned with surprise that the man who had just been talking with them so simply and showing such an interest in their affairs was the literary star of his time.

*Dr. A. B. Simpson*

## DON'T LOSE YOUR GLOW

The supreme height of spiritual loveliness is to be lovely and not to know it. Virtue is so apt to become self-conscious, and so to lose its glow.

*John Henry Jowett*

## THE SECRET OF CATCHING FISH

A little country boy was out fishing with only a switch for a pole and a bent pin for a hook, but he was catching many fish. A city fellow, who had all the best fishing equipment, was also fishing in the same lake. However, after several hours, he had not caught even one fish.

He finally gave up and was putting away his expensive gear when the country boy walked by with his long string of fish.

"You caught all those fish with that old stick?" asked the astounded city fellow. "How did you do that? What is your secret?"

The boy hitched up his jeans and replied, "The secret is that I keep myself out of sight."

*That secret is so true of ourselves if we desire to be a blessing to others.*

## DON'T GET TRAPPED

An old method of catching wild turkeys can be an excellent lesson to all of us. To trap the turkeys, corn was scattered on the ground. Then a net was stretched about two feet high over the grain. When the wild turkeys sensed that no human was near, they would approach the corn and lower their heads to eat it. Never lifting their heads, they would nibble their way beneath the net.

When they became full and tried to leave, instead of keeping their heads down, they lifted their heads and were immediately caught in the net.

*There must be a lesson here for the haughty. Could it be that when heads are held too high, getting trapped by self-centeredness is inevitable?*

## YOUR MANNERS SPEAK

George Washington shocked General Lafayette one morning by merely being a gentleman. It seems George Washington and Lafayette were talking together when a slave passed. The old colored man paused, tipped his hat and said, "Good mo'nin', Gen'l Washin'ton."

Immediately George Washington removed his hat, bowed, and answered, "Good morning to you, and I hope you have a pleasant day."

After a moment of shocked silence, General Lafayette exclaimed, "Why did you bow to a slave?"

Washington smiled and replied, "I would not allow him to be a better gentleman than I."

*Billie Avis Hoy*

# Kindness

*Kindness is more than deeds. It is an attitude, an expression, a look, a touch. It is anything that lifts another person.*

C. Neil Strait

29

When you are dog-tired at night, could it be that you've been growling all day long?

*Anonymous*

Do all the good you can
By all the means you can
In all the ways you can
In all the places you can
At all the times you can
To all the people you can
As long as ever you can!

*John Wesley*

Join the great company of those who make the barren places of life fruitful with kindness. Carry a vision of heaven in your hearts, and you shall make your name, your college, the world, correspond to that vision. Your success and happiness lie in you. External conditions are the accidents of life, its outer wrappings. The great, enduring realities are love and service. Joy is the holy fire that keeps our purpose warm and our intelligence aglow. Resolve to keep happy, and your joy and you shall form an invincible host against difficulty.

*Helen Keller*

Speak kind words and you will hear kind echoes.

*Bahn*

If someone were to pay you ten cents for every kind word you ever spoke and collect five cents for every unkind word, would you be rich or poor?

*Anonymous*

What you are speaks so loudly, I cannot hear what you are saying.

*Ralph Waldo Emerson*

Kindness always pays, but it pays most when you do not do it for pay. A youthful giant slouched into an Illinois schoolroom one day after school. The teacher, Mentor Graham, looked up and recognized the young husky standing there awkwardly as the new young buck who had recently moved to town and who had whipped the daylights out of all local toughs. Graham looked up and down the six-foot-four-inches of muscle and ignorance before him and offered to help him read and to lend him a few books. No one remembers Mentor Graham now-a-days. He was one of the quiet men, but his pupil will be remembered for a long time. His name was Abraham Lincoln.

*William P Barker*

Kindness is the oil that takes the friction out of life

*Anonymous*

That best portion of a good man's life—his little, nameless, unremembered acts of kindness and of love.

*William Wordsworth*

Benjamin Franklin, tactless in his youth, became so diplomatic, so adroit at handling people that he was made U.S. ambassador to France. The secret of his success? "I will speak ill of no man," he said, "and speak all the good I know of everybody."

A great man shows his greatness by the way he treats little men.

*Thomas Carlyle*

Compassion will cure more sins than condemnation.

*Henry Ward Beecher*

### I Shall Not Pass This Way Again

Through this toilsome world, alas!
Once and only once I pass;
If a kindness I may show,
If a good deed I may do
To a suffering fellow man,
Let me do it while I can.
No delay, for it is plain
I shall not pass this way again.

*Anonymous*

## YOU NEVER KNOW

One Sunday, a scholarly looking man, plainly dressed, went into a church in Holland and took a seat near the pulpit. In a few minutes, a lady approached the pew, and seeing the stranger in it, curtly asked him to leave. He took one of the seats reserved for the poor, and joined devoutly in the service.

When the service was over, one of the woman's friends asked her if she knew who it was whom she had ordered out of her seat. "No," she replied, "but it was only some stranger, I suppose." "It was King Oscar, of Sweden," replied her informant: "He is here visiting the queen."

*The Motor*

## FROM A KERNEL TO ABUNDANCE

My farmer friends expertly capitalize on the principle of geometric progression. For every kernel of corn planted, one stalk will grow. Each stalk produces an average of two ears of corn, each of which will yield approximately 200 kernels. Of course, these kernels will become 400 stalks of corn, each of which will have a couple of new ears of corn, with a total of 400 kernels. It's phenomenal. In just one season, one ear of corn becomes 160,000 kernels.

*I've learned plenty from my farming friends about the value of geometric progression. I've also learned that kindness reproduces itself in the very same way. One unselfish, kind act you do today may very well inspire the kindness of others. The Bible says, "Be not weary in well doing." Why? That which you sow, you will also reap; that which you send out, comes back; and what you give, you get. An abundance of kindness begins with one simple "kernel."*

## HOLD MY HAND

During the Civil War, Abraham Lincoln often visited the hospitals to cheer the wounded. On one occasion, he saw a young soldier who was very near death. Lincoln approached his bedside.

"Is there anything I can do for you?" asked the president. Not recognizing the compassionate man as President Lincoln, the badly wounded young man nodded quietly.

Struggling with severe pain, the soldier could hardly speak. "Would you please write a letter to my mother?" he whispered.

Abraham Lincoln placed his large hand gently on the soldier's arm and patted him softly. Finding paper and pen, he carefully wrote each word the youth told him.

The letter read: "My dearest mother, I was badly hurt while doing my duty. I'm afraid I am not going to recover. Don't grieve too much for me, please. Kiss Mary and John for me. May God bless you and father." The young man was too weak to go on, so Lincoln signed the letter for him and then added this postscript: "Written for your son by Abraham Lincoln."

Asking to see the note, the soldier was astonished to discover who had shown him such kindness. "Are you really the president?" he asked.

"Yes, I am," was the quiet answer, and Lincoln asked if there was anything else he could do.

The lad replied feebly, "Will you please hold my hand? I think it would help to see me through to the end." The tall, gaunt president granted his last request. In the small quiet hospital room, Lincoln offered warm words of encouragement until death stole in with the dawn.

## COMPASSION IN HIS EYES

It was a bitter, cold evening in northern Virginia several years ago. The old man's beard became glazed with winter's frost while he was waiting for a ride across the river. The wait seemed endless, and his body became numb from the frigid winter wind.

Suddenly, he heard the thunder of horse's hooves in the distance. Anxiously, he watched as several horsemen approached. He let the first one pass by without an effort to get his attention, and then another passed, and another. Finally, one horseman was left. As he drew near, the man caught the rider's eye and said, "Sir, would you mind giving me a ride to the other side? There seems to be no passage on foot."

"Sure, hop aboard," the rider responded. Unable to force the man's half-frozen body onto the horse, the horseman dismounted and assisted the old man. It was decided the horseman would take the old man to his destination just a few miles away. As they approached the small but cozy home, the horseman's curiosity caused him to ask, "Sir, I noticed that you allowed several others to pass without an effort to secure a ride. Then, when I drew beside you, you immediately asked me for a ride. I'm curious why, on a bitter winter night, you would wait and ask the last rider. What if I had refused?"

The old man gently got down from the horse, looked at the horseman, and replied, "I've been around for a while, son, and I know people pretty well. I looked into the other horsemen's eyes and immediately knew there was no concern for my condition. So it was useless to ask them for a ride. But, when I looked into your eyes, kindness and compassion were evident. I knew your loving spirit would welcome the opportunity to give me assistance."

Those heartwarming comments touched the horseman. "I am most grateful for what you are saying," he replied. "May I never get too busy in my own affairs that I fail to respond to the needs of others with kindness and compassion."

With that final comment, Thomas Jefferson turned and directed his horse back to the White House.

*Zig Ziglar*

# Leadership

*Take away my people, but leave my factories, and soon grass will grow on the factory floors. Take away my factories, but leave my people, and soon we will have a new and better factory.*

ANDREW CARNEGIE

30

The extent to which you are able to transform your "self-concern" into "other concern" will determine your effectiveness in getting others to follow along.

*Anonymous*

Who hath not served cannot command.

*John Florio*

You can only make others better by being good yourself.

*Hugh R. Hanels*

In any group of people, a small fraction will be leaders, a larger fraction will be followers, and a substantial proportion just won't want to get involved.

*Anonymous*

You need the ability to fail. I'm amazed at the number of organizations that set up an environment where they do not permit their people to be wrong. You cannot innovate unless you are willing to accept some mistakes.

*Charles Knight*

Instead of fitting round theories into square holes, we as managers should capitalize on the strengths of an individual's differences and the possibilities that are opened to us by different circumstances.

*William B. Miller*

What does it mean to be promoted into a leadership position? Frankly, it means we now have the authority to serve people in a special way.

*Anonymous*

A businessman's judgment is no better than his information.

*R. P. Lamont*

If you set the right example, you won't need to worry about the rules.

*Anonymous*

Leadership is a serving relationship that has the effect of facilitating human development.

*William Arthur Ward*

A prime function of a leader is to keep hope alive.

*John W. Gardner*

A good leader takes a little more than his share of the blame, a little less than his share of the credit.

*Arnold Glasow*

Treat people as if they were what they ought to be, and you help them become what they are capable of being.

*Johann Wolfgang von Goethe*

The buck stops here.

*Harry S. Truman*

When people are highly motivated, it's easy to accomplish the impossible. And when they're not, it's impossible to accomplish the easy. So how do we motivate them? Discard the mushroom theory of management—the one that says, keep your employees in the dark and throw a lot of manure on them. If you're going to manage a growing company, you have to concentrate on managing people, not ignoring them.

*Bob Collings*

An effective organization has a purpose that is shared by all its members and to which they will willingly commit their efforts. People working together can do almost anything.

*James L. Hayes*

I spend 60 percent of my time planning, 60 percent with people, and all other duties are completed with whatever time is left.

*A. W. Clausen*

There is something that is much more scarce, something finer far, something rarer than ability. It is the ability to recognize ability.

*Elbert Hubbard*

Great [corporate] leaders understand human behavior rather than the cybernetics of any functional specialty.

*James Schorr*

Many managers believe they are communicating with their employees when in reality they are only talking excessively and listening for their own words to be reflected in employees' statements.

*Jack Hulbert*

The secret of successful managing is to keep the five guys who hate you away from the four guys who haven't made up their minds.

*Casey Stengel*

The greatest genius will not be worth much if he pretends to draw exclusively from his own resources.

*Johann Wolfgang von Goethe*

There is nothing so unequal as the equal treatment of unequals. Individualize your leadership.

*Anonymous*

A foolish consistency is the hobgoblin of little minds.

*Ralph Waldo Emerson*

Everyone has peak performance potential—you just need to know where they are coming from and meet them there.

*Anonymous*

A man is fit to command another that cannot command himself.

*William Penn*

People ask the difference between a leader and a boss. The leader works in the open, and the boss is covert. The leader leads, and the boss drives.

*Theodore Roosevelt*

No man will work for your interests unless they are his.

*David Seabury*

If it were considered desirable to destroy a human being, the only thing necessary would be to give his work a character of uselessness.

*Fyodor Dostoyevsky*

You cannot push anyone up the ladder unless he is willing to climb himself.

*Andrew Carnegie*

The chief lesson I have learned in a long life is that the only way to make a man trustworthy is to trust him; and the surest way to make him untrustworthy is to distrust him and show your mistrust.

*Henry L. Stimson*

Our policy flows from the belief that men and women want to do a good job, a creative job, and that if they are provided with the proper environment, they will do so.

*William Hewlett*

The most effective leader is the one who satisfies the psychological needs of his followers.

*David Ogilvy*

The worker must feel that he is recognized in accordance with his contribution to success. If he does not have that feeling of self-respect and the respect of others because of his skill, he will think he is being "played for a sucker" if he increases his output so the owners can have more profit.

*James F. Lincoln*

A good manager is a man who isn't worried about his own career but rather the careers of those who work for him.

*H. S. M. Burns*

Never be associated with someone you can't be proud of, whether you work for him or he works for you.

*Victor Kiam*

Some of the most talented people are terrible leaders because they have a crippling need to be loved by everyone.

*James Schorr*

I hold it more important to have the players' confidence than their affection.

*Vince Lombardi*

Leaders must recognize what's popular isn't necessarily right and what's right isn't necessarily popular. Child psychologist, Haim Ginott, sees it this way: "A good parent must like his children, but he must not have an urgent need to be liked by them every minute of the day."

Don't seek to be 1000 percent better at anything. Strive to be 1 percent better at a thousand things.

*Anonymous*

A wise leader remembers that people perceive service in their own terms.

*Anonymous*

I've got to follow them; I am their leader.

*Ledru-Rollin*

Leadership is the ability to put the right people in the right jobs and then sit on the sidelines and be a rousing good cheerleader.

*Anonymous*

Action springs out of what we fundamentally desire . . . and the best piece of advice which can be given to would-be persuaders, whether in business, in the home, in the school, in politics, is: First arouse in the other person an eager want. He who can do this has the whole world with him. He who cannot walks a lonely way.

*Harry A. Overstreet*

The primary skill of a manager consists of knowing how to make assignments and picking the right people to carry out those assignments.

*Lee Iacocca*

A manager is not a person who can do the work better than his men; he is a person who can get his men to do the work better than he can.

*Fred Smith*

I will pay more for the ability to deal with people than for any other ability under the sun.

*John D. Rockefeller*

Our chief want is someone who will inspire us to be what we know we could be.

*Ralph Waldo Emerson*

The dream begins with a teacher who believes in you, who tugs and pushes and leads you to the next plateau, sometimes poking you with a sharp stick called "truth."

*Dan Rather*

Leadership: The art of getting someone else to do something that you want done because he wants to do it.

*Dwight D. Eisenhower*

The best way to motivate a subordinate is to show him that you are conscious of his needs, his ambitions, his fears, and himself as an individual. The insensitive manager who is perhaps unintentionally aloof, cold, impersonal, and uninterested in his staff usually finds it very difficult to get his people to put out extra effort.

*Dr. Mortimer R. Feinberg*

The supreme quality for a leader is unquestionable integrity. Without it, no real success is possible, no matter whether it is in a section gang, on a football field, in an army, or in an office. If his associates find him guilty of phoniness, if they find that he lacks forthright integrity, he will fail. His teachings and actions must square with each other. The first great need, therefore, is integrity and high purpose.

*Dwight D. Eisenhower*

Setting an example is not the main means of influencing another, it is the only means.

*Albert Einstein*

## WHAT DID YOU SEE?

An executive friend of mine did an amazing job of transforming a run-down agency into an outstanding success. His secret was to request each department head to submit a report every Monday morning of all the good things that had happened in his department during the preceding week. This was a simple enough way to turn organizational failure into dynamic success.

## TELL PEOPLE HOW THEY'RE DOING

There is a story of a man in a restaurant making a phone call.

"Mr. Smith?" he said. "I understand you have been looking for an assistant." He paused. "Oh, you hired one two months ago and are pleased with your choice. Well, thank you anyway. I hope you continue to be satisfied with your decision."

When he hung up the phone, the restaurant manager commented, "I happened to overhear your conversation. I'm sorry you didn't get a shot at the job."

"Oh, that's all right," the man replied. "That's my boss. I was hired as his assistant three months ago. I was just phoning to find out how I'm doing."

## WORTH A MILLION

When asked why he was worth $3,000 a day or $1 million a year in salary, Charles M. Schwab responded, "I consider my ability to arouse enthusiasm among men the greatest asset I possess, and the way to develop the best that is in a man is by appreciation and encouragement, so I am anxious to praise but loath to find fault. If I like anything, I am hearty in my appreciation and lavish in my praise."

In a later interview, responding to a comparable question about his success, Schwab reiterated his conviction. "In my wide association in life, meeting with many and great men in various parts of the world," Schwab declared, "I have yet to find a man, however great or exalted his station, who did no better work and put forth greater effort under the spirit of approval than he would ever do under a spirit of criticism."

## IT COULD HAVE BEEN WORSE

Understanding, willingness to accept failure, and sincere appreciation were a few of the qualities contributing to John D. Rockefeller's success. It was reported that when one of his partners, Edward T. Bedford, failed miserably and ended up losing the company a million dollars, Rockefeller responded with a classic statement. He didn't criticize Bedford because he knew he had done his best. However, he did call him into the office and said, "I think it is honorable that you were able to salvage 60 percent of the money you invested in the South America venture. That's not bad; in fact, it's splendid. We don't always do as well as that upstairs."

*Finding something good to say, even in the worst situations, is a true quality of a leader.*

## If I Were Leader

If I were leader I'd like to say:
"You did an excellent job today."
I'd look for a man, or woman, or boy
Whose heart would leap with a thrill of joy
At a word of praise and I'd pass it out
Where others could hear what I talked about.

If I were a leader, I'd like to find
The person whose work is the proper kind;
And whenever to me a good thing came
I'd like to be told the toiler's name,
And I'd go to the person who had toiled to win,
And I'd say, "That was perfectly splendid, Lynn!"

Now a bit of praise isn't much to give,
But it is dear to the hearts of all that live;
For there's never a person on this old earth
But is glad to know that one's been of worth;
And a kindly word, when the work is fair,
Is welcome and wanted everywhere.

If I were leader I'm sure I would
Say a kindly word whenever I could;
For those who have given their best by day
Want a little more than their weekly pay.
They like to know, with the setting sun,
That the leader's pleased with the work they've done.

*Anonymous*

## MAN OF STEEL AND VELVET

Not often in the story of mankind does a man arrive on earth who is both steel and velvet, who is as hard as rock and as soft as drifting fog, who holds in his heart and mind the paradox of terrible storm and peace unspeakable and perfect.

While the war winds howled, he insisted that the Mississippi was one river meant to belong to one country.

While the luck of war wavered and broke and came again, as generals failed and campaigns were lost, he held enough forces . . . together to raise new armies and supply them, until generals were found who made war as victorious war has always been made, with terror, frightfulness, destruction . . . valor and sacrifice past words of man to tell.

In the mixed shame and blame of the immense wrongs of two crashing civilizations, often with nothing to say, he said nothing, slept not at all, and on occasions he was seen to weep in a way that made weeping appropriate, decent, majestic.

*Carl Sandburg*

*Carl Sandburg held the joint session of Congress in the palm of his hand as he shared these eloquent thoughts concerning Abraham Lincoln. Sandburg, a student of Lincoln, helped everyone see the remarkable leader as both capable and vulnerable.*

## JUST TEN PERCENT MORE

The year was 1958. The Green Bay Packers ended their season with one win and ten losses. In 1959, new life was injected into this struggling football team. Vince Lombardi became their new coach and in the next nine years led the Packers to a 75 percent winning record. The Packers accumulated five NFL championships, including the nation's first two Superbowls.

How did they do it? Frank Gifford explained it this way: "It wasn't his knowledge of football strategy and tactics. No, it was his ability to motivate each player. Lombardi could get that extra 10 percent effort out of an individual." Gifford went on to explain the compounding effect: "Multiply 10 percent times forty men on the team times fourteen games in a season—and you're fast building a winning team."

### A Leader Is Best

A leader is best
When people barely know he exists,
Not so good, when people obey
and acclaim him,

Worse when they despise him.
But of a good leader, who talks little,
When his work is done, his aim fulfilled.

They will say:
"We did it ourselves."

*Chinese proverb*

## REMOVE THE DIRT TO FIND THE TREASURE

Andrew Carnegie was renowned for his ability to produce million-aires from among his employees. One day a reporter asked him, "How do you account for the fact you have forty-three millionaires working for you?"

Carnegie responded, "They weren't rich when they came. We work with people the same way you mine gold. You have to remove a lot of dirt before you find a small amount of gold."

Carnegie knew how to bring about change in people. He led them to a realization of their hidden treasure, inspired them to develop it, and watched their lives become transformed.

Carnegie activated the wisdom of philosopher and psychologist William James: "Compared to what we ought to be, we are only half awake. We are making use of only a small part of our physical and mental resources. Stating the thing broadly, the human individual thus lives far within his limits. He possesses powers of various sports which he habitually fails to use."

### A Supervisor's Prayer

Dear Lord, please help me
To accept human beings as they are—
not yearn for perfect creatures;
To recognize ability—and encourage it;
To understand shortcomings and make
allowance for them;
To work patiently for improvement
and not expect too much too quickly;
To appreciate what people do right—
not just criticize what they do wrong;
To be slow to anger and hard to
discourage;
To have the hide of an elephant and
the patience of Job;
In short, Lord, please help me be a
better boss!

*John Luther*

## LEADERSHIP BY IBM

Leadership is an invisible strand as mysterious as it is powerful. It pulls and it bonds. It is a catalyst that creates unity out of disorder. Yet it defies definition. No combination of talents can guarantee it. No process or training can create it where the spark does not exist. The qualities of leadership are universal: they are found in the poor and the rich, the humble and the proud, the common man, and the brilliant thinker; they are qualities that suggest paradox rather than pattern. But wherever they are found, leadership makes things happen.

The most precious and intangible quality of leadership is trust—the confidence that the one who leads will act in the best interest of those who follow—the assurance that he or she will serve the group without sacrificing the rights of the individual. Leadership's imperative is a "sense of rightness"—knowing when to advance and when to pause, when to criticize, and when to praise, how to encourage others to excel. From the leader's reserves of energy and optimism, his/her followers draw strength. In his/her determination and self-confidence, they find inspiration. In its highest sense, leadership is integrity. This command by conscience asserts itself more by commitment and example than by directive. Integrity recognizes external obligations, but it needs the quiet voice within, rather than the clamor without.

*International Business Machines Publications*

## BOSS VERSUS LEADER

H. Gordon Selfridge built one of the world's largest department stores in London. He achieved success by being a leader, not a boss. Here is his own comparison of the two types of executives:

The boss drives subordinates; the leader coaches them.

The boss depends upon authority; the leader on good will.

The boss says "I"; the leader, "we."

The boss fixes the blame for the breakdown; the leader fixes the breakdown.

The boss knows how it is done; the leader shows how.

The boss says "go"; the leader says "Let's go!"

*Anonymous*

## A GOOD QUESTION

One day a little girl asked her mother, "Mommy, why does daddy bring so much work home at night?"

"Because he doesn't have time to finish it at work," answered the mother.

"Then why don't they put him in a slower class?" asked the little girl.

Before you get put in a slower class, consider this list of conditions most advantageous for delegation:

1. Delegate when people are satisfied with the work.

2. Delegate when employees accept management objectives.

3. Delegate when consistency of effort and coordination are not all-important concerns.

4. Delegate when you are frequently with your employees.

5. Delegate when the technology allows.

6. Delegate details that recur to free you for the rest of your duties.

7. Delegate to help you develop.

8. Delegate to subordinates who desire responsibility.

*Management Information*


## LEADERS HELP OTHERS REACH GOALS

Paul "Bear" Bryant, the football coach who won more college football games than any other college coach in history (323), used a technique from which all leaders could benefit. At the beginning of each football season at Alabama, Bryant had every member of his squad write out his personal goals. Only after reading and studying those goals did Bryant design a game plan and objectives for his football team.

Why did this work so well? This simple technique had a threefold message. Bryant was conveying to his team (1) I care about you and what you want; (2) you should be thinking ahead; and (3) we are building a team in which each of you can pursue your personal goals, and I'm going to include those goals in our total team plan in as many ways as possible.

Knowing this, Bryant's squad gave their coach all they could give, and in so doing they strived for their own personal goals as well as producing strong, winning records year after year.

## WATER THE PERFORMANCE YOU WANT TO GROW

A young bride bought two rose bushes and planted them side by side in her backyard. One rose bush was big, beautiful, and healthy, but the other was scrawny and sick-looking. Each day the bride stood in front of the two rose bushes and watered only the scrawny rose bush.

Finally, a neighbor said to her, "What are you doing, only watering the one bush?"

"I'm trying to make that rose bush grow," said the bride, pointing to the healthy bush.

"Well," said the puzzled neighbor, "if you want that bush to grow, why are you watering this bush?"

"Because the pretty one oughta wanna grow anyhow!"

*Sounds silly, doesn't it? But how many times have you ignored your good performers, thinking they can survive by themselves. Don't forget, the good ones will also die from lack of attention. Since people tend to do those things that brighten their world, the moral is: Water the performance you want to grow.*

## GOOD LEADERS STAND UP FOR THEIR MEN

During the Civil War, General George McClellan was one of the Yankee's most outstanding officers. The war turned out to be longer and bloodier than either the North or the South had expected. At the height of that terrible war, Lincoln and his secretary of war visited the battlefield home of General McClellan. When they arrived, he was not at home, so they waited in the parlor for hours before McClellan finally stomped through the front door. He glanced at the president and the secretary of war but barely acknowledged them. Instead, he walked past them and on up the stairs to his room. Lincoln and the secretary of war looked at one another and decided to wait, thinking McClellan would soon be back down to see them. Finally, a maid approached them and said, "I'm sorry, Mr. President, but the general asked me to tell you that he is tired and has gone to bed."

The secretary of war was shocked and said, "Mr. President, I've never heard of anything so rude in my entire life. You must relieve General McClellan of his command immediately."

Lincoln remained silent for a moment and then answered, "No, I'd never do that. That man wins battles! And winning battles shortens this war, and if he can shorten this bloodshed by even one hour, I'd saddle his horse for him. I'd polish his boots for him. I'd do anything for him!"

## WE'RE ON THE SAME SIDE

Buddy was a small boy who was very wise and very clever for his age. What he lacked in physical stature, he made up for in his ability to think on his feet.

As he was eating his lunch in the school yard one day, three big bullies swaggered up to him and demanded he hand over his food. The small boy hesitated, and slowly stood up.

"Maybe you're hard of hearing," growled the largest of the three. "We said to hand over your lunch!"

The little guy backed up dramatically, then he drew a line in the dirt with the toe of his shoe. He looked the leader of the group right in the eye and said, "Now, you just step across that line."

The bully didn't hesitate for one moment at the challenge. He stomped defiantly across the line and barked, "I'm across, now what are you going to do about it!"

Smiling, the little guy looked the big bully right in the eye and said, "There, now we're on the same side!"

## LEADERS DON'T PUSH, THEY PULL!

Leadership isn't something that comes automatically just because you have people working for you. Leadership depends on followers. If people don't follow a manager's lead voluntarily—if they always have to be forced—that person is not a good leader.

General Dwight D. Eisenhower used to demonstrate the art of leadership with a simple piece of string. He'd place the string on a table and say, "Pull the string, and it will follow wherever you wish. Push it and it will go nowhere at all. It's just that way when it comes to leading people."

*Effective leaders know that they can get the best efforts out of people by working with them, by helping them to do their best, by showing them how to be more productive. But try to push or force efforts from people, and you bump up against a brick wall. Leaders don't push, they pull!*

## "I'M THE BOSS?"

Did you hear about the executive who was shamefully intimidated by a bossy, domineering secretary? During an argument, she began chasing him around the office with a broom. Finally, he dashed into a conference room, dove underneath the table, and slid back toward the wall as far as he could. Prodding him with the broom handle, his secretary shouted, "Pete P. Pushover, you come out from under there!" Cowering under the table, he cried out in a trembling voice, "I won't do it! I don't have to. I'm the boss in this business "

## THINK ABOUT IT

I wish you could know how it feels "to run" with all your heart and lose—horribly!

I wish that you could achieve some great good for mankind, but have nobody know about it except for you.

I wish you could find something so worthwhile that you deem it worthy of investing your life within it.

I hope you become frustrated and challenged enough to begin to push back the very barriers of your own personal limitations.

I hope you make a stupid mistake and get caught red-handed and are big enough to say those magic words: "I was wrong."

I hope you give so much of yourself that some days you wonder if it's worth all the effort.

I wish for you a magnificent obsession that will give you reason for living and purpose and direction and life.

I wish for you the worst kind of everything you do, because that makes you fight to achieve beyond what you normally would.

I wish for you the experience of leadership.

*Earl Reum*

## THE ESSENCE OF LEADERSHIP

I observe that there are two entirely different theories according to which individual men seek to get on in the world. One theory leads a man to pull down everybody around him in order to climb up on them to a higher place. The other leads a man to help everybody around him in order that he may go up with them.

*Elihu Root*

# Love

*Love begins when a person feels another person's need to be as important as his own.*

HARRY STACK SULLIVAN

31

Sign in the Republic Airlines headquarters: "God loves you, and I'm trying."

Love is only for the young, the middle-aged, and the old.

*Anonymous*

You can give without loving, but you cannot love without giving.

*Amy Carmichael*

Love is a fruit in season at all times, and within the reach of every hand.

*Mother Teresa*

Love cures people—both the ones who give it and the ones who receive it.

*Dr. Karl Menninger*

Home is the place where, when you have to go there, they have to take you in

*Robert Frost*

No one can deal with the hearts of men unless he has the sympathy which is given by love. You must have enough benevolence, not only for yourself, but for others, to pervade and fill them. This is what is meant by living a godly life.

*Henry Ward Beecher*

Love must be learned, and learned again and again; there is no end to it. Hate needs no instruction, but wants only to be provoked.

*Katherine Anne Porter*

The greatest happiness of life is the conviction that we are loved, loved for ourselves, or rather loved in spite of ourselves.

*Victor Hugo*

Someday after we have mastered the air, the winds, the tides, and gravity, we will harness for God the energies of love. And then for the second time in the history of the world, man will have discovered fire.

*Teilhard de Chardin*

Life's greatest happiness is to be convinced we are loved.

*Victor Hugo*

There is no fear in love; but perfect love casteth out fear.

*I John 4:18*

'Tis better to have loved and lost
Than never to have loved at all.

*Alfred, Lord Tennyson*

How far you go in life depends on your being tender with the young, compassionate with the aged, sympathetic with the striving, and tolerant of the weak and the strong. Because someday in life you will have been all of these.

*George Washington Carver*

It is this intangible thing *love,* love in many forms, which enters into every therapeutic relationship. It is an element of which the physician may be the carrier, the vessel. And it is an element which finds and heals, which comforts and restores, which works what we have to call, for now, miracles.

*Dr. Karl Menninger*

A mother who had raised an exceptional family of three sons and two daughters, all achievers, was asked her formula for being a successful parent. She answered, "I really don't know. I just love them and trust them."

Men have often found that the basis of success in influencing a boy lies in respecting him. You have to believe in the boy and in his possibilities so wholeheartedly that you convey that idea of confidence and respect to him as you use patience and skill and understanding in dealing with him. Sure, it takes faith, too.

*Walter MacPeek*

The roots of the deepest love die in the heart if not tenderly cherished.

*Von Herder*

'Tis not love's going hurts my days, but that it went in little ways.

*Edna St. Vincent Millay*

We are shaped and fashioned by what we love.

*Goethe*

Love is the basic need of human nature, for without it, life is disrupted emotionally, mentally, spiritually, and physically.

*Dr. Karl Menninger*

## IT'S NOT THE SAME

The young desperately crave physical affection. Howard Maxwell of Los Angeles is a man in tune with his times. So when his four-year-old daughter Melinda acquired a fixation for "The Three Little Pigs" and demanded that he read it to her night after night, Maxwell, very pleased with himself, tape-recorded the story. When Melinda next asked for it, he simply switched on the playback. This worked for a couple of nights, but then one evening Melinda pushed the storybook at her father.

"Now, honey," he said, "you know how to turn on the recorder."

"Yes," said Melinda, "but I can't sit on its lap."

*Anonymous*

### The Wire Fence

The wires are holding hands around the holes
To avoid breaking the ring, they hold tight the
neighboring wrist,
And it's thus that with holes they make a fence.

Lord, there are lots of holes in my life.
There are some in the lives of my neighbors.
But, if you wish, we shall hold hands,
We shall hold very tight,
And together we shall make a fine roll of fence
to adorn paradise.

*Anonymous*

### The Legend of the Blarney Stone

One night the King of Leprechauns
Saw a handsome Irish lad
Seated by an emerald pond
And looking very sad.

The king approached the gloomy boy
And tipped his little crown,
"Good evening, lad, what troubles ye
And causes ye to frown?"

The lad sighed, "Sir, I love a girl,
She's lovely as can be,
But when I try to tell her so
She always laughs at me.

"For I can't talk in fancy words
Or sing a lover's song,
And everything I say to her
Just seems to come out wrong!"

The king had listened carefully,
And when the lad was done,
He said, "The Gift of Flattery
Is all ye need, my son.

"But Ye must promise first
To never catch a leprechaun."
"I promise!" said the happy lad,
So the little king went on.
"Way yon in Blarney Castle
There's a stone with a magic spell,
And if ye'll only kiss it,
Ye can flatter very well."

So he found the stone and kissed it
And was happy all his life,
For his magic Gift of Flattery
Won him a lovely wife!

And people to this very day
Still kiss the Blarney Stone,
Hoping that this magic gift
Will be their very own.

*Anonymous*

## ME, TOO

I heard a story about a man who had been married for over thirty years. Returning home from work one evening, he found his wife packing. "What in the world are you doing?" he asked.

"I can't handle it anymore!" she cried. "We've done nothing but fight, argue, complain, and bicker at each other. I've decided to leave."

The man stood in shock and bewilderment as his wife walked out of the house—out of his life. Suddenly, he dashed to the bedroom and pulled a suitcase down from the closet shelf. Running outside, he yelled to his wife, "I can't handle it anymore, either. Wait for me, and I'll go with you."

## LOVE ACTIONS SPEAK LOUDEST

A great example of one who related out of love instead of out of fear was Father Damien, a courageous Roman Catholic missionary, who, from 1873 to 1889, worked for God in a leper colony. The colony was located on the Hawaiian Island of Molokai.

A recent television program told the story, beginning with Father

Damien's arrival by ship. Before the missionary got off the ship, the captain, with a scornful laugh, told him he wouldn't stay long in the leper colony but, like all other clergymen, would return soon to the ship.

As the priest prepared to step from the large ship to a small rowboat that would take him ashore, the leper at the oars held out his hand to help the priest into the boat. Seized by the fear of leprosy, the priest refused the man's hand. Hurt and separation showed in the leper's eyes as he held out the oar for the priest to grasp.

Arriving at the colony, Father Damien found his church building in shambles and his congregation nonexistent. The lepers wanted nothing to do with him and his touch-me-not brand of Christianity. The priest beat on the bell to summon people to the church, but the lepers turned deaf ears to all his pleas and calls.

Beaten and giving up, Father Damien made his way back to the ship, which had returned to the colony. On board, however, something happened that changed his life and to literally transform the leper colony.

A load of lumber intended for another Catholic parish was on board. Seeing it, the priest demanded that the captain drop the lumber off here for the lepers. The captain refused.

Also on board was a fresh band of untouchable lepers to be dropped at the colony. Father Damien, caught up in a cause greater than himself, forgot about his fear and, in love, picked up a little girl who had leprosy. Holding her close, he gently kissed her little cheek. Then he threatened the captain that unless he lowered the lumber and left it for the leper colony, the little girl would kiss him. The fearful captain immediately agreed to the priest's demand.

Word spread quickly that the priest had touched the little girl with leprosy. By the time Father Damien arrived back in the colony with the load of lumber and the new band of lepers, the colony's citizens had gathered excitedly to see what was happening.

Father Damien announced that instead of using the lumber to build the church first, they would together build a hospital to care for the needs of the people. Isn't that what a church is supposed to be anyway—a hospital to care for the needs of the hurting, the wounded, and the broken?

In the story you see the transforming miracle of love. As Father Damien reached out and touched the untouchable, love came alive, and worked the miracle. Estranged, suffering, lonely people drew together in serving, caring, healing love for one another.

*Dale Galloway*

## SEEING THROUGH ANOTHER'S EYES

Seeing John Jones through John Jones' eyes is a story that exemplifies empathy.


Before I can sell John Jones
What John Jones buys
I must see John Jones
Through John Jones' eyes.


A sign in a pet store indicated there were puppies for sale. John Jones walked into that pet store and as he produced fifty cents, he said to the manager, "I'd like to buy one of the puppies."

The manager replied, "I'm sorry, son, these puppies are a special breed of dog and cost $75."

"I could give you fifty cents just to look at your puppies," John said in a disappointed voice.

The pet store manager said, "Son, you can look at my puppies anytime, and it won't cost you anything." He whistled to the mother dog, and she came trotting out of the back room with four little puppies right behind her.

And then there was another puppy four or five paces behind its sisters and brothers—limping and struggling to keep up. John pointed to the lame puppy and said, "I want to buy that puppy."

The pet store owner replied, "I don't think you would want that puppy because, you see, our veterinarian has told us she was born without a hip socket and will never be able to run, jump, and do all the fun things that puppies and boys like to do as they grow up together."

John looked at the pet store owner as he pulled up his trousers legs and pointed to heavy steel braces on either side of his legs and joined together with heavy leather caps over the knees. John was suffering from the residual effects of polio, and as he pointed at his legs, he said, "I need that puppy because I feel she can understand me, and she needs me because I would have a special feeling and understanding for her. So, I'll give you fifty cents now and fifty cents a week until I've paid the $75."


Before I can sell John Jones
What John Jones buys

I have to begin to see John Jones
Through John Jones' eyes.

*This is more than a story about a boy and a puppy—it is a story about
people; people who work with other people, who are significant
influences in the lives of those others, and who can see things through
their eyes.*

*Anonymous*

## EMPTY-HANDED

A negotiator likes to tell the story of a businessman who was fishing
in a lake and caught a strange fish. The fish was a brilliant blue and
glimmered in the sunlight as it thrashed about in the boat. Suddenly the
fish spoke to the man.

"Please throw me back in the lake," begged the fish, "and I'll grant
you three wishes."

The businessman considered the request and replied, "Make it five
and we've got a deal."

"I can grant only three," gasped the fish.

"Four and a half," the man suggested.

"Three," the fish replied faintly.

"Okay, we'll compromise on four wishes," the businessman conced-
ed.

The fish did not reply. It lay dead on the bottom of the boat.

## THANK YOU FOR LOVING ME

Robert Browning, the poet, knew how to stimulate growth in people.
His undying love for Elizabeth Barrett was proof of this. Elizabeth Barrett
endured hell on earth during her young formative years. She was one of
eleven children and grew up under the seige of an oppressive, dictatorial,
controlling father. His angry rages during her childhood forced the frail,
sensitive Elizabeth to be frequently confined to her bed with an accumu-
lation of ills.

This was the saga of her sad life until she was nearly forty years old.
Then she met Robert Browning. Browning did not see Elizabeth as a
sickly middle-aged invalid. He saw her as a beautiful, talented spirit
waiting to blossom. He loved her with all of his heart and gave her an
irresistible invitation to grow and become all she was capable of becoming.

Browning lifted her from her pathetic and stunted existence, and after brutal confrontations with Elizabeth's father, they were married.

Glowing in their love for one another, they traveled the European continent, drinking in the wonders of God's world. Their union transformed Elizabeth into the beautiful, special person her husband knew she was. At forty-three, she bore Browning a healthy child. Their lives were full and beautiful. Growing and blossoming in her life with Browning, Elizabeth's unique artistry for literary expression produced works such as *Sonnets from the Portuguese*. This collection included the incomparable "How Do I Love Thee?", an artistic word–portrait of the transformation Robert Browning had created in her life.

*This beautiful story exemplifies the fact that the way you see people is the way you treat them, and the way you treat them is what they become.*

## ROOTS AND BONDS OF LOVE

Albert Einstein's wife died in 1936. His sister Maja agreed to assist the great genius with his household affairs. Fourteen years later, she suffered a stroke and lapsed into a coma. From that point on, Einstein spent two hours each afternoon with her, reading aloud from Plato. Maja gave no sign of understanding one word that was read. Einstein believed that a part of her mind lived, and he knew how much love could be communicated through consistent, attentive acts.

## POWER OF LOVE

In James Hilton's novel *Goodbye, Mr. Chips,* the hero is a shy, inept schoolteacher, bungling and unattractive in every way. And then something spectacular happens. He meets a woman who loves him and whom he loves, and they are married. Because of her, he becomes a kind, gracious, friendly man with everyone—so much so, in fact, that he becomes the most beloved teacher in the school. He experienced the positive, potential power of love.

## A "REVOLUTIONARY" METHOD

In 1925, two young medical school graduates and their father started a tiny sanitarium for mental patients on a farm outside Topeka, Kansas. At a time when the "rest cure" was in vogue in psychiatry, this father-and-son team determined to create a family atmosphere among their patients. The nurses were given specific training on how they were to behave toward specific patients: "Let him know that you value and like him." "Be kind but firm with this woman—don't let her become worse."

Those young doctors were Karl and William Menninger, and the Menninger Clinic, using such "revolutionary" methods, has become world famous.

Karl Menninger, summing up, said, "Love is the medicine for the sickness of mankind. We can live if we have love."

# Marriage

*Happy marriages begin when we marry the ones we love, and they blossom when we love the ones we marry.*

TOM MULLEN

32

A message to all brides: "If any of you happen to marry an archeologist, you're in luck. The older you get, the more he'll be interested in you."

*Arthur F. Lenehan*

A good marriage is that in which each appoints the other guardian of his solitude. Once the realization is accepted that even between the closest human beings infinite distances continue to exist, a wonderful living side-by-side can grow up, if they succeed in loving the distance between them which makes it possible for each to see the other whole against a wide sky.

*Rainer Maria Rilke*

Marrying a man is like buying something you've been admiring for a long time in a shop window. You may love it when you get it home, but it doesn't always go with everything else in the house.

*Jason Kerr*

My wife is always trying to get rid of me. The other day she told me to put the garbage out. I told her I had already put out the garbage. She suggested I go out and keep an eye on it.

*Rodney Dangerfield*

My wife is a very religious cook. Everything she serves is a burnt offering.

*Anonymous*

By all means marry. If you get a good wife, you will become very happy; if you get a bad one, you will become a philosopher—and that is good for any man.

*Socrates*

"I'd die for you, my love."
     "Oh, Harry. You're always saying that, but you never do anything about it."

*Anonymous*

My wife and I pledged we would never go to bed mad. Of course, we have gone without sleep for three weeks.

*Anonymous*

Love has been described as a three-ring circus: First comes the engagement ring, then the wedding ring, and after that the suffering.

*Bob Phillips*


All deep relationships, especially marriage relationships, must be based on absolute openness and honesty.

*Dr. H. Norman Wright*


Marriage—as its veterans know well—is the continuous process of getting used to things you hadn't expected.

*Anonymous*


Success in life is more than finding the right person. Being the right person is even more important.

*Elof Nelson*


Adam and Eve had an ideal marriage. He didn't have to hear about all the men she could have married—and she didn't have to hear about the way his mother cooked.

*Bob Orben*


Don't marry someone you can live with. Marry someone you cannot live without.

*Josh McDowell*


Marriage resembles a pair of shears, so joined they cannot be separated; often moving in opposite directions, yet always punishing anyone who comes between them.

*Dr. H. Norman Wright*


Love at first sight is easy to understand; it's when two people have been looking at each other for a lifetime that it becomes a miracle.

*Sam Levenson*

## GROUNDS FOR DIVORCE

In a House debate, the cry was raised that the Administration was not giving Congress the full story. This reminded Rep. Pat Swindall of an experience when he was a lawyer. "There was a lady who came to my office and wanted a divorce. I decided it might be helpful if I found out if she had grounds for divorce. I asked her and she said, 'Yes, as a matter of fact about an acre and a half.'

"I replied, 'Perhaps I am not communicating well. Let me try again.'

"I then asked her if she had a grudge. She said no, she didn't have a grudge but she did have a double carport. I said, let me try this one more time, a little more to the point: 'Does your husband beat you up?' She answered, 'No, I generally get up earlier than he does.'

"At this point I began to recognize that I was going to have to try a different track entirely and said, 'Are you sure you really want a divorce?'

"She said, 'No, I don't want a divorce at all. It's my husband who wants it. He contends that we have difficulty communicating.'"

*Washington Spectator*

## "I CANNOT UNDERSTAND"

Theodore Roosevelt was a passionate romanticist. While attending Harvard, he met Alice Hathaway. The woman of his dreams, she was a seventeen-year-old cousin of Teddy's best friend. If ever there was love at first sight, this relationship exemplified it. Roosevelt's January 25, 1880, entry in his diary reveals his love: "A year ago last Thanksgiving I made a vow that win her I would if it were possible. And now that I have done so, the aim of my whole life shall be to make her happy and to shield her and guard her from every trial. And oh, how I will cherish my sweet queen! How she, so pure and sweet and beautiful, can think of marrying me, I cannot understand, but I praise and thank God it is so."

## WIFE TALK

I love the story of two men who, while playing golf together, began talking about their wives.

Joe said, "If all men could be like me, they would all want to be married to my wife."

Alan quickly replied, "On the other hand, if they were all like me, none of them would want to be married to her."

*Different strokes for different folks.*

## HAVE FUN TOGETHER

A middle-aged couple had just gone to sleep when their smoke alarm went off. The husband jumped out of bed, dashed into the hall, and then back into the bedroom. "The whole back end of the house is on fire!" he shouted.

Grabbing his wife by the arm, he led her down the smoke-filled hallway and out the front door. As the husband opened the door to safety, he glanced at his wife and saw a smile on her face. "Good grief!" he inquired. "What have you got to be smiling about now!"

"I can't help it," she replied. "This is the first night we've gone out together in five years!"

A termite eats away at the joy of marriage when a couple no longer makes the time to have fun together. It's all too easy to allow responsibilities and routines to completely take over our lives.

*Dale Galloway*

## DOUBLE DILEMMA

"My husband is a real do-it-yourselfer," one wife lamented. "Every time I ask him to do something, he responds with, 'Do it yourself.'"

"Well, I'm seeking a divorce from my husband," responded her friend.

"He's very careless about his appearance. In fact, he hasn't made an appearance in over a year."

"One good husband is worth two good wives; for the scarcer things are, the more they are valued."

*Benjamin Franklin*

## "I WAS!"

Shortly after the honeymoon, the new bride started to complain about family finances. "When we were courting," she nagged, "you led me to believe you were well off."

"Oh, I was," the husband sighed. "I was."

*Lane Olinghouse*

## TREAT HER LIKE A QUEEN

The past two and one half years had seemed like a lifetime. Pete had taken all he could take. He no longer saw his wife as interesting, fun to be with, attractive, or someone he wanted to continue living with. She had become a sloppy housekeeper, overweight (in Pete's mind anyway), and had developed a nitpicking, fault-finding personality. Overwhelmed with it all, Pete sought advice from a divorce attorney on how he could make life miserable for his soon-to-be ex-wife.

The attorney listened to Pete's heartrending story and then offered this advice: "Pete, I have got the perfect plan for you. Now listen carefully. Starting when you get home this afternoon, I want you to begin treating your wife like a queen. I mean a *queen!* Do everything in your power to serve her, please her, and make her feel like royalty. Listen to her every thought with sincerity, give her a hand around the house, take her out for a few unexpected candlelight dinners, and even pick up flowers for her on your way home from work. Then, after two or three months of this royal treatment, just pack your bags and leave her. That will surely get to her. In fact, I can't think of anything that would hurt more than that."

Pete thought about the advice for a few brief moments. "It sounds like a fantastic idea. She would never expect anything like this from me." Pete couldn't wait to get home and get started. He even picked up a dozen roses on his way home. That night, he helped his wife with the dinner dishes and then brought her breakfast in bed the next morning. Pete began complimenting her on her clothes, cooking, and housekeeping habits. The two of them even went on a couple of weekend getaways. Old Pete really knew how to stick it to her.

After three weeks, Pete received a call from his divorce attorney. "Pete," he said, "I have the divorce papers ready if you're ready. In a matter of minutes, we can make you a happy bachelor again."

"Are you kidding?" Pete responded. "Why, I am married to an absolute queen. You wouldn't believe the changes she has made. In fact, her attitude and behavior has made a complete turnaround. I wouldn't divorce her in a million years."

*Marriage is an amazing thing. Loving your spouse begins with deciding that you want to fall madly in love with that person. Successful marriages are not something that come to you out of the blue. A happy life together is something you make happen.*

## KISS AND HUG

Remember the childhood lyrics:

Kiss and hug,
Kiss and hug,
Kiss your sweety
On the mug.

Of course, we didn't know it at the time, but that puppy-love activity holds the secret to some positive affects as an adult. Some time ago, a West German magazine released its fascinating results of a study conducted by a life insurance company. This study found that husbands who kiss their wives every morning:

- live an average of five years longer,
- are involved in fewer auto accidents,
- are ill 50 percent less time,
- earn 20 to 30 percent more money.

## GOLDEN ADVICE

A small-town newspaper was interviewing a couple who were celebrating fifty years of married life. The reporter asked the routine question: "To what do you attribute the success of your marriage?" The husband lovingly glanced at his wife and responded, "The secret of our fifty years of marital harmony is quite simple. My wife and I made an agreement the day we were married. If she was bothered or upset about something, she was to get it off her chest and out in the open. We felt it was important for her to get it out of her system. And if I was mad at her about something, we agreed I would take a walk. So, I guess you can attribute our marital success to the fact that I have largely led an outdoor life."

Albert Einstein was asked the same question on the occasion of his golden anniversary. Professor Einstein offered this profound response: "When we first got married, we made a pact. It was this: In our life together, it was decided I would make all the big decisions and my wife would make all the little decisions. For fifty years, we have held true to that agreement. I believe that is the reason for the success in our marriage. However, the strange thing is that in fifty years, there hasn't been one big decision!"

# Mind

*What the human mind can conceive and believe, it can accomplish.*

DAVID SARNOFF

33

To think is to live

*Cicero*

Nurture your mind with great thoughts.

*Benjamin Disraeli*

Conductor Arturo Toscanini conditioned his mind to store, organize, and recall musical information. He memorized every note for every musical instrument in 250 symphonies and 100 operas.

The mind is like a clock that is constantly running down and must be wound up daily with good thoughts.

*Bishop Fulton J. Sheen*

## UNTAPPED CAPACITY

The brain is a fabulous mechanism. About the size of a half of grapefruit, it is capable of recording eight hundred memories per second for seventy-five years without exhausting itself. It is the storehouse for between ten billion and one hundred billion pieces of information. Even the most powerful computers in the world have memories that hold only a few million items of accessible information. The human brain retains everything it takes in and never forgets anything; even though we don't recall all the information received, everything is on permanent file in our brain.

Building a computer to match the brain's potential is possible, I think. However, it would occupy space comparable to the size of the Empire State Building and need one billion watts of electrical power to run. The cost would be billions of dollars.

The mind is one of God's most amazing gifts to man. Scientists tell us we use approximately 2 percent of the brain power available to us. Condition your mind and yourself to use the fabulous power available.

# Opportunity

*A wise man will make more opportunities than he finds.*

SIR FRANCIS BACON

34

God helps them who help themselves.

*Benjamin Franklin*

Great minds must be ready not only to take the opportunities, but to make them.

*C. C. Colton*

Opportunity comes to those who look for it.

*Anonymous*

Today's opportunity is yesterday's dream and tomorrow's memory.

*Anonymous*

There is no security on this earth; there is only opportunity.

*General Douglas MacArthur*

All of us do not have equal talent, but all of us should have an equal opportunity to develop our talents.

*John F. Kennedy*

Some people get the breaks; some people make their own.

*Anonymous*

It is a paradox that in our time of drastic rapid change, when the future is in our midst devouring the present before our eyes, we have never been less certain about what is ahead of us.

*Eric Hoffer*

## ACRES OF DIAMONDS

Years ago, when the first diamonds were being discovered in Africa, diamond fever spread across the continent like wildfire. Many people struck it rich in their search for the sparkling beauties, and they became millionaires overnight.

At this time, Lamar, a young black farmer in central Africa, was scratching out a moderate living on the land that he owned. However, the promise of great diamond wealth soon possessed Lamar, and one day he could no longer restrain his insatiable desire for diamonds and the lust to become a wealthy man. He sold his farm, packed a few essentials, and left his family in search of the magnificent stones.

His search was long and painful. He wandered throughout the African continent, fighting insects and wild beasts. Sleeping in the elements, fighting the damp and cold, Lamar searched day after day, week after week, but found no diamonds. He became sick, penniless, and utterly discouraged. He felt there was nothing more to live for, so he threw himself in a raging river and drowned.

Meanwhile, back on the farm that Lamar had sold, the farmer who bought the land was working the soil one day and found a strange-looking stone in the small creek that ran across the farm. The farmer brought it in to his farmhouse and placed it on the fireplace mantle as a curio.

Later, a visitor came to the farmer's home and noticed the unusual stone. He grasped the stone quickly and shouted excitedly at the farmer, "Do you know this is a diamond? It's one of the largest diamonds I've ever seen." Further investigation revealed that the entire farm was covered with magnificent diamonds. In fact, this farm turned out to be one of the richest and most productive diamond mines in the world, and the farmer became one of the wealthiest men in Africa.

*How sad that Lamar had not taken the time to investigate what he had in his own backyard. Instead, he gave up everything he had to search for wealth he could have had right at home.*

*This amazing story was a favorite of Dr. Russell Conwell (1843 –1925), founder of Temple University in Philadelphia, a first-class university for poor but deserving young people who would otherwise be unable to attend college.*

# Perseverance

*Tribulation brings about perseverance; and perseverance proven character; and proven character, hope.*

Romans 5:3–4

35

There is no poverty that can overtake diligence.

*Japanese proverb*

Triumph is just an "ump" ahead of "try."

*Anonymous*

Austere perseverance, harsh and continuous, may be employed by the smallest of us and rarely fails of its purpose, for its silent power grows irresistibly greater with time.

*Goethe*

No one would ever have crossed the ocean if he could have gotten off the ship in a storm.

*Charles F. Kettering*

If you consistently do your best, the worst won't happen.

*B. C. Forbes*

Energy and perseverance can fit a man for almost any kind of position.

*Theodore F. Merseles*

Great works are performed not by strength but by perseverance

*Samuel Johnson*

When nothing seems to help, I go and look at a stonecutter hammering away at his rock, perhaps a hundred times without as much as a crack showing in it. Yet, at the hundred and first blow, it will split in two, and I know it was not that blow that did it, but all that had gone before.

*Jacob A. Riis*

The next mile is the only one a person really has to make.

*Danish proverb*

Great works are performed, not by strength, but by perseverance.

*Samuel Johnson*

When I was a young man, I observed that nine out of ten things I did were failures. I didn't want to be a failure, so I did ten times more work.

*George Bernard Shaw*

"I am not concerned that you have fallen. I am concerned that you arise," said President Abraham Lincoln to his nation divided by the Civil War. By perseverance, the snail reached the ark.

*Charles H. Spurgeon*

## CHALLENGE OF THE GOLDEN ARCHES

I stopped for a cup of coffee this morning at the Golden Arches. The phenomenal success of McDonalds is evident throughout the world. How was such a dynasty built? Why is Ronald McDonald a household name? The answer rests in the motto adopted by McDonald's executives. It simply reads: "Press On."

As Calvin Coolidge said, "Nothing in the world can take the place of persistence. Talent will not; nothing is more common than unsuccessful people with talent. Genius will not; unrewarded genius is almost a proverb. Education will not; the world is full of educated derelicts. Persistence and determination alone are omnipotent."

*A solid base for success is perseverance. It separates the winners from the losers. Those who persevere understand that luck is something only failures believe in.*

## CODE OF PERSISTENCE

1. I will never give up so long as I know I am right.
2. I will believe that all things will work out for me if I hang on until the end.
3. I will be courageous and undismayed in the face of odds.

4. I will not permit anyone to intimidate me or deter me from my goals.

5. I will fight to overcome all physical handicaps and setbacks.

6. I will try again and again and yet again to accomplish what I desire.

7. I will take new faith and resolution from the knowledge that all successful men and women have had to fight defeat and adversity.

8. I will never surrender to discouragement or despair no matter what seeming obstacles may confront me.

*Herman Sherman*

### Don't Quit

When things go wrong, as they sometimes will,
When the road you're trudging seems all up hill,
When the funds are low and the debts are high,
And you want to smile, but you have to sigh,
When care is pressing you down a bit,
Rest, if you must—but don't you quit.

Life is queer with its twists and turns,
As every one of us sometimes learns,
And many a failure turns about
When he might have won had he stuck it out;
Don't give up, though the pace seems slow—
You might succeed with another blow.

Often the goal is nearer than
It seems to a faint and faltering man,
Often the struggler has given up
When he might have captured the victor's cup.
And he learned too late, when the night slipped down,
How close he was to the golden crown.

Success is failure turned inside out—
The silver tint of the clouds of doubt—
And you never can tell how close you are,
It may be near when it seems afar;
So stick to the fight when you're hardest hit—
It's when things seem worst that you mustn't quit.

*Clinton Howell*

## PEOPLE WHO PERSEVERED

Shakespeare said, "We are such stuff as dreams are made on." History rings with people who believed in their dreams and persevered to see those dreams come true.

Plato labored over his *Republic* masterpiece. In fact, he rewrote the first sentence nine different ways before he was satisfied.

As a young boy, Jesse Owens went to hear the speedster Charlie Paddock speak. Young Jesse approached Paddock after the speech and said, "Sir, I've got a dream! I want to be the fastest human being alive." Developing his scrawny legs, Jesse Owens persevered to become the fastest man ever to run the 100-meter dash; the fastest to run the 200-meter. He won four gold medals. His name was inscribed in the charter list of the American Hall of Athletic Fame.

Franklin D. Roosevelt was struck down by polio, but he persevered. Unable to walk, he proved to people across the world he could lead as president of the United States. FDR never made excuses because of his disability. He just kept on pressing on.

Adam Clark labored forty years writing his commentary on the holy scriptures. Milton rose every morning at 4:00 A.M. to write *Paradise Lost.* The *Decline and Fall of the Roman Empire* took Gibbon twenty-six painstaking years to complete. Ernest Hemingway is said to have reviewed *The Old Man and the Sea* manuscript eighty times before submitting it for publication. It took Noah Webster thirty-six years to compile *Webster's Dictionary.*

As a boy, he dreamed of drawing comic strips. As a young man, he was advised by an editor in Kansas City to give up drawing. He kept knocking on doors, only to be rejected. He persevered until finally a church hired him to draw publicity material. Working out of an old garage, he befriended a little mouse who ultimately became famous. The man was Walt Disney, and his friend became Mickey Mouse. A 1931 nervous breakdown, rejections, and setbacks could not steal Disney's dreams.

Totally deaf and blind, Helen Keller became a famous author and lecturer. Instead of wallowing in grief, Helen Keller lived life fully in spite of her handicaps. She even graduated *cum laude* from Radcliffe College. Helen Keller had perfect perseverance.

Leonardo Da Vinci spent ten years perfecting *The Last Supper.* He reportedly became so engrossed in his work he would forget to eat for several days. *The Last Judgment,* considered one of the twelve master paintings of all time, consumed eight years of Michelangelo's life.

The Chicago fire of 1871 inspired Dwight L. Moody to build a school that would train young people to know the Bible and spread its teachings.

And how about Lindbergh's commitment to cross the Atlantic in a single-engine plane?

Finally, there was Fritz Kreisler. As a young boy, he wanted to play the violin. His parents encouraged his interest by paying for his lessons. Kreisler didn't progress as he had hoped and finally quit. Fritz Kreisler tried to study medicine and failed, and joined the army and went nowhere. He tried and quit many other pursuits. Desperate for a successful experience, Kreisler went back to his violin instructor.

"I want to play," he told her.

"Fine," his instructor responded. "But you must acquire one irreplaceable quality. You must exhibit undefeatable determination."

Fritz Kreisler persevered until his music filled the walls of Carnegie Hall.

*It is true. Nothing can take the place of perseverance.*

## NEVER GIVE UP!

Sir Winston Churchill took three years getting through eighth grade because he had trouble learning English. It seems ironic that years later Oxford University asked him to address its commencement exercises. He arrived with his usual props. A cigar, a cane, and a top hat accompanied Churchill wherever he went. As Churchill approached the podium, the crowd rose in appreciative applause. With unmatched dignity, he settled the crowd and stood confident before his admirers. Removing the cigar and carefully placing the top hat on the podium, Churchill gazed at his waiting audience. Authority rang in Churchill's voice as he shouted, "Never give up!" Several seconds passed before he rose to his toes and repeated: "Never give up!" His words thundered in their ears. There was a deafening silence as Churchill reached for his hat and cigar, steadied himself with his cane, and left the platform. His commencement address was finished.

*Never give up! That's no doubt the shortest and most eloquent commencement address ever given. Those words should echo in our ears whenever challenges, tribulations, and opportunities come our way.*

## The Quitter

It's the plugging away that will win you the day,
So don't be a piker, old pard!

Just draw on your grit; it's so easy to quit:
It's the keeping-your-chin-up that's hard.
It's easy to cry that you're beaten—and die;
It's easy to crawfish and crawl;
But to fight and to fight when hope's out of sight—
Why, that's the best game of them all!
And though you come out of each grueling bout,
All broken and beaten and scarred,
Just have one more try—it's dead easy to die,
It's the keeping-on-living that's hard.

*Robert W. Service*

## TRY, TRY AGAIN

Struggling with a volunteer assignment, Mother threw up her arms in desperation.

"Don't give up," her son admonished. "Don't ever give up."

"In most cases I would agree, son, but this problem can't be solved."

Now catch the wisdom of this fourteen-year-old boy. "Remember, Mom, people won't remember you for what you were going to do. They will only remember those who keep pressing on. Abraham Lincoln didn't give up. Thomas Edison kept pressing on. Benjamin Franklin always kept hope alive—and look at Victor McNasson."

Mother questioned, "Who is Victor McNasson?"

"See," said her son, "You never heard of him. He gave up."

Susie, overhearing the conversation piped in, "It's like we learn at school, Mommy. If at first you don't *conceive*, try, try again."

## "I WANT TO BE AN ADMIRAL"

The newspapers carried a remarkable story of a junior naval officer who was discharged from the service because he had cancer. He survived bout after bout with this treacherous disease. At one point, he was given only two weeks to live, but with dogged determination and faith, he won the battle. His cancer was brought under control.

Now what? He wanted, more than anything else, to be a naval officer. However, regulations forbade reinstatement of an individual with a history of cancer. "Give up," they told him. "It would take an act of Congress to get reinstated." Inspired by his lifelong goal, Irwin W. Rosenberg pursued that act of Congress.

President Harry S. Truman ultimately signed into law a special bill that ensured Rosenberg's reinstatement. That paved the way for Irwin W. Rosenberg to become rear admiral in the United States' Seventh Fleet. What was once a seemingly impossible feat became a glittering reality. Admiral Rosenberg typifies outstanding achievement realized by those who activate a life-style of persistence and undying commitment to their goals.

# Personalities

*No man, for any considerable period, can wear one face to himself and another to the multitude without finally getting bewildered as to which may be true.*

NATHANIEL HAWTHORNE

36

Years of research tell us that an expert is a person who will know tomorrow why the things they predicted yesterday didn't happen.

*Anonymous*


Neurotics are sure that no one understands them, and they wouldn't have it any other way.

*Mignon McLaughlin*


Extremely nervous people can even keep coffee awake at night.

*Anonymous*


Be a comfortable person so there is no strain in being with you—be an old-shoe, old-hat kind of person  Be homey

*Norman Vincent Peale*


It's easy to have a well-rounded personality. Just remember your blessings as easily as you do your troubles.

*Glenn Van Ekeren*


I always wanted to be a procrastinator but never got around to it.

*Anonymous*


A tart temper never mellows with age, and a sharp tongue is the only edged tool that grows keener with constant use.

*Washington Irving*


A miser isn't much fun to live with, but he makes a wonderful ancestor.

*Modern Maturity*


An intellectual is a man who takes more words than is necessary to tell more than he knows.

*Dwight D. Eisenhower*

The most important thing about you is what you think about God.

*A W Tozer*

## WHAT YOUR DOODLES MEAN

Are you a doodler? Have you ever wondered what—if anything—those peculiar scribblings you unconsciously make during telephone conversations tell about yourself?

At long last, they've been classified. According to one group of psychologists:

If you make boats, you are energetic, long to be free to do as you please.

If you draw arrows, you have a high goal in life.

If you make alternate squares and checkerboards, you are logical and emotionally stable.

Do you draw circles? Then you are a daydreamer who wants to escape from the sordid details of life.

If you draw flowers and trees, you are lonely.

Do you make stairsteps? You are extremely ambitious.

If you frequently draw eyes, noses, and other features, then you possess an appreciation of beauty.

And if you are always filling in open spaces of o's, then you are indecisive.

*Telephony via Sunshine Magazine*

# Problems

*I always view problems as opportunities in work clothes.*

HENRY J. KAISER

37

I am not surprised at what men suffer, but I am surprised at what men miss.

*John Ruskin*

Those things that hurt, instruct.

*Benjamin Franklin*

Part of the problem today is that we have a surplus of simple answers and a shortage of simple problems.

*Syracuse Herald*

Even when confronted with a hopeless situation, you still have a chance to make life meaningful . . . in turning personal tragedy into a triumph or by transforming your predicament to an accomplishment.

*Victor Frankl*

Don't ever let your problems become an excuse

*Anonymous*

Do not bring me your successes; they weaken me. Bring me your problems; they strengthen me.

*Charles F. Kettering*

When a man makes up his mind to solve any problems, he may at first meet with dogged opposition, but if he holds on and keeps on searching, he will be sure to find some sort of solution. The trouble with most people is that they quit before they start.

*Anonymous*

Every problem contains within itself the seeds of its own solution.

*Stanley Arnold*

No one can become strong without struggle with adversity, resistance, and problems. Struggle makes us strong, and in the process of overcoming, we achieve happiness. We learn thereby how, despite everything, life can become a joyous adventure.

*Anonymous*

There is less to this than meets the eye.

*Tallulah Bankhead*

This tendency to avoid problems and the emotional suffering inherent in them is the primary basis of all human mental illness.

*Charles Swindoll*

It is in the whole process of meeting and solving problems that life has meaning. Problems are the cutting edge that distinguishes between success and failure. Problems call forth our courage and our wisdom; indeed, they create our courage and our wisdom. It is only because of problems that we grow mentally and spiritually. It is through the pain of confronting and resolving problems that we learn.

*Scott Peck*

When Noah sailed the waters blue, he had his troubles same as you; for forty days he drove the ark, before he found a place to park.

*Anonymous*

The most glorious moments in your life are not the so-called days of success, but rather those days when out of dejection and despair, you feel rise in you a challenge to life, and the promise of future accomplishments.

*Gustave Flaubert*

Find the essence of each situation, like a logger clearing a log jam. The pro climbs a tall tree and locates the key log, blows it, and lets the stream do the rest. An amateur would start at the edge of the jam and move all the logs, eventually moving the key log. Both approaches work, but the "essence" concept saves time and effort. Almost all problems have a "key" log if we learn to find it.

*Fred Smith*

It's all important that you develop a positive attitude toward problems. Let me suggest four attitudinal philosophies toward problems. Two are positive and two are negative. You have four choices when you run into any problem. Your first choice is to resent it. Your second choice is to simply consent to it. Your third choice is to invent a solution. And your fourth possibility is to prevent the problem from getting worse and from coming back at you later.

*Robert Schuller*

A danger foreseen is half avoided.

*Thomas Fuller*

Make the most of the best and the least of the worst.

*Robert Louis Stevenson*

### GET TO THE SOURCE OF THE PROBLEM

Old Barney was a perfectionist when it came to his yard. His grass was manicured with nary a weed in sight. He had the best-looking yard in town, and he was proud of it.

One morning, he put up the window shade to survey his beautiful lawn, and the sight shocked and devastated the old man. Little piles of dirt and humps in the turf had riddled his beautiful yard. Barney knew instantly what the problem was—he had a yard full of moles. Barney rolled up his sleeves and immediately began war against the underground enemy. He tried to drown them, trap them, and poison them. However, just when he thought he'd gotten rid of them, more moles appeared.

Finally, a neighbor, who had been watching Barney battle his moles, came to the rescue. "Barney, you're attacking the wrong problem," he explained. "The moles aren't your real problem. The real problem is the grubs in your lawn that the moles are feeding on. Get rid of the grubs and the moles will leave."

At his wits' end, Barney took his neighbor's advice and applied insecticide to his lawn. It worked. With the grubs gone, the moles left. Soon Barney had a beautiful, healthy lawn again.

## PRETEND IT ISN'T THERE

A father and his son were on their annual fishing weekend. Mother had sent along sack lunches for them to eat in the boat. The son became hungry and pulled out an apple and took a big bite. It had a worm in it, so the boy instantly spit it out and threw the apple in the lake.

Again, he reached in and pulled out another apple and took a bite. Once again, there was a worm. Making a terrible face, he spit it out and threw the apple away.

Finally, he took a third apple, shined it on his sleeve, closed his eyes, and then ate the entire apple. When he had finished, he opened his eyes, and smiling at his father he said, "I just pretended the worm wasn't there, and it tasted good."

## LEARN TO LAUGH AT YOURSELF

Jessica, a cute little five-year-old, simply could not pronounce the word *spaghetti*. The harder she tried, the funnier the word would come out. "Pasghetti—no, I mean saphetti," she would stammer, and usually end up crying because she was so humiliated.

One day, her father advised, "Jessica, don't take it so seriously. If you make a mistake, so what! Just laugh about it, and you won't be embarrassed about it."

What excellent advice! The next time Jessica mispronounced *spaghetti,* she laughed at herself. She was amazed that others around her began to laugh with her. She discovered that she, as well as the others, were genuinely having good fun over it. In fact, as Jessica grew older and finally pronounced *spaghetti* correctly, it almost became a disappointment. She missed the good times she and her friends had laughing over *pasghetti.*

## LOOK FOR THE RAYS OF SUNSHINE

Robert Louis Stevenson was well known as a great Scottish novelist and author of *Treasure Island.* He was very productive, even though often bedridden with poor health. However, his disease never seemed to stifle his optimism. Stevenson made it a point to always look for the good in everything.

Even his wife was amazed at his constant optimistic attitude. One day Stevenson had to put his work aside; he was extremely ill and had body-wrenching coughing spells. During one of his roughest coughing spells, his wife was gently treating him with a home remedy.

"Robert," she smiled at him. "I expect you still believe it's a wonderful day."

Stevenson smiled back at her, and noticed rays of sunshine bouncing off his bedroom walls. "I do believe it's a wonderful day," he replied. "I will never allow a row of medicine bottles to block my horizon."

## DON'T PANIC THE SKUNKS

Marlene, a mother of six children, walked into the house one day and spotted her children huddled together in a circle. When Marlene approached her children to see what the intense interest was, she could hardly believe her eyes. In the middle of the circle of attention were several baby skunks.

The shocked mother screamed at the top of her voice, "Children! Run, run, run!"

At the sound of their mother's alarmed voice, each child grabbed a skunk and ran. The screaming and panicking set off the danger alarm in the skunks, and each of them dispelled its horrible scent. Each child became mercilessly doused with the hideous smell.

*The lesson here is quite simple. The mother had caused the very chaos that she feared simply by overreacting to the situation. We can learn a lot about people and their reactions from this story. Allowing situations to be blown out of proportion does not help to handle difficult people. Allowing another's difficult behavior to consume your life can cause double stress.*

## AN IMPORTANT LESSON FROM AN ANT

In southwest Asia during the fourteenth century, Emperor Tamerlane's army suffered a devastating defeat. His army dispersed in retreat. Tamerlane escaped and hid in a deserted manger while enemy troops scoured the countryside.

As he lay there in the mud, desperate and dejected, Tamerlane noticed an ant trying to carry a grain of corn over a perpendicular wall. The kernel was larger than the ant itself. Fascinated, the emperor counted how many times the little ant tried to carry the corn up the wall but failed. The tenacious little ant tried sixty-nine times, and sixty-nine times he fell back, but did he give up? No! On the seventieth try, the ant pushed the grain of corn over the top.

Catching the little ant's spirit, Tamerlane leaped out of the mud with a shout. He, too, would triumph in the end. Gathering up his army, reorganizing them, and with renewed spirit, they attacked the enemy and won the battle. Tamerlane had been successful, too, just like the tiny ant.

## TURNING A PROBLEM INTO AN OPPORTUNITY

Once upon a time, there was a railroad express clerk in Minnesota. He was a nice young man who went to work every day, doing his job. One day, he received a large box of watches that were to go to the local jeweler. However, the jeweler did not want them. The young express clerk contacted the distributor who had sent the watches in the first place, but he did not want them back because the return postage was too expensive.

The railroad clerk had a problem. What was he going to do with the box of watches? An idea dawned on him, and he devised a creative solution by drawing pictures of the watches, adding written descriptions of them, and putting together a small catalog of watches. He then sent the catalog to other railroad clerks. In just a few weeks, they bought all the watches he had. His catalog plan was so successful that he ordered more watches and enlarged the catalog.

The clerk's name? Sears. His catalog? Sears, Roebuck, and Company. Sears turned his problem into opportunity and became one of the most successful men in America.

## TOO BUSY TREATING VICTIMS

Two teenage boys were fishing by a stream one day when they noticed someone floating downstream. They both jumped in, pulled the person out of the water, gave mouth-to-mouth resuscitation, and saved his life.

The next day, they were fishing in the same spot and noticed another person floating down the stream. Again, they jumped in and saved that person's life.

From then on, people floating downstream happened quite consistently, and many died en route to the hospital. The city council decided to build a hospital on that very spot so that they wouldn't have to transport the nearly drowned patients to the nearest hospital, which was eighty miles away.

The hospital became very busy and began to grow and expand. In fact, the hospital became very well-known across the country. Many interns came there to serve their residencies. One day, one of those interns approached the administrator and thanked him for the opportunity to do his internship with the hospital.

"There is one thing that bothers me, though," the intern said to the administrator. "Has anyone ever gone upstream to see why people are jumping into the river?"

"No," the administrator answered. "We just don't have time. We are too busy treating the victims."

## TO MOURN OR TO CELEBRATE

A man in China raised horses for a living, and one day one of his prized stallions ran away. His friends all gathered at his home to mourn his great loss. The next week, the runaway horse returned with several strays following close behind. The same acquaintances again assembled at their friend's home, but this time to celebrate his good fortune.

That very afternoon the horse kicked the owner's son and broke his back. Once more, the crowd came to express their sorrow and concern about the son's injury. However, during the next month, war broke out, and the man's son was exempt from military service because of his broken back.

*This story could go on and on. However, the point is that from our limited human perspective, it is impossible to know for certain how to interpret the experiences of life. Unless we can somehow see the total plan of our life, we cannot know if an experience is good or bad.*

## Keep Kicking

Two frogs fell into a can of cream—
Or so I've heard it told.
The sides of the can were shiny and steep,
The cream was deep and cold.
"Oh, what's the use?" said Number 1,
"'Tis fate—no help's around—
Good-bye, my friend! Good-bye, sad world!"
And weeping still, he drowned.
But Number 2 of sterner stuff,
Dogpaddled in surprise,
The while he wiped his creamy face
And dried his creamy eyes.
"I'll swim awhile, at least," he said—
Or so it has been said—
"It wouldn't really help the world
If one more frog was dead."
An hour or two he kicked and swam—
Not once he stopped to mutter,
But kicked and swam, and swam and kicked,
Then hopped out, via butter.

*Anonymous*

## THE BIG POT: REAL AND STRAW ISSUES

Once upon a time, there was a wise man who lived in a Russian village. An unhappy woman came to him seeking advice. She told him that she lived in a small hut barely large enough for her husband and two children. Hard times had befallen her husband's parents, and now they had moved into the already crowded hut.

"I can't stand it!" she cried to the wise man. "It's getting on my nerves. What should I do?"

He stroked his beard, thought awhile, and finally asked, "Do you have a cow, dear lady?" When she told him that indeed she did have a cow, he advised her to take the cow into the hut for a week and then come back. So she followed his advice.

A week passed and things were impossible. Every time the cow turned, the six occupants had to change seats. It was impossible to sleep, and the smell became unbearable. The lady returned to the wise man in tears. "I am more miserable than ever!" she said. "Your advice did not work."

Again he stroked his beard and asked, "Do you have any chickens, dear lady?" When she told him she did, he advised her to take the chickens into the hut also. "Then in a week, come back and see me again." More skeptical than ever, she again took his advice, for he was known as the greatest wise man in Russia.

A week later, hysterical, she returned. "You are insane!" she shouted. "Your advice is horrible. My hut is now absolutely impossible to live in. The cow turns, the chickens fly, the in-laws cough and whine, the children find feathers in their soup, and I fight constantly with my husband. It's all your fault!"

"Well, my dear lady," he answered thoughtfully. "I want you to try one more thing. Go home and take the cow and chickens out of your hut. Then, come back in a week." So the embittered woman decided to follow his advice one last time.

One week later she returned. "Oh, dear wise man, thank you so much. Since I took the cow and chickens out of our home, I am so very happy," she told the wise man. The old man only smiled, and the lady went home and lived happily ever after with her husband, her children, and her in-laws.

## A CLASSIC PROBLEM-SOLVER

Charlie Steinmetz is not a household word. However, in the field of scientific research and technology, the name Charlie Steinmetz is significant. Steinmetz has described himself as an ugly, deformed immigrant blessed with an "electronic" mind.

Steinmetz built the electrical generators for Henry Ford's first plant in Dearborn, Michigan. One day those generators failed to function, and production in the plant came to a halt. Ordinary mechanics and electricians were brought in to assess the problem. Unfortunately, they were unable to get the generators going, and Henry Ford was losing money.

Desperate to resume production, Ford called Steinmetz. The genius arrived and seemed to just tinker around. He would tinker with one part, then move to another. Ford's employees stood in disbelief at the incompetence of this unusual-looking man. After a few hours of tinkering, Steinmetz threw the main generator switch, and instantly power was revived.

Returning home, Steinmetz forwarded a bill to Henry Ford for

$10,000. Although a very rich man, Ford considered the amount outrageous and returned it to Steinmetz with this note: "Charlie, isn't this a little steep for a few hours of tinkering?"

Steinmetz reworked the bill and sent it back to Ford. This time the bill read: "$10 for tinkering around; $9,990 for knowing where to tinker. Total = $10,000."

Henry Ford paid the bill.

*It is tough to determine the value of people who know* how *to deal with problems, as well as* where *adjustments are needed.*

## "WHAT'S YOUR PROBLEM, LOUIE?"

At age twenty-seven, my friend Louie began experiencing an irritating problem. By 9:00 A.M. every morning, his ears began ringing, and his eyeballs popped out. Because Louie was experiencing tremendous job stress, his supervisor suggested that he see a psychologist.

"There's no doubt in my mind, Louie," the psychologist said. "Quit your job, find a new line of work, and your problem will be solved." So Louie submitted his resignation.

Within twenty-four hours, his ears started ringing again, and his eyeballs popped out. He was checked by a doctor, who suggested the source of his problem was his teeth. So he arranged to have all his teeth pulled. But that didn't work either. His ears still rang, and his eyeballs continued to pop.

Frustrated, Louie set up an appointment with a specialist who worked primarily with ringing ears and popping eyeballs. After a week of tests, Louie heard the sad verdict. "Louie," the specialist said, "it's bad news. You've got only three months to live."

What a shock! "I've quit my job, had all my teeth removed," said Louie in despair, "and now I find out I'm going to die." Resigned to his fate, Louie decided to enjoy his final three months. Selling his house and withdrawing all of his life's savings, Louie went on a spending spree. He bought a sports car, a boat, and even decided to have his suits tailored.

The tailor meticulously determined Louie's measurements. "That will be a 34 sleeve," the tailor determined, "and, let's see, a 16-inch neck."

"No, no," Louie interrupted. "I've always worn a 15-inch neck. Make my collars size 15."

"Whatever you say," replied the tailor. "But I'll tell you one thing; if you keep wearing size 15 collars, your ears will ring and your eyeballs will begin popping out."

Louie found the source of his problem. Ironically, a one-inch adjustment could have saved him a lot of unnecessary trouble.

## CALHOUN DIDN'T WANT THE BALL!

Two Alabama college football teams, archrivals on the field, were in the midst of one of the scrappiest games in the history of both teams. Even though the teams were unequally matched, one team was made up of unusually huge players, and the other team was quite small in stature. The score was fairly even.

It was a scary game for the little guys, but miraculously they were behind by only one touchdown. Calhoun, the small team's running back, had played a great game even though he had been nearly demolished on every play he'd carried the ball.

There were just a few seconds left in the game, and as the small team huddled up for their last play, the coach ran up and down the sidelines, screaming, "Give the ball to Calhoun! Give the ball to Calhoun!"

Calhoun did not get the ball. They lost yardage and lost the game. The coach ran onto the field shouting furiously at the quarterback, "Why didn't you give the ball to Calhoun?"

The quarterback just shook his head and said, "But coach, Calhoun didn't want the ball no more!"

*Some people are like Calhoun. They look at the big guys, the mountains, and they give up.*

## DON'T PANIC

During the Korean War, an American destroyer was lying at anchor off Korea. It was a still, moonlit night, and the tide was going out.

The quartermaster was making his midnight rounds of the ship when he noticed a cylindrical black object in the water. He knew immediately it was a live mine drifting in a direction that would result in the ship's destruction. Fear struck. He panicked, seized the ship's intercom, and called the duty officer and the captain.

The general alarm was sounded, ringing throughout the quiet air. Suddenly the entire crew was bursting into action. Quickly they considered the options. Can we pull up anchor? There was no time for that. Reverse the engines? The propeller might suck in the mine. Blow up the mine with gunfire? It was already too close for that to be a safe option. The crew was faced with the ultimate fear of total destruction.

However, one of the seamen on deck drew from his experiences as a volunteer fireman. "Get the firehoses!" he shouted. "We'll create a current by shooting the water between the ship and the mine. That way we can get it far enough away to explode it harmlessly."

*That simple and practical idea averted a terrible tragedy. Faced with a problem? Draw on your experiences to determine the most practical options available to you.*

## ENOUGH IS ENOUGH

The first thirty-five years of Harry's life were picture perfect. Everything seemed to go his way. Even when trials and tribulations entered his life, he was quick to view them as matters of divine Providence. And who was he to question that power?

Overnight, misfortune began to knock at his door. His wife for fifteen years ran off and married his best friend. His precious daughter married a loser and was left with large debts to pay. His son was gored by a bull while working on his father's farm. A couple of weeks later, a tornado devastated the farm, ruining his crops and blowing his house away. An electrical line was snapped to the ground, igniting a fire in his straw stack, resulting in Harry's barn being burned to the ground. The banker foreclosed on his mortgage, taking the farm away. Yet, in the midst of this terrible catastrophe, Harry continued to have faith that everything would be all right.

Penniless Harry landed a job as a greenskeeper at the community golf course. One day he was out mowing the fairways. A thunderstorm was brewing in the west but seemed to be passing to the north. Without warning, the wind switched directions and brought the storm directly on him. Suddenly, a bolt of lightning descended from the sky. It melted the mower and tractor, stripped the clothes from Harry's back, singed off his hair, and threw Harry against a tree.

When he recovered consciousness, Harry slowly rose to his knees, folded his hands, and looked toward heaven. Then, for the first time, Harry had a little different attitude about his circumstances. "God," he said, "don't you think enough is enough?"

# Relationships

*The world is full of lonely people,*
*each isolated in a private, secret dungeon.*

LORETTA GIRZARTIS

38

No man is an island, entire of itself; every man is a piece of the continent, a part of the main; . . . any man's death diminishes me, because I am involved in mankind; and therefore never send to know for whom the bell tolls; it tolls for thee.

*John Donne*

What is success if, when you're standing at the top, having achieved everything you wanted to achieve, you have no one to share it with? Make love your number one aim. Love is your greatest possibility in the one life you have to live.

*Anonymous*

Everyone has a right to his own opinion. It's generally no use to anyone else.

*Dublin Opinion*

The famous doctor and humanitarian, Dr. Albert Schweitzer, was right when he said, "We are all so much together, but we are all dying of loneliness."

If someone listens, or stretches out a hand, or whispers a word of encouragement, or attempts to understand a lonely person, extraordinary things begin to happen.

*Loretta Girzartis*

It is not who is right but what is right.

*Anonymous*

A frog has a wonderful advantage in life—he can eat everything that bugs him.

*Anonymous*

If it be possible, as much as lieth in you, live peaceably with all men.

*Romans 12:18*

Often a hostile person tries to roll right over others. He is an expert on anything and everything. I am right, and you are wrong, his attitude cries. This aggressive, pushy, manipulating person may victimize you and then turn around and make you feel like a crook.

*Robert M. Bramson*

Handle your anger by preventing its buildup.

*Dale Galloway*

I've had a few arguments with people, but I never carry a grudge. You know why? While you're carrying a grudge, they're out dancing.

*Buddy Hackett*

Associate yourself with men of good quality if you esteem your own reputation; for 'tis better to be alone than in bad company.

*George Washington*

We need each other! Two cows grazing in a pasture saw a milk truck pass. On the side of the truck were the words, "Pasturized, homogenized, standardized, Vitamin A added." One cow sighed and said to the other, "Makes you feel sort of inadequate, doesn't it?" We, too, are inadequate without quality, cooperative relationships. People are the supplement that make our life better.

*Anonymous*

Most of us like people who come right out and say what they think —unless they disagree with us.

*Grit*

Little happens in a relationship until the individuals learn to trust each other.

*David W. Johnson*

Of all my relatives, I like me best.

*Anonymous*

Jealousy can be caused by your concern over your ability to gain and maintain the affection and attention of another.

*Anonymous*

Before introducing him, Sir Winston Churchill's aunt told the following to a man applying for the job of private secretary: "Remember, you will see all of Winston's faults in the first five hours. It will take you a lifetime to discover his virtues."

## TAKE A STAND, COUNSELOR

A high school counselor wanted everyone to like him, so he began trying to please everyone. When he was asked to intervene in a difference of opinion between two students, he asked the most verbal student to state her case first. When she had completed her story, the counselor nodded his head and said to her, "I can see why you feel that way. You're right!"

Then it was the second student's turn to tell her side of the story. When she finished, the counselor again nodded his head and said, "Yes, you have a point there. You're right!"

A bystander who had witnessed the entire incident approached the counselor and said indignantly, "Sir, they can't both be right!"

The counselor stammered and stuttered and finally answered, "You're right, too!"

*There is just no way we can agree with everyone and please them, and still be real, authentic people. In the end, nothing will create more stress and tension than trying to please everyone.*

## KEY TO SUCCESS

When Andrew Carnegie was a boy in Scotland, he caught a mother rabbit. Presto! Shortly, he had a whole nest of little rabbits, but nothing to feed them; but he had a brilliant idea. He told the boys in the neighborhood that if they would go out and pull enough clover and dandelions to feed the rabbits, he would name the bunnies in their honor. The plan worked like magic!

Even as a boy, Carnegie knew how to handle people. He had a flair for organization and a genius for leadership. He also knew the astonishing importance people place on their own names. The business world knew Carnegie as the Steel King, even though there were many men who worked for him who knew far more about steel than he did. His ability to organize and understand what was important to people made him a successful and wealthy man.

## TRUE FRIENDS ENCOURAGE STRENGTHS

Someone once said, "True friends don't coddle your weaknesses; they encourage your strengths."

Not only friends but also parents, teachers, and supervisors would do well to follow the same advice.

Take this situation, for example. Parents were called in to visit with the principal concerning their daughter.

"I'm sorry, but Julie is not making the grade in German. She is flunking the class. I feel she is just too dumb to learn German."

Julie's father replied, "I don't know much about teaching, and I'm not well versed in German, but tell me, how do the dumb kids in Germany learn German?"

## THE GOLDEN RULES

Every major religion and philosophical following in the world understands the value of treating people as you want to be treated. Consider the following eight golden rules:

1. "So whatever you wish that men would do to you, do so to them."—Christianity

2. "That which is hateful to you, do not to your fellow man." —Judaism

3. "One precept to be acted upon throughout one's whole life. . . . Do not unto others what you would not have them do to you."—Confucianism

4. "Do not hurt others in ways that you yourself would find hurtful."—Buddhism

5. "Not one of you is a believer until he desires for his brother that which he desires for himself."—Muhammadanism

6. "This is the sum of duty: Do nothing to others which would cause you pain if done to you."—Hinduism

7. "Regard your neighbor's gain as your own gain, and your neighbor's loss as your own loss."—Taoism

8. "That nature alone is good which keeps from doing unto another whatever is not good for itself."—Zoroastrianism

*It's putting into practice the principle of treating others as we'd want to be treated that results in productive relationships.*

## AN EARFUL

The always tense director of a large agency had just finished a stormy session with his board of directors. Unfortunately, he took it out on his secretary. "Miss Smith," he demanded, "where is my pencil?"

"Why, Mr. Jones," the frightened girl replied. "It's behind your ear."

"You know how busy I am!" shouted the director. "Which ear?"

## TOUCH THE EMOTIONS

Envision a young woman poised on a bridge, preparing to end it all by plunging into the depths of a swirling river far below.

A psychologist, a police officer, and a pastor pleaded with her, giving all the reasons to go on living, but to no avail.

Then another young woman happened by and shouted, "You don't want to jump into that stinkin' dirty water. It's absolutely filthy!" The would-be suicide victim promptly responded by climbing down from the bridge.

*Words are not effective in influencing others unless they touch what's important to them. People respond when you use words that touch their emotions, their lives.*

## TRUE FRIENDS GIVE FREELY

A healthy tree may consist of up to 80 percent moisture. It draws large quantities of water through its root system or absorbs it from dew and rain. But did you know that the tree does not hoard this moisture for itself? Vast quantities of water are lifted through the trunk, branches, and leaves to be transpired into the surrounding air. This precious moisture, along with the discharge of oxygen, gives the surrounding forest a lovely fresh fragrance.

*True friends are very much like a healthy tree. When they do not hoard their love and feelings, but give of it freely, something lovely and precious happens. Other people are automatically drawn to them because of the loving and caring attitude that surrounds them.*

## PRAYER FOR TONGUE CONTROL

O Lord, keep me from getting talkative. And particularly from the fatal habit that I must say something on every subject on every occasion.

Release me from the craving to straighten out everybody's affairs.

Keep my mind free from the recital of endless details; give me wings to get to the point. Seal my lips when inclined to tell of my aches and pains.

They are increasing with the years and my love of rehearing them grows sweeter as the years go by.

Teach me the glorious lesson that occasionally it is possible that I may be mistaken.

Keep me reasonably sweet. I do not want to be a saint. Some of them are hard to live with, but a sour old woman is one of the crowning works of the devil.

Help me to extract all possible fun out of life. There are so many funny things around us, and I do not want to miss any of them.

Make me thoughtful but not moody, helpful but not bossy.

With my vast store of wisdom, it seems a pity not to use it all, but Thou, my Lord, knoweth that I want a few friends left at the end.

*Anonymous*

## ROUTINE ASSISTANCE

Sir Edmund Hillary and his guide Tenzing Norkay made history in 1953 by climbing Mount Everest. Their accomplishment required remarkable skill and courage, but there was another element that ensured their success.

Descending from mighty Mount Everest, Hillary lost his footing and feared for his life. Instinctively, Tenzing held the line taut, firmly planted his ax into the ice, thereby preventing their otherwise unavoidable deaths. Hillary soon recovered his footing, and the two adventurers completed their descent.

Learning about the climbers' perils, the press later called Tenzing a hero. He refuted the glory and refused to take any credit. Instead, he was quoted as saying: "Mountain climbers always help one another. It's a routine part of their profession."

*Other professions would do well to master this commendable quality.*

## DON'T TAKE PEOPLE FOR GRANTED

Dr. E. Schuyler English relates a story about the Philadelphia Orchestra's visit to China. At one stop, they listened to the Chinese Philharmonic Orchestra perform Beethoven's Fifth Symphony. American visitors were quietly unimpressed with the production. With the completion of the first movement, the Chinese conductor graciously offered the baton to the American conductor, Eugene Ormandy. What followed was an impressive transformation. It seemed as though the American conductor had been working with the Chinese Philharmonic for years. Even the performers appeared impressed with their improved performance. The smiles on their faces revealed an enlightened enthusiasm in their work. But a more important revelation took place during the concert. The members of the Philadelphia Orchestra were inspired in a new way with their own conductor's abilities, talent, and directing genius. They began to realize that they had been taking his competence for granted. Suddenly, his musical greatness was reinstated in the minds of his hometown performers.

# Procrastination

*Mr. Meant-To*

*Mr. Meant-To has a comrade,*
*And his name is Didn't-Do.*
*Have you ever chanced to meet them?*
*Have they ever called on you?*
*These two fellows live together*
*In the house of Never Win,*
*And I'm told that it is haunted*
*By the ghost of Might-Have-Been.*

ANONYMOUS

39

# EXCELLENT EXCUSES

The next time you need an excuse, try one of the following. It will surely impress the people around you and keep you from accomplishing anything worthwhile.

1. That's the way we've always done it around here.
2. I'm so busy, I just forgot.
3. It didn't appear that important.
4. That's someone else's job, not mine.
5. No one gave me the go-ahead.
6. I just work here. I'm not paid to make decisions.
7. I didn't realize you were in a hurry for it.
8. I've got better things to do with my time.
9. That's not part of my department.
10. You'll have to ask the boss.
11. I didn't think it would make any difference.
12. Let someone else do the dirty work.

## ANY EXCUSE WILL DO

Someone has said, "Where the heart is willing, it will find a thousand ways, but where the heart is weak, it will find a thousand excuses."

It's like the man who asked his farming neighbor if he could borrow his rope.

"I'm sorry," said the farmer. "I'm using it right now to tie up my milk."

"You can't use a rope to tie up milk," laughed the neighbor.

"I know that," replied the farmer, "but when you don't want to do something, one excuse is as good as another."

*Benjamin Franklin said, "I never knew a man who was good at making excuses who was good at anything else."*

### How and When

We are often greatly bothered
By two fussy little men,
Who sometimes block our pathway—

Their names are How and When.

If we have a task or duty
Which we can put off awhile,
And we do not go and do it—
You should see those two rogues smile.

But there is a way to beat them,
And I will tell you how:
If you have a task or duty,
Do it well, and do it now.

*Anonymous*

## TO CHANGE OR NOT TO CHANGE

Thomas Harris said there are three things that give people the "Wantivation" to change: They must hurt sufficiently; they must experience despair or boredom; or they must suddenly discover they can change.

*Until one of those three is realized, any excuse not to change will suffice. As Mark Twain once said, "Why put off until tomorrow that which you can put off until the day after tomorrow?"*

# Self

*Some people are going to like me and some people aren't, so I might as well be me. Then, at least, I will know that the people who like, like me.*

HUGH PRATHER

40

## What Would You Be?

If you'd never been born, well then what would you be?
You might be a fish? Or a toad in a tree!
You might be a doorknob! Or three baked potatoes!
You might be a bag full of hard green tomatoes!
Or worse than all that—why, you might be a WASN'T!
A WASN'T has no fun at all. No, he doesn't.
A WASN'T just isn't. He just isn't present.
But you—you ARE YOU! And now, isn't that pleasant?

Today you are you! That is truer than true!
There is no one alive who is you-er than you!
Shout loud, "I am lucky to be what I am!
Thank goodness I'm not just a clam or a ham!
Or a dusty old jar of sour gooseberry jam!
I am what I am! That's a great thing to be!
If I say so myself, "HAPPY BIRTHDAY TO ME!"

*Dr. Seuss (Theodore Geisel)*

## YOU ARE IMPORTANT

When God made you, he threw the mold away. There never has been or ever will be another person just like you. Now I know that your husband, or wife, or friends might exclaim: "Well, thank God for that!" but the fact remains, you are the only one in the world who can do your thing! What is it? What would you like to accomplish in life? Here is a beautiful quotation from the late Robert Kennedy's address to the young people of South Africa on their Day of Affirmation in 1966. It was used by Ted Kennedy in his eulogy at Robert's funeral. It bears study and repetition time and time again.

"Some believe there is nothing one man or one woman can do against the enormous array of the world's ills. Yet many of the world's great movements, of thought and action, have flowed from the work of a single person. A young monk began the Protestant Reformation, a young general extended an empire from Macedonia to the borders of the earth, and a young woman reclaimed the territory of France. It was a young Italian explorer who discovered the New World, and the thirty-two-year-old Thomas Jefferson who proclaimed that all men are created equal.

"These people moved the world, and so can we all. Few will have the greatness to bend history itself, but each of us can work to change a small portion of events, and in the total of all those acts will be written the history of this generation.

"It is from numberless diverse acts of courage and belief that human history is shaped. Each time a person stands up for an ideal, or acts to improve the lot of others, or strikes out against injustice, he or she sends forth a tin. ripple of hope, and crossing each other from a million different ʌnters of energy and daring, those ripples build a current that can sweep down the mightiest walls of oppression and resistance."

*Anonymous*

## Build a Better World

God said, "Let's build a better world,"
and I said, "How?
The world is such a cold, dark place,
and so complicated now,
And I'm so afraid and helpless,
there's nothing I can do!"
But God in all His wisdom said,
"Just build a better *you!*"

*Anonymous*

## "DOORMATS" GIVE THE YELLOW LIGHT

According to Bill Farmer's newspaper column, J. Upton Dickson was a fun-loving fellow who said he was writing a book titled *Cower Power*. He also founded a group for submissive people. It was called "Doormats." That stands for "Dependent Organization of Really Meek and Timid Souls—If There Are No Objections." Their motto was: "The meek shall inherit the earth—if that's okay with everybody." Their symbol was the yellow traffic light.

## INTERVAL IMPRISONMENT

Remember Rapunzel? Her experience as a young girl, imprisoned in a tower with an old witch, contains valuable truths for us.

Rapunzel was beautiful. However, the old witch consistently told her she was ugly. The witch was a genius. By convincing the young girl she was ugly, she knew Rapunzel would never gain the confidence to step outside the castle walls.

Enter Prince Charming! Standing at the base of the tower, he convinced Rapunzel of her attractiveness and desirability. She hung her hair, long and beautiful, out of the window, and Prince Charming braided the ends into a ladder and climbed to her rescue. Suddenly, Rapunzel realized she had never been imprisoned by the tower, but by the fear of her own ugliness. She had allowed herself to be trapped by the witch's insistence of her ugliness.

*Oh, the blessing and curse of a vivid imagination! It can free us or cause us to be locked inside the prison tower of ourselves. How you see yourself will ultimately determine how others see you.*

### WHOM ARE YOU DECEIVING?

I love the story of the man who was promoted into a management position. He felt very insecure being ushered into his new office. Nevertheless, he looked proudly at his new surroundings as he settled into his overstuffed office chair. Suddenly, there was a knock at the door. The new manager, wanting to look busy, picked up the receiver of his phone. Then he asked the visitor in. When the young man entered, the new manager nodded toward him saying, "Just a minute. I have to finish this call." Positioning the receiver, he continued into the phone, "Yes sir, I can handle that account. I know it's the largest this company has ever had. You can count on me. You're welcome, sir. Good-bye." The manager put the phone down and turned to his visitor. He smiled and asked, "Now, what can I do for you?" The young man smiled and answered, "Well, I just came in to connect your telephone."

### TWICE MINE

Oh, he was proud. The little boy held up his boat and declared, "It's all mine. I made every part of you." Then he made his way to the shore of the lake. This was the day he had been waiting for. His handmade masterpiece skipped along the clear, blue water as the gentle breeze caught the sails. Suddenly, a gust of wind caught the boat and snapped the string the little boy was holding. It was out of control and beyond the boy's reach, until finally it disappeared in the middle of the lake. Heartbroken, the little boy made his way home—without his prized sailboat. It was gone!

Several weeks later, the little boy was walking down Main Street. As he passed the toy shop, something caught his eye. There it was! How could it be? There in the window was his toy boat. He rushed into the store and told the owner the story of his boat. "It really is mine," he said. "I made it with my own two hands." The shopkeeper shook his head and said, "I am sorry. That is my boat now. If you want it back, you'll have to pay the price."

Dejected, yet hopeful, the boy left the toy shop, determined to buy back his boat  He worked and saved doing any job that friends, neighbors, and family would provide

Finally, the day came. His heart danced as he entered the toy shop and spread his hard-earned money on the counter. "I want to buy my boat back," the boy said. The owner carefully counted all the change and a few dollar bills. There was enough. Reaching into the showcase window, the store owner carefully retrieved the little boat and placed it in the boy's outstretched hands.

The little boy walked into the afternoon sun and hugged his boat. "You're mine," he said. "Twice mine. First I made you, and then I bought you."

*Why are we important? Because first God made us, and then He bought us.*

# Self-Confidence

*As is our confidence, so is our capacity.*

WILLIAM HAZLITT

41

How silent the woods would be if only the best birds sang.

*Anonymous*

Self-confidence, in itself, is of no value. It is useful only when put to work.

*Anonymous*

Do what you can, with what you have, where you are.

*Theodore Roosevelt*

Think you can or think you can't, either way you will be right.

*Henry Ford*

No one can make you feel inferior without your consent.

*Eleanor Roosevelt*

An inferiority complex would be a blessing, if only the right people had it.

*Alan Reed*

Sign in a London employment agency waiting room: "Never think of yourself as inferior. Leave this to the experts."

They conquer who believe they can.

*Ralph Waldo Emerson*

I can do all things through Christ who strengtheneth me.

*Philippians 4:13*

## "I FINALLY KNOW, I THINK!?"

There is a pointed story of a man who, after years of evaluation and self-study, emerged in a state of elation. He went to everyone he knew, and even those he didn't know, shouting, "I finally figured myself out! I'm in touch with my emotions! I know myself!"

A stranger stopped him in the middle of his declaration one day. "I am excited for you," he said. "But tell me, what you have found?"

"I am one with the world," the man exclaimed.

"You are one with the world?" the stranger repeated.

"You mean I'm not?" asked the man.

*There is never an end to building self-confidence. The process does not end when we realize we are one with the world. Healthy self-confidence means cultivating and maintaining a caring relationship with our-selves in spite of the disbelief, discouragement, and influence of others.*

# Self-Discipline

*The tough thing about learning self-discipline is that
we need self-discipline in order to learn it.*

GLENN VAN EKEREN

42

# FINISH WHAT YOU START

Henry Ford was often asked, "How can I make my life a success?" He would always reply, "If you start something, finish it!"

Ford had worked long but exciting hours in a little brick building behind his home. When he was building his first car, enthusiasm overtook him, and he found he could hardly take time out to sleep and eat. Then, before he had completed his first Ford automobile, he became acutely aware that it could be built even better. Ford felt positive he could create a second car superior to his first one. The thrill and enthusiasm of his first car began to wane.

Why spend all that time finishing a car that he already knew was inferior? But something inside him pressed on, as if he realized that he must focus his total energy on the first car and finish what he had started. In addition to discovering this fantastic principle, he learned more and more about the second car by finishing every detail of his original dream. If he had succumbed to the temptation of quitting on the first one, he might never have made a car at all.

*It requires discipline to keep our attention on one thing at a time.*

# MASTER YOURSELF

Bobby Jones was a master at golf, but he was also a master at mastering himself. Jones was only five when he first swung a golf club, and by twelve he was beating everyone at the local golf club. However, Jones was also noted for his hot temper and soon picked up the nickname "Club Thrower" by those who knew him.

Jones became good friends with Grandpa Bart, who helped out part-time in the club pro shop. Bart, an excellent golfer in his day, retired from the game because of arthritis, but working in the pro shop kept him in touch with the game he loved.

At fourteen Jones entered the National Amateur Tournament but came home a loser. "Bobby, you are good enough to win that tournament," Grandpa Bart told him. "But you'll never win until you can control that temper of yours. You miss a shot—you get upset—and then you lose."

Jones knew Grandpa Bart was right, but Jones was twenty-one years old before he won a tournament.

Grandpa Bart smiled when Jones finally won. "Bobby was fourteen years old when he mastered the game of golf," Bart chuckled, "but he was twenty-one years old before he mastered himself!"

# Self-Image

*All psychological problems, from the slightest neurosis to the deepest psychosis, are merely symptoms of the frustration of the fundamental need for a sense of personal worth. Self-esteem is the basic element in the health of any human personality.*

DR. WILLIAM GLASSER

43

# WHAT DO YOU BELIEVE?

The image we have of ourselves exists largely because of our past experiences. However, those experiences have not made you the way you are; they have made you believe you are the way you are.

It is thought that by the time you and I reached the age of two, 50 percent of what we ever believed about ourselves had been formed; by six, 60 percent of our self-belief had been established, and by eight, about 80 percent. By the time we reached the age of fourteen, over 99 percent of us had a well-developed sense of who and what we believed ourselves to be.

*Ultimately, however, we have the power to decide what we believe about ourselves. Don't allow people to impose limitations on what you can do or become. Take the bumble bee. Biologists have determined that, technically speaking, the bumble bee cannot fly. Fortunately, the bumble bee doesn't believe a word of it. Remember: People rise no higher than their expectation level. If you expect little or nothing from yourself, don't be surprised if you amount to nothing.*

## Believe It!

Believe it, you are a real find,
A joy in someone's heart.
You're a jewel, unique and priceless.
I don't care how you feel.
Believe it, God don't make no junk.

*Herbert Barks*

Thank you for making me so wonderfully complex! It is amazing to think about. Your workmanship is marvelous—and how well I know it.

*Psalms 139:14*

We should not live like cringing, fearful slaves, but we should behave like God's very own children, adopted into the bosom of his family, and calling to Him, "Father, Father."

*Romans 8:15*

The maintenance and enhancement of the perceived self are the motives behind all behavior.

*A. W. Combs*

Your worth consists in what you are and not in what you have; what you are will show in what you do.

*Thomas Davidson*

If you think you're a second-class citizen, you are.

*Ted Turner*

It is myself I am weary of and find intolerable. I want to fall asleep and forget myself and cannot.

*Leo Tolstoy*

The deepest urge in human nature is the desire to be important.

*John Dewey*

The will to self-love is the deepest of all desires.

*Robert Schuller*

Everybody needs to feel like somebody.

*Anonymous*

You are embarking on the greatest adventure of your life—to improve your self-image, to create more meaning in your life and in the lives of others. This is your responsibility. Accept it, now!

*Dr. Maxwell Maltz*

## FROM DUNCE TO GENIUS

People expressed little faith in him. Most of his teachers believed he had no chance of ever finishing school. At fifteen he succumbed to the destiny others had prescribed for him. Victor Seribriakoff spent the next seventeen years trying to find his niche in life. The term "dunce" was indelibly printed in his mind, and thus he lived. Working odd jobs here and there, Victor became an itinerant. One day an amazing transformation took place. At thirty-two an evaluation revealed that Victor had an IQ of 161. He was a genius! Victor wondered how that could be, yet he believed the written results. He lived, performed, and acted like a genius. Victor began writing, inventing, and eventually found himself in various successful business ventures. The highlight for this former dropout came with his election as chairman of the international Mensa Society. What is the Mensa Society? The group's membership requires an IQ of 140 or more. That was quite an accomplishment for a "dunce" to attain.

*The wise sage of long ago said, "As a man thinketh in his heart, so is he." How do you see yourself? Are you allowing the perception of others to blur your own vision? Bring out the genius in yourself by believing in who you are and what you can do.*

### LITTLE MARTHA TAFT WAS A PROUD SCOUT

When Martha Taft was in elementary school in Cincinnati, her teacher asked her to introduce herself and tell the class a little about her family.

Remembering that her family had taught her to be proud of her accomplishments, Martha stood straight and tall and announced to the class, "My name is Martha Bowers Taft. My great-grandfather was president of the United States. My grandfather was a United States senator, and my daddy is ambassador to Ireland."

Then smiling proudly, she added, "And I am a Brownie Scout!"

**Me**

I keep my mask right with me
Everywhere I go.
In case I need to wear it,
So ME doesn't show.

I'm so afraid to show you ME,
Afraid of what you'll do.
You might laugh at me and say mean things
Or I might lose you.

I'd like to take my mask off
To let you look at ME.
I want you to try and understand,
And please, love what you see.

So if you'll be patient and close your eyes,
I'll pull it off so slow.
Please understand how much it hurts
To let the REAL ME show.

Now my mask is taken off.

I feel naked! Bare! So cold!
If you still love all that you see,
You're my friend, pure as gold!

I want to save my mask,
And hold it in my hand.
I need to keep it handy in case,
Someone doesn't understand.

Please protect me, my new friend,
And thank you for loving ME true.
But please let me keep my mask with me
Until I love ME too.

*Anonymous*

### The Man in the Glass

When you get what you want in your struggle for self,
And the world makes you king for a day,
Just go to a mirror and look at yourself,
And see what that man has to say.

For it isn't your father or mother or wife,
Whose judgment upon you must pass;
The fellow whose verdict counts most in your life,
Is the one staring back from the glass.

Some people may think you are a straight-shooting chum,
And call you a wonderful guy,
But the man in the glass says you're only a bum,
If you can't look him straight in the eye.

He's the fellow to please, never mind all the rest,
For he's with you clear up to the end,
And you have passed your most dangerous, difficult test,
If the man in the glass is your friend.

You may fool the whole world down your pathway of years,
And get pats on the back as you pass
But your final reward will be heartache and tears,
If you've cheated the man in the glass.

*Anonymous*

## DULCINEA LEARNS TO LOVE HERSELF

In the musical drama *The Man of La Mancha,* Don Quixote acquaints himself with a woman of the streets. Her name is Aldonza. She is wild and wanton, but Quixote is attracted to her. The man of La Mancha stops short, looks at her intently, and announces that she is his lady and that he will call her Dulcinea.

She responds with mocking laughter, "I'm hardly a lady," she sneers. Still, Don Quixote sees the seed of potential greatness and tries desperately to give her a new self-image. He tries to get her to believe it. He insists that she is his lady. Angered and wild, with hair flying over nearly naked breasts, she screams at the top of her lungs that she is only a kitchen maid—a strumpet—a nothing. "I am Aldonza, not Dulcinea," she says as she runs from the stage, while the man from La Mancha whispers again that she is his lady.

At the close of the play, Don Quixote is dying. He feels he has failed Dulcinea, his lady. Then to his side comes Aldonza—Dulcinea—now lovely in a new gentleness. Confused, he does not recognize this lovely stranger until in a warm, soft voice she tells him that she is his Dulcinea. She has been saved from self-hate. Don Quixote had taught Dulcinea self-love. She truly was a new person.

# Self-Talk

*Your life is an expression of all your thoughts.*

MARCUS AURELIUS

44

Nothing can work me damage except myself. The harm that I sustain I carry about with me, and I am never a real sufferer but by my own fault.

*Saint Bernard*

We become what we habitually contemplate.

*George Russell*

What we are, is what we have thought for years.

*Buddha*

Take charge of your thoughts. You can do what you will with them.

*Plato*

There is no illness of the body except for the mind

*Socrates*

As a man thinketh in his heart, so is he.

*King Solomon*

You will draw to yourself that which you most persistently think about.

*Robert Anthony*

No person is what he thinks he is, but what he *thinks* he is.

*Robert Anthony*

What the human mind can conceive and believe, it can accomplish.

*David Sarnoff*

Nurture your mind with great thoughts.

*Benjamin Disraeli*

You will draw to yourself that which you most persistently think about.

*Anonymous*

Dr. David Schwartz, in *The Magic of Thinking Big,* says that over 80 percent of our hospital beds are filled with people with "EII," or Emotionally Induced Illness. This does not mean that the people are not sick, just that their illnesses began in their minds.

Nothing is good or bad, but thinking makes it so.

*William Shakespeare*

Men are not troubled by things themselves, but by their thoughts about them.

*Epictetus*

For they can conquer who believe they can.

*John Dryden*

## YOU ARE WHAT YOU THINK

Have you ever seen the breathtaking pillars in Mammoth Cave in Kentucky? These solid, enormous "icicles of stone" have taken centuries to form. A single drop of water finds its ways through the roof of the cavern to deposit its tiny sediment on the floor of the cave. Another drop follows, and still another, until a marble-like finger begins to grow. Ultimately, this process forms a tremendous pillar.

A similar process goes on in each of us. Each of our thoughts sinks into our soul, inadvertently forming our own pillars—pillars of character. If we let dishonest, immoral, selfish, and violent thoughts constantly fill our minds, we will form decaying pillars of weakness and evil. If we fill our minds with ideas, truth, love, and sincerity, we build strong and beautiful pillars within our souls. For it is the sum total of our daily thoughts that paint the portrait of our true character.

For as a man thinketh in his heart, so is he.

*Proverbs 23:7*

# Servanthood

*It is one of the most
beautiful compensations
of this life that no man
can sincerely try to help
another without helping
himself.*

RALPH WALDO EMERSON

45

The only gift is a portion of thyself.

*Ralph Waldo Emerson*

It is well to give when asked, but it is better to give unasked, through understanding.

*Kahlil Gibran*

Doing nothing for others is the undoing of one's self. We must be purposely kind and generous or we miss the best part of existence. The heart that goes out of itself gets large and full of joy. This is the great secret of the inner life. We do ourselves the most good by doing something for others.

*Horace Mann*

The world is full of two kinds of people, the givers and the takers. The takers eat well—but the givers sleep well.

*Modern Maturity*

We make a living by what we get; we make a life by what we give.

*Duane Hulse*

I expect to pass through this world but once. Any good things, therefore, that I can do, any kindness that I can show a fellow being, let me do it now. Let me not defer or neglect it, for I shall not pass this way again.

*Stephen Grellet*

He that gives should never remember; he that receives should never forget.

*The Talmud*

No man can live happily who regards himself alone, who turns everything to his own advantage. Thou must live for another, if thou wishest to live for thyself.

*Seneca*

Shared joy is double joy, and shared sorrow is half-sorrow.

*Swedish proverb*

You have not lived a perfect day, even though you have earned your money, unless you have done something for someone who will never be able to repay you.

*Ruth Smeltzer*

The game of life is a game of boomerangs. Our thoughts, deeds, and words return to us sooner or later, with astounding accuracy.

*Anonymous*

All of us are born for a reason, but all of us don't discover why. Success in life has nothing to do with what you gain in life or accomplish for yourself. It's what you do for others.

*Danny Thomas*

In thanking God for our own good fortune, each of us must render in return some sacrifice of our life for another life.

*Albert Schweitzer*

It is possible to give away and become richer. It is also possible to hold on too tightly and lose everything. Yes, the liberal man shall be rich. By watering others, he waters himself.

*Proverbs 11:24, 25*

The reason rivers and seas receive the homage of a hundred mountain streams is that they keep below them. Thus, they are able to reign over all the mountain streams. So the sage, wishing to be above men, putteth himself below them; wishing to be before them, he putteth himself behind them. Thus, though his place be above men, they do not feel his weight; though his place be before them, they do not count it an injury.

*Lao-tzu*

No person was ever honored for what he received. Honor has been the reward for what he gave.

*Calvin Coolidge*

One of the surest ways to find happiness for yourself is to devote your energies toward making someone else happy. Happiness is an elusive, transitory thing. And if you set out to search for it, you will find it evasive. But if you try to bring happiness to someone else, then it comes to you.

*Napoleon Hill*

We can be cured of depression in only fourteen days if every day we will try to think of how we can be helpful to others.

*Alfred Adler*

Rings and jewels are not gifts, but apologies for gifts. The only gift is a portion of thyself.

*Ralph Waldo Emerson*

He gives nothing who does not give himself.

*French proverb*

## DECIDING OUR PEOPLE PRIORITIES

Dr. Charles Mayo and his brother William are remembered for founding the famous Mayo Clinic. Dr. Charlie, as he was called, once was host to an English visitor in his home at Rochester, Minnesota, for several days. Before retiring for the night, the visitor put his shoes outside the door, expecting a servant to shine them. Dr. Charlie shined them himself. That's serving!

## "WIDE-LIKED"

John A. Andrew was well-liked and respected by the people of Massachusetts. He was reelected to the governor's office four times. On his death, Andrew's pastor, James Freeman Clarke, wrote an article about his life, in which he summarized the secret of the governor's success in four words: "He was a wide-liked." Clarke meant that Andrew was a man who deeply loved and cared for others, and he demonstrated that love effectively. It extended beyond his immediate friends and contacts. Andrew actively searched out and gave assistance to those who were disadvantaged. Because of that, many people mourned his death. On the day of the funeral, the procession route was lined with huge crowds. It is reported that some people ran beside the coffin for the entire five miles from Boston to Mount Auburn.

## JOY OF GIVING

In his book, *The Art of Loving,* the renowned psychologist Erich Fromm summarizes what life for him is all about. "For the productive character, giving has an entirely different meaning. Giving is the highest expression of potency. In the very act of giving, I experience my strength, my wealth, my power. This experience of heightened vitality and potency fills me with joy. I experience myself as overflowing, spending, alive, hence as joyous. Giving is more joyous than receiving, not because it is a deprivation, but because in the act of giving lies the expression of my aliveness."

## WHY ARE WE HERE?

Albert Einstein reflected on the purpose of man's existence when he said, "Strange is our situation here upon earth. Each of us comes for a short visit, not knowing why, yet sometimes seeming to a divine purpose. From the standpoint of daily life, however, there is one thing we do know: That we are here for the sake of others, . . . for the countless unknown souls with whose fate we are connected by a bond of sympathy. Many times a day, I realize how much my own outer and inner life is built upon the labors of people, both living and dead, and how earnestly I must exert myself in order to give in return as much as I have received."

## "NOT ONE!"

Dale Galloway, in his book *Dream a New Dream,* tells the story of a young man who can teach us all a lesson about giving and serving others.

Little Chad was a shy, quiet young man. One day he came home and told his mother that he'd like to make a valentine for everyone in his class. Her heart sank. She thought, "I wish he wouldn't do that!" because she had watched the children when they walked home from school. Her Chad was always behind them. They laughed and hung on to each other and talked to each other. But Chad was never included. Nevertheless, she decided she would go along with her son. So she purchased the paper and glue and crayons. For three weeks, night after night, Chad painstakingly made thirty-five valentines.

Valentine's Day dawned, and Chad was beside himself with excitement. He carefully stacked them up, put them in a bag, and bolted out the door. His mother decided to bake him his favorite cookies and serve them nice and warm with a cool glass of milk when he came home from school. She just knew he would be disappointed and maybe that would ease the pain a little. It hurt her to think that he wouldn't get many valentines—maybe none at all.

That afternoon she had the cookies and milk on the table. When she heard the children outside, she looked out the window. Sure enough there they came, laughing and having the best time. And, as always, there was Chad in the rear. He walked a little faster than usual. She fully expected him to burst into tears as soon as he got inside. His arms were empty, she noticed, and when the door opened she choked back the tears.

"Mommy has some cookies and milk for you," she said.

But he hardly heard her words. He just marched right on by, his face aglow, and all he could say was: "Not a one. Not a one."

Her heart sank.

And then he added, "I didn't forget a one, not a single one!"

It isn't a song until it's sung.
It isn't a bell until it's rung.
It isn't love until it's given away!

## ANGEL OF MERCY

According to Malcolm Muggeridge, in *Something Beautiful for God,* Calcutta's Angel of Mercy, Mother Teresa, shared her insight into the true value and meaning of friendship:

When I was homeless, you opened your doors,

When I was naked, you gave me your coat,

When I was weary, you helped me find rest,

When I was anxious, you calmed all my fears,

When I was little, you taught me to read,

When I was lonely, you gave me your love,

When in a prison, you came to my cell,

When on sick bed, you cared for my needs,

In a strange country, you made me at home,

Seeking employment, you found me a job,

Hurt in a battle, you bound up my wounds,

Searching for kindness, you held out your hand,

When I was Negro, or Chinese, or White,

Mocked and insulted, you carried my cross,

When I was aged, you bothered to smile,

When I was restless, you listened and cared,

You saw me covered with spittle and blood,

You knew my features, though grimy with sweat,

When I was laughed at, you stood by my side,

When I was happy, you shared in my joy.

## "I WANT YOU"

A wealthy woman was so caught up in her love for worldly pleasures that she had little time for her daughter. Even when her child became bedridden because of an illness, her mother's attitude remained the same. She felt she could shower gifts on her daughter to compensate for her lack of personal attention. Intent on her own plans, she left the girl in the care of a nurse and went to Europe to see the sights. While there, she remembered her daughter's birthday and sent her a rare and beautiful vase. When it arrived, the nurse brought it to the girl, saying, "Wasn't it thoughtful of your mother to remember you with another vase?" Refusing even to look at the present, the girl cried, "Take it away, take it away!" And then, as if her mother were in the room, she tearfully exclaimed, "Oh, Mother! Don't send me any more things. I have enough flowers, vases, and pictures. Send me no more! I want you—YOU!"

*Our Daily Bread*

## THE GOOD SAMARITAN

This happened nearly one hundred years ago. Germany was experiencing one of its worst snowstorms in history. Snow, waist deep, swirled angrily in the raging wind. The temperature dropped dangerously below zero, causing human flesh to freeze within minutes.

Not realizing how bad the snowstorm had become, Oberlin, a well-known German philanthropist, started out on foot to his home near Strasbourg. Trudging through the deep snow, frozen to the bone, and unable to see his hand before his face in the blinding snow, Oberlin soon lost his way.

Sinking deeper into a bottomless drift, Oberlin panicked. He could not move. His body was numb, and his screams became lost in the angry wind. Finally, he ceased to struggle and simply waited to die.

Within a few yards of Oberlin, a farmer was checking his livestock and heard Oberlin's screams. The farmer rescued Oberlin from his snowy grave and carried him into a safe, warm farmhouse. Oberlin soon revived. He thanked the farmer for saving his life and offered him a sizable reward. But the farmer refused the reward.

"At least tell me your name," Oberlin said.

The farmer smiled warmly and said, "You tell me the name of the Good Samaritan."

Oberlin thought for a moment and said, "I don't think his name was ever recorded."

"Then let me withhold mine," smiled the farmer.

## MORE THAN A PICTURE

The story is told of a wealthy man who lost his wife when their only child was young. The father hired a housekeeper to take care of the boy, who lived only into his teens. Heartbroken from this second loss, the father died a short time later. No will could be located, and since there were no relatives, the state was about to assume his fortune. The man's personal belongings, including his mansion, were put up for auction. The old housekeeper had very little money, but there was one thing she was determined to buy. It was a picture that had hung on a stairway wall in the house—a large painting of the boy she had loved and nurtured. When the items were sold, nobody else wanted the painting, so she bought it for just a few pennies. Taking it home, she began to clean it and to cherish the memories it brought. As she took it apart, a paper fell out. It was the man's will, and in it he stated that all his wealth should go to the one who loved his son enough to buy that picture.

## WHAT ECHO DO YOU HEAR?

I'm sure you've heard the story of the little boy who, in an outburst of temper, shouted to his mother that he hated her. Then, fearing punishment, he fled from the house to the hillside and shouted into the valley, "I hate you! I hate you! I hate you!" Back from the valley came the echo, "I hate you! I hate you! I hate you!" Startled by the response, the little boy ran back into the house and told his mother there was a mean little boy in the valley shouting that he hated him. His mother took him back to the hillside and told him to shout, "I love you! I love you!" The little boy did as his mother said, and this time he discovered there was another boy in the valley saying, "I love you! I love you!"

*The natural laws of life tell us that what we give, we get; what we sow, we shall also reap; and what we send out, comes back.*

## WHILE WE'RE LIVING

A pig was depressed about his lack of popularity. He complained to the cow that people were always talking about her gentleness and her kind eyes, while his name was used in a derogatory manner. He admitted that cows give milk and cream, but he was convinced that pigs gave more. "Why, we give bacon and ham and pork chops, and people even pickle our feet," he grumbled. "I don't see why you cows are held in such high esteem."

The cow thought for a while and then said gently, "Maybe it's because we cows are giving while we're living."

## ACTIONS SPEAK LOUDER THAN WORDS

In *Treasury of Quotations,* F. B. Proctor told the following story: A man was trying to get financial help for a widow who was in dire need, but his efforts were meeting with very little success. Even so, most of the people he contacted did express their regret over the sad situation of the poverty-stricken woman. The concerned man, refusing to give up, had high hopes as he approached a wealthy acquaintance, but he too refused to offer help. In declining the request, the rich man said, "I do want you to know, however, that I really feel sorry for that poor woman." The one who was asking for the money responded, "I'm sure you do. But I'm afraid you don't feel it in the right place." "Oh, yes, I do," the man replied. "I feel it very deeply in my heart." The other responded, "That's the problem. You feel it in the wrong place. I just wish those feelings were also in your pocket."

## CREATE A LITTLE HEAVEN

One night in his dreams, a man was given a tour of heaven and hell. As he entered the first room, his eyes immediately focused on a beautiful banquet table. People were seated around this feast of every food imaginable, including selections from every corner of the globe. It was an awesome sight.

However, as the touring dreamer took a closer look, he noted that not one person had a smile. In fact, the entire atmosphere of the place was gloomy and dull. Even with this abundance of food, every person there was literally skin and bones. Suddenly, he realized the reason for this depressing sight. Each person in the room had a fork strapped to the left arm and a knife strapped to the right arm. So with the abundance of delicacies at their fingertips, they were starving. There was no doubt in the man's mind that this was truly hell.

His next stop produced a scenario identical to his visit in hell. The same foods were prepared, and the knives and forks had the same four-foot handles. However, the inhabitants were joyful, laughing, singing, and having a wonderful time. They were not skin and bones but well fed and in excellent health. How could the conditions be so similar and produce such drastically different results?

Then the answer became clear. The people in hell had been trying to feed themselves with four-foot utensils. It was impossible. In heaven people were using the same knife and fork; however, they were feeding one another. Each person would reach across the table and feed the opposite person. By feeding one another, they were fed themselves.

*The moral is clear, by serving one another we can create a little heaven here on earth.*

## SIMPLE—BUT POWERFUL

I am told about a wise and beloved shah who once ruled the land of Persia. He cared greatly for his people and wanted only what was best for them. The Persians knew this shah took a personal interest in their affairs and tried to understand how his decisions affected their lives. Periodically he would disguise himself and wander through the streets, trying to see life from their perspective.

One day he disguised himself as a poor village man and went to visit the public baths. Many people were there enjoying the fellowship and relaxation. The water for the baths was heated by a furnace in the cellar, where one man was responsible for maintaining the comfort level of the water. The shah made his way to the basement to visit with the man who tirelessly tended the fire.

The two men shared a meal together, and the shah befriended this lonely man. Day after day, week in and week out, the ruler went to visit the firetender. The stranger soon became attached to his visitor because he came to where he was. No other person had showed that kind of caring or concern.

One day the shah revealed his true identity. It was a risky move, for he feared the man would ask him for special favors or for a gift. Instead, the leader's new friend looked into his eyes and said, "You left your comfortable palace and your glory to sit with me in this dungeon of darkness. You ate my bitter food and genuinely showed you cared about what happens to me. On other people you might bestow rich gifts, but to me you have given the best gift of all. You have given yourself."

*For thousands of years, people have been speculating on what constitutes quality human relationships. With all the philosophies, theories, and speculations, only one principle seems to stand strong. It is not new at all. In fact, it is almost as old as history itself. It was taught in Persia over three thousand years ago by Zoroaster to his fire worshipers. Confucius asserted the principle in China twenty-four centuries ago. In the Valley of Han lived the followers of Taoism. Their leader Lao-tzu taught the principle incessantly. Five hundred years before Christ, Buddha taught it to his disciples on the banks of the holy Ganges. The collections of Hinduism contained this principle over fifteen hundred years before Christ. Nineteen centuries ago, Jesus taught his disciples and followers much the same principle. He summed it up in one thought: "Do unto others as you would have them do unto you."*

## A TRANSFORMATION

A hurried businessman plunked a dollar into the cup of a man selling flowers and hurriedly went his way. Half a block down the street, he turned around and made his way back to the beggar. "I'm sorry," he said picking out his favorite flower. "In my haste I failed to make my purchase. After all, you are a businessman just like me. Your merchandise is fairly priced and of good quality. I trust you won't be upset with my failure to pick out my purchase." With that he smiled and quickly went his way.

At lunch a few weeks later, a neatly dressed, handsome man approached his table and introduced himself. "I'm sure you don't remember me, and I don't even know your name, but your face I will never forget. You are the man who inspired me to make something of myself. I was a vagrant selling dried flowers until you gave me back my self-respect. Now I believe I am a businessman."

*A lot of people have accomplished more in their lives than they thought they could. Servants don't share their wealth with others but rather reveal their own wealth to them.*

## YOU HAVE GOT TO BE KIDDING!

It was a stormy night several years ago when an elderly couple entered the hotel lobby and asked for a room. "I am sorry," responded the clerk. "There are several business conventions in town, and we are entirely booked." A few moments of silence followed as the hotel clerk noticed the disappointed look on the elderly couple's faces. "I just can't send a nice couple like you out into this weather," the clerk began, not knowing what to say next. "How about staying in my room?" The couple were uncomfortable at inconveniencing the clerk this way but after a few moments accepted his hospitality.

The man paid his bill the next morning, and before leaving he told the clerk, "You are the kind of person that every hotel owner dreams about having as an employee. Maybe someday I'll build a motel for you." The hotel clerk was flattered, but the idea sounded so outrageous he chuckled at the old man's joke.

A few years passed. Then one day the hotel clerk received a registered letter from the elderly man. His comments reflected his vivid recollection of that stormy night. He invited the hotel clerk to visit him in New York. The elderly man had even enclosed a round-trip ticket.

Arriving a few days later in New York, the clerk was met by his friend at the corner of Fifth Avenue and Thirty-fourth Street, where a magnificent new building stood. "That," exclaimed the old man, "is the hotel I have built for you to run! I told you a few years ago it might happen, and today you must know I am serious."

"You *must* be joking," said the clerk. "What is the catch? Why me? Who are you anyway?" stammered the flustered man.

"My name is William Waldorf-Astor. There is no catch, and you are the person I want." That hotel was the original Waldorf-Astoria, and the young clerk who accepted the first managerial position was George C. Boldt.

*It is true. When you meet the needs of other people, your needs will be met. Even when it might first seem to be a joke.*

## THE LOVE OF TWO BROTHERS

The beautiful story of two brothers who farmed together is a perfect example of unselfish love. The brothers lived in separate houses but met each day in the fields and worked together. One brother was married and had a large family. The other lived alone. However, they divided the harvest from the fields equally.

Each night one brother gave serious thought to the other. The brother without a family asked himself why he was taking half the harvest when his brother was struggling to support a large family. With sincere love in his heart, this brother had a plan to help out his married brother. Each night he filled a huge basket with a portion of his own share of the harvest, slipped over to his brother's storage areas, and unloaded the basket there.

The married brother with the large family often wondered why his single brother took his full half of the harvest, but reasoned that his brother would not have children to care for him in his old age. He would be alone. The married brother's heart went out to his brother because he loved him very much. So each night he also filled a basket with a good measure of his share of the yield and sneaked quietly to his brother's storage sheds and there left it as a silent offering.

One night in their passage, the brothers met. When each told the other what he was doing, they both cried and embraced there in the dark. Perhaps they both realized that their greatest wealth lay in the respect and love that they had for one another.

## "WHEN DO I DIE?"

In 1910, Dr. George Crane's daily newspaper column carried the following story: Jimmy, age ten, was devoted to his little sister, age six. He nearly panicked when his little sister fell off her bicycle and cut a large artery in her leg. The bleeding was profuse, and by the time the doctor arrived at their house, the little girl was failing fast.

In the early 1900s blood transfusions and other medical miracles were not yet common. However, the doctor managed to clamp the cut ends of the artery with his hemostat. The little girl's heart was still failing. In desperation, the doctor turned to Jimmy and asked, "Jimmy, will you give your blood to help save your little sister's life?"

Jimmy swallowed hard but nodded his head. So the doctor lay him on the kitchen table and began withdrawing blood from one of his veins. Then he injected the blood directly into the little girl's vein.

For the next thirty minutes, the doctor and the family watched over the little girl anxiously and prayerfully. The doctor kept his stethoscope over her heart to note its beating. Finally, she was over the crisis. The doctor wiped the perspiration off his forehead. Only then did he notice that Jimmy was still stretched out on the kitchen table, tense and trembling.

"What's the matter, Jimmy?" asked the doctor. "W-w-when do I die?" Jimmy replied through his clenched teeth.

The doctor realized that Jimmy had misunderstood what the request for his blood really meant. Jimmy had imagined that his sister was going to need all his blood. Which meant that Jimmy, though hesitating a moment and swallowing hard at the doctor's original request, had silently agreed to die for his little sister!

The doctor had tears in his eyes as he reassured Jimmy that he had extracted only a little of his blood for his sister, and that Jimmy was not going to die. Jimmy was willing to die so that his sister might live.

## GIVING VANISHES PROBLEMS

There is an old Chinese story about a woman who lost her only son and went to the holy man in her village and said, "What mystic powers do you have that will lift the ache from my heart?"

"Well, my dear woman," he said gently. "There is a wonderful thing you can do. I want you to go and get me a mustard seed from a home that has no problems. Such a mustard seed can ward off your own problems."

So she traveled to a beautiful mansion. Nothing could possibly be wrong there, she thought. She knocked at the door and said, "I have to find a mustard seed from a home where there are no problems. It's very important to me."

"Oh," they said, "you have come to the wrong house." They began listing all of their family problems, and the list went on and on.

She thought to herself, "Well, I certainly know something about problems, for I have my own. Maybe I can be of help to them." And she was. She listened and comforted them. The fact that she listened and cared helped them.

She then went on in her search to find the magic mustard seed. She went from house to house. But no matter where she went, to the wealthy or to the poor, she could not find that seed. It simply was not to be found.

The woman found that troubles are universal and she learned that in giving herself in love and compassion to help others, her own pain vanished.

## THE MAGIC DRAGON

A few weeks after his parents learned their son, "P.J." Dragon, had leukemia, the child began receiving a variety of get-well messages. He received gifts, cleverly written letters, poems, and drawings. The presents all came from an unnamed party called "Magic Dragon." The special trademark of Magic Dragon's gifts was a big green bow.

As the weeks and months wore on, little P.J.'s treatments grew long and painful. But there was one consolation. Magic Dragon's favorite gift was a stuffed dragon. The stuffed dragon became a friend that he depended on as his disease progressed. P.J.'s father was a Detroit policeman. At one point, he tried to track down Magic Dragon's hidden identity. However, he soon changed his mind when he discovered the trouble that Magic Dragon had gone to in order to cover his or her tracks.

When little P.J. went into the hospital, the prized toy dragon received the same treatment the boy did. When a bandage was put on P.J., the dragon got one too. That little stuffed toy with the big green bow pulled P.J. through some of the most difficult times of his illness.

Unfortunately, five-year-old P.J. lost his battle. Shortly after listening to his favorite record, "Puff the Magic Dragon," the brave little boy died. Hundreds of friends and relatives paid their final respects to P.J. and contributed to the vast array of flowers that occupied most of the room where his little body lay. In the middle of the display was a gigantic bouquet of daisies tied affectionately together with a big green bow. Magic Dragon was a true friend—always giving and not demanding anything in return.

*United Press International*

## A TRULY HUMBLE MAN

Booker T. Washington, the renowned black educator, was an outstanding example of a truly humble man. Shortly after he took over the presidency of Tuskegee Institute in Alabama, he was walking in an exclusive section of town when he was stopped by a wealthy white woman. Not knowing the famous Washington by sight, she asked if he would like to earn a few dollars by chopping wood for her. Professor Washington smiled, rolled up his sleeves, and proceeded to do the humble chore she had requested.

When he was finished, he carried the logs into the house and stacked them by the fireplace. The woman's daughter recognized him and later revealed his identity to her mother. The next morning the embarrassed woman went to see Washington in his office at the Institute and apologized profusely.

"It's perfectly all right, madam," he replied. "Occasionally I enjoy a little manual labor. Besides, it's always a delight to do something for a friend." She shook his hand warmly and assured him that his meek and gracious attitude would never be forgotten. Not long afterward, she showed her admiration by persuading wealthy acquaintances to join her in donating thousands of dollars to the Tuskegee Institute.

*Booker T. Washington had learned that doing a task with a selfless attitude will bring both the respect of men and the favor of God.*

## A LITTLE BIT OF GOD

The war was over, but the fight had just begun. World War II devastated Europe, and the fight was on to pick up the pieces and go on with life. Undoubtedly, the saddest sight were the numbers of children who had been orphaned. Many were without clothes and starving in the streets. Their present existence was unfortunate, but their future looked hopeless.

Early one foggy morning, an American soldier was making his way back to base when he spotted a young boy with his nose pressed against a bakeshop window. The little boy's hunger was evident as he watched every move the baker made preparing the day's goods. Taken in by the emotional sight, the soldier pulled his jeep over, got out, and quietly approached the young boy. There was a silent plea on the boy's face.

Suddenly, the soldier's heart was heavy. He asked the boy if he would like one of the tasty morsels.

Startled, the boy replied, "I sure would!"

The soldier made his way inside and purchased a dozen pastries for the young boy. Stepping back into the chilly morning air, he smiled as he approached his smiling friend.

"Here you are, son."

Turning to leave, he felt a tug at his coat. He looked back and heard the little boy softly ask, "Mister, are you God?"

*The willingness to give of ourselves enhances the opinions others have of us.*

## THE GREATEST THING IN THE WORLD

Henry Drummond beautifully comments on servanthood in his book *The Greatest Thing in the World:* "There is no happiness in having or getting, but only in giving. Half of the world is on the wrong scent in the pursuit of happiness. They think it consists of having and getting and in being served by others. It consists of giving and serving others."

# Success

*There are two kinds of success. One*
*is the very rare kind that comes to the*
*man who has the power to do what no one else*
*has the power to do. That is genius. But*
*the average man who wins what we call success*
*is not a genius. He is a man who has merely*
*the ordinary qualities that he shares with his fellows,*
*but who has developed those ordinary qualities*
*to a more than ordinary degree.*

THEODORE ROOSEVELT

46

I would rather fail in a cause that will ultimately succeed than succeed in a cause that will ultimately fail.

*Woodrow Wilson*

Men never plan to be failures; they simply fail to plan to be successful.

*William A. Ward*

I can give you a six-word formula for success: "Think things through —then follow through."

*Edward Rickenbacker*

Most people would succeed in small things if they were not troubled with great ambitions.

*Henry Wadsworth Longfellow*

Nothing is so commonplace as the wish to be remarkable

*Oliver Wendell Holmes, Jr.*

Where there's a will, there's a way.

*Anonymous*

Personal success is simply the fulfillment of what makes you happiest.

*Anonymous*

It's good to have money and the things that money can buy, but it's good, too, to check once in a while and make sure that you haven't lost the things that money can't buy.

*George Horace Lorimer*

The toughest thing about success is that you have got to keep on being a success.

*Irving Berlin*

Heroes are symbolic figures whose deeds are out of the ordinary, but not too far out. They show—often dramatically—that the idea of success lies within human capacity.

*Corporate Cultures*

If you want a place in the sun, you have to put up with a few blisters.

*Abigail Van Buren*

The secret of success is to do the common things uncommonly well.

*John D. Rockefeller, Jr.*

The secret of success is to be like a duck—smooth and unruffled on top, but paddling furiously underneath.

*Anonymous*

The road to success is dotted with many tempting parking places.

*Anonymous*

He who wants milk should not sit himself in the middle of a pasture waiting for a cow to back up to him.

*Anonymous*

Sometimes it is not good enough to do your best; you have to do what's required.

*Sir Winston Churchill*

Success is knowing what your values are and living in a way consistent with your values.

*Danny Cox*

"It has always seemed strange to me," said Doc. "The things we admire in men, kindness and generosity, openness, honesty, understanding, and feeling are the concomitants of failure in our system. And those traits we detest, sharpness, egotism, and self-interest are the traits of success. And while men admire the quality of the first, they love the product of the second."

*John Steinbeck*

Self-trust is the first secret of success.

*Ralph Waldo Emerson*

Success, if it is to be—is up to me.

*Anonymous*

Shoot for the moon—if you fail, you land in the stars. That is not bad company. Most people shoot for the barn door, and if they fail—it is not a rose-colored landing.

*Anonymous*

I have learned that success is to be measured not so much by the position that one has reached in life as by the obstacles which he has overcome while trying to succeed.

*Booker T. Washington*

You cannot be anything if you want to be everything.

*Solomon Schechter*

Some men succeed because they are destined to, but most men because they are determined to.

*Anonymous*

To accomplish great things, we must not only act but also dream, not only dream but also believe.

*Anatole France*

Small opportunities are often the beginnings of great enterprises.

*Demosthenes*

There exist limitless opportunities in every industry. Where there is an open mind, there will always be a frontier.

*Charles F. Kettering*

There is a four-word formula for success that applies equally well to organizations or individuals: Make yourself more useful.

*Anonymous*

The rung of a ladder was never meant to rest upon, but only to hold a man's foot long enough to enable him to put the other somewhat higher.

*Thomas H. Huxley*

All things come to him who goes after them

*Anonymous*

Success or failure is caused more by mental attitude than by mental capacity.

*Sir Walter Scott*

Becoming number one is easier than remaining number one.

*Senator Bill Bradley*

For when the one great scorer comes
   to write against your name,
He marks—not that you won or lost—
   but how you played the game.

*Grantland Rice*

There's always room at the top.

*Daniel Webster*

Let us be thankful for the fools, but for them the rest of us could not succeed.

*Mark Twain*

The difference between failure and success is doing a thing nearly right and doing a thing exactly right.

*Edward Simmons*

The wealthy man is the man who *is* much, not the one who has much.

*Karl Marx*

It's great to be great, but it's greater to be human.

*Will Rogers*

The worst part of success is to try finding someone who is happy for you.

*Bette Midler*

It takes twenty years to make an overnight success.

*Eddie Cantor*

Contrary to the cliché, genuinely nice guys most often finish first, or very near it.

*Malcolm Forbes*

Success often comes from taking a misstep in the right direction.

*Anonymous*

Eighty percent of success is showing up.

*Woody Allen*

If at first you don't succeed, then quit. There's no use in being a fool about it.

*W. C. Fields*

### It's Up To You!

If you think you're a winner you'll win.
If you dare to step out you'll succeed.
Believe in your heart, have a purpose to start.
Aim to help fellow man in his need.
Thoughts of faith must replace every doubt.
Words of courage and you cannot fail.
If you stumble and fall, rise and stand ten feet tall,
You determine the course that you sail.
For in life as in death, don't you see,
It's the man who has nothing to fear,
Who approaches the gates, stands for a moment and waits,
Feels the presence of God oh so near.
You've been given the power to see,
What it takes to be a real man,
Let your thinking be pure, it will make you secure,
If you want to, you know that you can.

*Anonymous*

## IT'S AN UPHILL CLIMB

Paul Harvey has said, "You can tell when you are on the road to success. It's uphill all the way."

A young man in Kansas City, with a burning desire to draw, understood the uphill climb to success. He went from newspaper to newspaper trying to sell his cartoons. But each editor coldly and quickly suggested that he had no talent and implied that he might want to choose another line of work. But he persevered, determined to make his dream a reality. He wanted to draw, and draw he would.

For several months, the rejections came. Finally, in a move of "grace," he was hired by a minister to draw pictures advertising church events. This young artist was not discouraged by his unusual opportunity. Rather, he remembered the wise words of Benjamin Disraeli: "The secret of success in life is for a man to be ready for his opportunity when it comes."

Working out of a small, mouse-infested shed owned by the church, he struggled to be creative. Ironically, this less-than-ideal working environment stimulated his most famous work. He called it Mickey Mouse. And, of course, the man of whom we are talking was Walt Disney.

Walt Disney made it happen because he realized the uphill climb to success contained the opportunities he would capitalize on.

## What Is Success?

To laugh often and love much;
To win the respect of intelligent persons
and the affection of children;
To earn the approval of honest critics
and endure the betrayal of false friends;
To appreciate beauty;
To find the best in others;
To give of one's self without the
slightest thought of return;
To have accomplished a task, whether
by a healthy child, a rescued soul, a
garden patch, or a redeemed social
condition;
To have played and laughed with
enthusiasm and sung with exaltation;
To know that even one life has breathed
easier because you have lived;
This is to have succeeded.

*Anonymous*

## SUCCESS TRIVIA

The following are eight illustrations that will test your awareness of people who have overcome their setbacks to achieve impressive success:

1. Who ran for public office seven times, was defeated every time, and still went on to become president?—Abraham Lincoln

2. Who struggled through thousands of experiments before perfecting one invention and was awarded over one thousand patents for his inventions?—Thomas Alva Edison

3. Who flunked the first grade and went on to become attorney general?—Robert F. Kennedy

4. Who didn't learn to talk until he was four years old but ultimately communicated fabulous scientific theories throughout the world?—Albert Einstein

5. Who was dismissed from the psychiatric society in Vienna, Austria, only to become a world respected, prominent psychiatrist?—Victor Frankl

6. Who was told at an early age that he had no talent for music but whose name is synonymous with music quality?—Ludwig van Beethoven

7. Who flunked first and fourth grades yet went on to become an astronaut?—Ed Gibson

8. Who worked as a water boy in a mine, as a lumberjack, a garage mechanic, and spent two years acting with a tent show before achieving acting success?—Clark Gable

Ralph Waldo Emerson once said, "Self-trust is the first secret of success." Imagine how difficult it must have been for the people mentioned above to continue trusting themselves. Through failure, adversity, and overwhelming obstacles, they maintained a clear picture of what they wanted and then applied their efforts toward the attainment of their goals.

Success: If it is to be—is up to me.

## HOW BADLY DO YOU WANT SUCCESS?

There is a story about Paderewski and a woman he met at a reception who said, "Mr. Paderewski, I would give anything if I could play like you."

"No, madam," he replied. "I don't believe you would, for I doubt that you want to badly enough to make the effort."

*The first step to experiencing success is to want it with all our heart. Then, of course, we need to commit ourselves to achieving it.*

## COMMITTED FOR LIFE

A woman rushed up to famed violinist Fritz Kreisler after a concert and cried, "I'd give my life to play as beautifully as you do."

Kreisler replied, "I did."

## "HOW CAN I?" RATHER THAN "WHY NOT?"

In his great self-help classic, *I Dare You*, William Danforth indicates that 95 percent of all individuals lack the determination to call on their untapped potential. This overwhelming majority quickly settles on the status quo of mediocrity and reflects on their misfortune and bad breaks for the rest of their lives, while the daring 5 percent continue on to successful levels. He speaks to that small group of forward-moving individuals when he says, "The day of defending your present possessions is gone. From now on, you are not going to worry about holding your job. Put the worry on the fellow above you about holding his. From this day onward, wrong things are put on the defense. You have marshaled right things for the attack. Your eyes are turned toward your strength, not your weakness. Henceforth, you will wake in the morning thinking of ways to do things, rather than reasons why they cannot be done!"

## THE TEN COMMANDMENTS OF SUCCESS

1. WORK HARD: Hard work is the best investment a man can make.

2. STUDY HARD: Knowledge enables a man to work more intelligently and effectively.

3. HAVE INITIATIVE: Ruts often deepen into graves.

4. LOVE YOUR WORK: Then you will find pleasure in mastering it.

5. BE EXACT: Slipshod methods bring slipshod results.

6. HAVE THE SPIRIT OF CONQUEST: Thus you can successfully battle and overcome difficulties.

7. CULTIVATE PERSONALITY: Personality is to a man what perfume is to the flower.

8. HELP AND SHARE WITH OTHERS: The real test of business greatness lies in giving opportunity to others.

9. BE DEMOCRATIC: Unless you feel right toward your fellow men, you can never be a successful leader of men.

10. IN ALL THINGS DO YOUR BEST: The man who has done his best has done everything. The man who has done less than his best has done nothing.

*Charles M. Schwab*

## DAY BY DAY

Remember Aesop's fable about the goose and the golden egg? It's a story about a farmer who visits the nest of his goose one day and finds a glittering yellow egg. He was tempted to throw it away, but a second thought caused him to take it home and look it over more carefully. Much to his surprise, this strange egg turned out to be pure gold. Morning after morning, he gathered one golden egg from the goose, thereby becoming very rich. The richer he became, the greedier he got, until one day he became impatient with his gradual wealth. Hoping to get all the gold from the goose at once, he butchered it, only to find the goose empty.

*Success is not a get-rich-quick scheme. It is, however, a day-by-day process. Short-term personal profits are not synonymous with long-term prosperity. Like the farmer, we too can ruin our chances for getting long-term results by becoming impatient and unwilling to pay the daily price.*

### THERE IS MORE

In Valladolid, Spain, Christopher Columbus died in 1506. There stands a monument commemorating the great discoverer. An interesting feature of the memorial is a statue of a lion destroying one of the Latin words that had been part of Spain's motto for centuries. Before Columbus made his voyages, the Spaniards thought they had reached the outer limits of earth. Thus, their motto was *"Ne Plus Ultra,"* which means, "No more beyond." The word being torn away by the lion was "Ne" or "No," making it read *"Plus Ultra."* Columbus had proved that there was indeed "more beyond."

*Our Daily Bread*

### WHAT'S THE KEY?

When asked if there was a key to his company's success, Kemmons Wilson, founder of Holiday Inns, quickly responded, "I believe, to be successful, that you have to work at least half a day—it doesn't make any difference which half, the first twelve hours or the last twelve."

That same principle drove Althea Gibson to become a tennis star. In her book, *I Always Wanted To Be Somebody,* Gibson speaks of the road she traveled to athletic success: "I was determined that I was going to be somebody too—if it killed me." Hard work and perseverance landed her a place in tennis history.

James J. Corbett, the great prizefighter, provided a visual picture of the key to success: "When your feet are so tired that you have to shuffle back to the center of the ring, fight one more round. When your arms are so tired that you can hardly lift your hands to come on guard, fight one more round. When your nose is bleeding and your eyes are black and you are so tired that you wish your opponent would crack you on the jaw and put you to sleep, fight one more round—remembering that the man who always fights one more round is never whipped."

Calvin Coolidge, never a man to waste words, said there was one main ingredient needed in our lives to ensure success. What is it? *Perseverance.*

## MEASURING SUCCESS

I measure success by how well I sleep on a given night. If I have not had to question my motives for any particular action I might have undertaken, or knowingly caused another human being trouble or discomfort, then I am at peace with my God and myself and I fall asleep easily. If sleep comes hard, then I know the day has been a personal failure.

*Rod McKuen*

## YOU MAKE THE POSITION

How many times have you heard people lament that if only they had a more prestigious position, then they could really feel important?

President Woodrow Wilson experienced that attitude with one of his maids. She approached him one day after the secretary of labor had resigned from the cabinet. "President Wilson," she said, "my husband is perfect for this vacant position. He is a laboring man, knows what labor is, and understands laboring people. Please consider him when you appoint the new secretary of labor."

Wilson replied, "I appreciate your recommendation, but you must remember, the secretary of labor is an important position. It requires an influential person."

"But," the maid replied, "if you made my husband the secretary of labor, he would be an influential person!"

*A position can never make a person successful. A person makes the position and the success of that position.*

## A CLASSIC SUCCESS

With little more than a high school diploma, Harlow Curtice landed a bookkeeper's job with a subsidiary of General Motors. This country boy became president of the company at thirty-five, and by the time he was forty, Curtice was appointed general manager of General Motors' prized and prestigious Buick division.

Curtice, a man with a flair for action and new ideas, dared to design new styles and models. He personally traveled throughout the United States to inspire dealers and give them a renewed faith in their product.

The result? Although it was in the middle of the Depression, sales of Buick cars quadrupled. His division became the second biggest money-maker in General Motors' industrial history. That was the success he dreamed of when he was first employed in 1914.

To what did Harlow Curtice attribute his success? Three things seem to stand out. First, he set goals for himself and required the same of the people around him. Second, he took great pride in confronting and overcoming obstacles that blinded his vision. Finally, he made winning a habit. He was willing to do the things losers refused to do.

## DOING WHAT YOU WANT TO DO

Albert Schweitzer was born in 1875. He was a sickly child who was slow to read and write, and was a poor scholar. As he grew up, he forced himself to master subjects that were particularly difficult, such as Hebrew. He turned out to be a genuine music prodigy, playing the organ at eight, and by nine, he was substituting for the regular organist in a church service.

By early manhood, Schweitzer had several professional lives proceeding concurrently. At the University of Strasbourg, he earned his first Ph.D. in philosophy, then another in theology, followed by one in music theory. By the time he was thirty, he had a successful career as a concert organist and was publishing a stream of books in selected fields. Suddenly, one day, he decided to stop his academic career in order to study medicine. It was a dramatic move inspired by a decision to devote the rest of his life to being a missionary. His decision was made after he read a magazine article about the Congo. "While we are preaching to these people about religion," the article had said, "they are suffering and dying before our eyes from physical maladies."

Schweitzer knew what he wanted to do and began to lay plans to go to Africa. Friends and academicians protested: If Africa needed help, let Schweitzer raise the money necessary to increase their quality of living. He certainly had more ability than to wash lepers with his own hands, they believed.

Someone wise once said, "Success is doing what you want to do because you feel called to do it." Schweitzer's dreams were questioned by others, but he maintained a plan of action that he knew would enhance his life. No one could take away what he believed was right for him.

Schweitzer fell in love with Helen Bresslau, the daughter of a Jewish historian. His proposal to her was, to say the least, unique: "I am studying to be a doctor in Africa. Would you be willing to grow old with me and spend the rest of your life with me in the jungle?"

Helen's response was not of the usual nature. "I love you, Albert. Therefore, I will become a nurse. You will not be able to go without me." So, on Good Friday of 1913, Schweitzer and his wife departed for a lifetime of service in French Equatorial Africa. In over fifty years of service, Albert Schweitzer became a legend in his own time.

## A WINNER IN THE GAME OF LIFE

He was an unknown when his first book was published in 1936. He had been a successful salesman but was determined to teach people what he felt were important principles in the world of human relations and public speaking. Leaving Warrensburg, Missouri, he approached the directors of the Twenty-third Street YMCA in New York with his dream for teaching. The course was untried and unknown, so the directors were wary of its possibility for success. Finally, they agreed to pay him on a commission basis.

Within a few years, the course was so popular that the young man was making $30 a night in commission rather than the usual $2 teaching fee. While teaching in Larchmont, New York, he met a publishing executive who had enrolled in the course. The publisher was so impressed with the material that he suggested the instructor gather it into a book. And that he did.

After this young man, Dale Carnegie was his name, published *How To Win Friends and Influence People,* it stayed on the *New York Times* best-seller list for ten straight years. No other author can claim such an accomplishment. The final numbers are not yet in, but more than 10 million copies have been sold, and an additional 200,000 copies are purchased every year.

> *Voltaire said, "Life is like a game of cards. Each player must accept the cards that life deals to him or her. With cards in hand, each person must decide how the hand will be played in order to win the game." Dale Carnegie understood the necessity to play the hand he had been dealt. It would certainly be fair to say that Dale Carnegie was successful in the card game of life.*

## A HOME RUN EFFORT

If Pete Gray were here, he would tell you that self-motivation, determination, and action are the keys to personal success. And he should know. At six years old, Pete lost his arm in a freak farm accident. While trying to jump onto a slow-moving wagon, he missed, fell off, and caught his right arm in the wheel spokes. The arm was badly mangled. Doctors said there was no way to save it, so the arm was amputated just above the elbow.

The accident literally cut off the key to his dreams—or did it? Pete Gray was right-handed and desired more than anything to become a major league baseball player. Did he give up his dream? Not on your life!

Pete Gray learned to bat from the left side. He focused all his efforts on strengthening that left arm and mastering its control. His sharp eye and brilliant "magic" produced well-laid bunts, screaming line drives, and unbelievable distance.

As a semi-pro, his fielding acrobatics entertained the crowds. Pete Gray wore his glove on his fingertips. After catching the ball, he would quickly stick the glove under the stump of his right arm, grab the ball with his left arm, and throw. Amazing as it may seem, very little time was lost in this systematic approach.

While playing for the Memphis Chicks, Pete Gray began making a reputation for himself. In 1944, he batted .333, stole sixty-three bases, and was named the league's most valuable player. In two seasons of play, he struck out only fifteen times. His determination and baseball success made Pete Gray a household word. Even the U.S. government began filming his unusual yet effective style of play to show to wounded veterans. His story became an inspiration to many.

Finally, in 1945, Pete Gray's dream became a reality. Despite periodic personal doubts, discouragement from others, and, of course, his physical disability, Pete Gray signed a major league contract with the St. Louis Browns. If success really is doing what makes you happy, then Pete Gray was a successful man.

## SO HERE IT IS

Some wise person has written: "Success is a journey, not a destination. Happiness is to be found along the way, not at the end of the road—for then the journey is over and it is too late. The time for happiness is today, not tomorrow."

# Understanding

*Every man takes the limits of his own field of vision for the limits of the world.*

**ARTHUR SCHOPENHAUER**

47

If there is any one secret to success, it lies in the ability to get the other person's point of view and see things from his angle as well as from your own.

*Henry Ford*

You can make more friends in two months by becoming interested in other people than you can in two years by trying to get other people interested in you.

*Dale Carnegie*

When you want to convert someone to your view, you go over to where he is standing, take him by the hand, and guide him. You don't stand across the room and shout at him; you don't call him a dummy; you don't order him to come over to where you are. You start where he is and work from that position. That's the only way to get him to budge.

*Saint Thomas Aquinas*

Most people believe they see the world as it is. However, we really see the world as we are.

*Anonymous*

No one can develop freely in this world and find a full life without feeling understood by at least one person.

*Dr. Paul Tournier*

When we all think alike, no one thinks very much.

*Walter Lippmann*

Successful collaborative negotiation lies in finding out what the other side really wants and showing them a way to get it—while you get what you want.

*Herb Cohen*

The ability to see the situation as the other side sees it is one of the most important skills a negotiator can possess.

*Roger Fisher and William Ury*

## YOU CAN TAX IT

Michael Faraday knew that successful selling was a product of understanding what was important to other people. Faraday wanted the backing of Prime Minister William Gladstone for his invention of the first electric motor. Gladstone was not impressed with Faraday's crudely made invention. It was just a little wire revolving around a magnet.

"Of what possible good is it?" Gladstone asked.

"Of great benefit to our country," Faraday responded. "For some day you will be able to tax it!"

The minds of Gladstone and the inventive genius became one. Faraday did not go on to boast about his creativity, describe his product, or convince the world it needed an electric motor.

Faraday's success is attributed to his ability to understand Gladstone's world.

### The Other Side of the Desk

Have you ever thought just a wee little bit,
Of how it would seem to be a misfit,
And how you would feel if *you* had to sit,
On the other side of the desk?

Have you ever looked at the man who seemed a bum,
As he sat before you, nervous—dumb—
And thought of the courage it took to come,
To the other side of the desk?

Have you thought of his dreams that went astray,
Of the hard, real facts of his every day,
Of the things in his life that make him stray,
On the other side of the desk?

Have you thought to yourself, "It could be I,
If the good things of life had passed me by,
And maybe I'd bluster and maybe I'd lie,
From the other side of the desk?"

Did you make him feel he was full of greed,

Make him ashamed of his race or creed,
Or did you reach out to him in his need,
To the other side of the desk?

May God give us wisdom and lots of it,
And much compassion and plenty of grit,
So that we may be kinder to those who sit,
On the other side of the desk.

*Anonymous*

## PEOPLE DO THINGS FOR THEIR REASONS

Ralph Waldo Emerson was a great historian, noted poet, and respected philosopher. Emerson, however, knew little about persuading a female calf into the barn. His personal experience with this endeavor proved frustrating.

Emerson and his son, Edward, were engrossed in this effort one sultry afternoon. With Edward circling an arm about the neck of the calf and Ralph pushing from behind, they struggled to get the obstinate heifer to move, but with each push and pull, the stubborn calf locked its knees and firmly planted all four feet into the ground.

The sweat now streaming from his face and his clothing soaked with bovine smell, the great Ralph Waldo Emerson lost his persistent spirit.

A young Irish peasant woman happened by and sensed the Emersons' predicament. Smiling sweetly, she asked Emerson if she could be of some assistance. Rather sarcastically, the exasperated sage replied, "If you think you can do anything, go right ahead."

The young woman walked around to the front of the calf, thrust her finger into the calf's mouth, and the calf peacefully followed her into the barn.

Edward was amused. However, Ralph Waldo Emerson was intrigued with the simple lesson this young peasant woman had taught him. That night he recorded the incident in his journal with this thought: "I like people who know how to make things happen."

*People possess some comparable characteristics displayed by the young calf. You can push them, pull them, prod them, or even kick them, and they won't move, but give them a reason they can understand, one that will prove beneficial to them, and people will peacefully follow along. People don't do things because you want them to. They perform a certain way because they want to. When I learn what is important to others, it makes working with them simpler.*

## TRUTH IS TRUTH

Involved in a dispute concerning undisputable facts, Abraham Lincoln used his common sense to illustrate the point.

"How many legs has a cow?" questioned Lincoln of his disputer.

"Four, of course," came the disgusted reply.

"Exactly," agreed Lincoln. "Now let's suppose you call the cow's tail a leg; then how many legs would a cow have?"

"Why, five, of course," the man replied.

"I beckon to differ with you there," said Lincoln. "Calling a cow's tail a leg doesn't make it a leg."

*Before disputing what others say, get the facts. There can be a giant gap between what is and what is perceived.*

## CONSIDER BOTH SIDES

I read about an executive who kept a little ball in his desk. He would display the ball when differences of opinions surfaced with his employees. Holding the ball between two people, he would ask, "What color is this little ball?"

The person on his left would quickly respond, "White."

Now the person on the right was a little confused and would sputter, "Black."

As the two parties stared at the ball, they could never agree on the color. The executive would then tell his confused employees, "Unless you know each other's point of view, there will be no agreement on the color of the ball."

*How many disagreements could be quickly resolved if people would only look at both sides of the ball?*

# Values

*When you know what your values are, making decisions becomes easier.*

GLENN VAN EKEREN

48

The height of your accomplishment will equal the depth of your convictions.

*William F. Scolavino*

One person with a belief is equal to a force of ninety-nine who only have interests.

*Anonymous*

Once you believe something is true, whether or not it is, you will then act as if it is.

*Anonymous*

What you value is what you think about. What you think about is what you become.

*Joel Weldon*

Your values have validity if you adhere to them and they don't infringe on the rights of others.

*Anonymous*

Keep pace with the drummer you hear, however measured or far away.

*Henry David Thoreau*

A good conscience is a continual feast.

*Sir Francis Bacon*

## VALUABLE VALUES

Marshall Field once indicated the following twelve reminders that can be helpful in obtaining a sound sense of values:

1. The value of time.
2. The success of perseverance.
3. The pleasure of working.
4. The dignity of simplicity.
5. The worth of character.
6. The power of kindness.
7. The influence of example.

8. The obligation of duty.

9. The wisdom of economy.

10. The virtue of patience.

11. The improvement of talent.

12. The joy of originating.

# Work

*The dictionary is the only place that success comes
before work. Hard work is the price we must pay for
success. I think you can accomplish almost anything if
you're willing to pay the price.*

VINCE LOMBARDI

49

Choose a job you love, and you will never have to work a day in your life.

*Confucius*

Each morning sees some task begun,
Each evening sees its close.
Something attempted, something done,
Has earned a night's repose

*Henry Wadsworth Longfellow*

Work expands so as to fill the time available for its completion.

*C. Northcote Parkinson*

God gives us the nuts, but he does not crack them

*Proverbs*

Opportunities are usually disguised as hard work, so most people don't recognize them.

*Ann Landers*

The biggest things are always the easiest to do because there is no competition.

*William Van Horne*

Hard work without talent is a shame, but talent without hard work is a tragedy.

*Robert Half*

Hard work means prosperity; only a fool idles away his time.

*Proverbs 12:11*

If you love sleep, you will end in poverty. Stay awake, work hard, and there will be plenty to eat!

*Proverbs 20:13*

My parents always told me that people will never know how long it takes you to do something. They will only know how well it is done.

*Nancy Hanks*

The best-kept secret in America today is that people would rather work hard for something they believe in than enjoy a pampered idleness.

*John W. Gardner*

Far and away the best price that life offers is the chance to work hard at work worth doing.

*Theodore Roosevelt*

In order that people may be happy in their work, these three things are needed: They must be fit for it, they must not do too much of it, and they must have a sense of success in it.

*John Ruskin*

Work saves us from three great evils: boredom, vice, and need.

*Voltaire*

One thing you can learn by watching the clock is that it passes the time by keeping its hands busy.

*York Trade Compositor*

*Employer:* I'm sorry, things are tight right now, and I have no job for you. I doubt that I could find enough work to keep you busy.
*Applicant:* But you have no idea how little work it takes to keep me busy.

*Anonymous*

The number of people who are unemployed isn't as great as the number who aren't working.

*Frank A. Clark*

Thank God—every morning when you get up—that you have something to do which must be done, whether you like it or not. Being forced to work, and forced to do your best, will breed in you a hundred virtues which the idle never know.

*Charles Kingsley*

Make yourself indispensable, and you will move up. Act as though you are indispensable, and you will move out.

*Jules Ormont*

Never have we had so little time in which to do so much.

*Franklin D. Roosevelt*

When the grass looks greener on the other side of the fence, it may be that they take better care of it there

*Cecil Selig*

There is no limit to what can be accomplished if it doesn't matter who gets the credit.

*Ralph Waldo Emerson*

I like work. It fascinates me. I can sit and look at it for hours.

*Jerome K. Jerome*

I am a great believer in luck, and I find the harder I work, the more I have of it.

*Stephen Leacock*

Two laborers were watching a new computerized steam shovel at work in an open-pit mine. The shovel took in a truckload of dirt in one big bite. After just a few bites, the truck was full. One laborer said to the other,

"Man, that machine has put five hundred of us out of work. It's our enemy!" The other man said, "Yes, and if we got rid of our shovels, we could create a million jobs for people to dig the mine with spoons."

*Anonymous*

"Visited the zoo recently?" asked the supervisor.
"No, sir," answered the young delivery boy.
"Well, you should," said the supervisor. "You'd enjoy it and get a big kick out of watching the turtles zip by."

*Anonymous*

Those persons who want by the yard and try by the inch need to be kicked by the foot.

*W. Willard Wirtz*

What is happening to our drive, to our spirit, to our initiative? This morning, I saw two robins standing in line for worm stamps.

*Bob Orben*

Ask God's blessing on your work, but do not also ask Him to do it.

*Waggerl*

Work for the Lord. The pay isn't much, but the retirement plan is out of this world.

*church bulletin*

If God simply handed us everything we want, He'd be taking from us our greatest prize—the job of accomplishment.

*Frank A. Clark*

Business is a lot like a game of tennis—those who serve well usually end up winning.

*Anonymous*

No man goes before his time—unless the boss leaves early.

*Groucho Marx*

We are judged by what we finish, not by what we start.

*Anonymous*

I venture to say that at the bottom of most fears, both mild and severe, will be found an overactive mind and an underactive body. Hence, I have advised many people, in their quest for happiness, to use their heads less and their arms and legs more—in useful work or play.

*Dr. Henry C. Link*

What is the use of health, or of life, if not to do some work therewith?

*Thomas Carlyle*

The secret of success is to do the common things uncommonly well.

*John D. Rockefeller, Jr.*

Do a disagreeable job today instead of tomorrow. You will save twenty-four hours of dreading to do it, while having twenty-four hours to savor the feeling that the job is behind you.

*Communication Briefings*

Everybody should be paid what he is worth, no matter how big a cut he might have to take.

*Anonymous*

The young carry-out boy was asked, "How long have you been working here?" He replied, "Ever since they threatened to fire me."

*Anonymous*

Some people quit working as soon as they find a job.

*Anonymous*

I loathe drudgery as much as any man, but I have learned that the only way to conquer drudgery is to get through it as neatly, as efficiently, as one can. You know perfectly well that a dull job slackly done becomes twice as dull; whereas a dull job which you try to do just as well as you can becomes half as dull. Here again, effort appears to me the main art of living.

*Harold Nicolson*

Winners are people who do jobs uncommonly well even when they don't feel like doing them at all.

*Anonymous*

My grandfather once told me that there were two kinds of people: those who do the work and those who take the credit. He told me to try to be in the first group; there was much less competition.

*Indira Gandhi*

There is no such thing as a big job. Any job, regardless of size, can be broken down into small jobs which, when done, complete the larger job.

*Walter P. Chrysler*

I never did a day's work in my life—it was all fun.

*Thomas Alva Edison*

When your work speaks for itself, don't interrupt.

*Henry J. Kaiser*

The record of historical achievement cries out in loud, condemning tones against laziness. Gibbon spent twenty-six years writing *The Decline and Fall of the Roman Empire*. Milton used to rise at four o'clock every morning in writing *Paradise Lost*. Bryant rewrote one of his essays ninety-nine times. Webster worked thirty-six years to produce the first edition of the dictionary that bears his name. Cicero practiced speaking before friends every day for thirty years to perfect his elocution.

*Help and Food*

A horse can't pull while kicking,
This fact we merely mention;
And he can't kick while pulling,
Which is our chief contention.
Let's imitate the good horse
And lead a life that's fitting;
Just pull an honest load, and then
There'll be no time for kicking.

*The Trumpeter*

Our grand business in life is not to see what lies dimly at a distance, but to do what clearly lies at hand.

*Thomas Carlyle*

You can't build a reputation on what you're going to do.

*Henry Ford*

Professionalism is knowing how to do it, when to do it, and doing it.

*Frank Tyger*

Some people remind us of blisters—they don't show up until the work is done.

*Paul Carruth*

Inspiration is engendered by participation. Participation is sustained by perspiration.

*Dr. Clay Risley*

I work with unbroken concentration, but without hurry. However much I am at the mercy of the world, I never let myself get lost by brooding over its misery. I hold firmly to the thought that each one of us can do a little to bring some portion of that misery to an end.

*Albert Schweitzer*

If you're an adult of average weight, here is what you accomplish in 24 hours: Your heart beats 103,689 times. Your blood travels 168,000,000 miles. You breathe 23,040 times. You inhale 438 cubic feet of air. You eat 3¼ pounds of food. You drink 2.9 quarts of liquids. You lose ⅞ pound of waste. You speak 25,000 words, including some unnecessary ones. You move 750 muscles. Your nails grow .000046 inch. Your hair grows .01714 inch. You exercise 7,000,000 brain cells. Feel tired?

*Anonymous*

I never knew a person who suffered from overwork. There are many, however, who suffered from too much ambition, and not enough action.

*Dr. James Mantague*

I have never known a person who died from overwork. But there are many who died from doubt.

*Dr. Charles Mayo*

*It's not so much how busy you are—but why you are busy. The bee is praised. The mosquito is swatted.*

*Marie O'Connor*

## WISDOM ON WORK

Thomas Alva Edison was once quoted as saying, "I am wondering what would have happened to me if some fluent talker had converted me to the theory of the eight-hour day, and convinced me that it was not fair to my fellow workers to put forth my best efforts in my work. I am glad that the eight-hour day had not been invented when I was a young man. If my life had been made up of eight-hour days, I do not believe I could have accomplished a great deal. This country would not amount to as much as it does if the young men had been afraid that they might earn more than they were paid."

Edison believed that rewarding efforts called for 2 percent inspiration and 98 percent perspiration.

David Livingston activated this work philosophy. He worked in a factory from 6:00 A.M. until 8:00 P.M. Then he attended night school for two hours, followed by studying far into the night. It could be said Livingston's accomplishments were the result of inspired perspiration.

Leonardo DaVinci understood the need for hard work as well as the benefits involved. "Thou, Oh God, doth sell to us all good things at the price of labor. Work is the seed from which grows all good things you hope for. A man who's afraid of hard work better be brave enough to accept poverty."

The honey bee provides a splendid example, visiting 125 clover heads to make one gram of honey. That means 3 million trips to make one pound of honey.

Michelangelo disputed the wonder of his own talent by saying, "If people knew how hard I have had to work to gain my mastery, it wouldn't seem wonderful at all "

*Is it any wonder that ancient and present sages suggest that success is always preceded by hard work?*

## BELIEVE IN WHAT YOU DO

A carpenter whose brother was a famous musician was visiting with the foreman of the construction company where he worked. "You must feel honored to have a brother who is known around the world for his musical abilities," the foreman commented. And then, failing to recognize that he might have hurt his worker's feelings, he continued, "Of course, not everyone in the same family can enjoy an equal amount of talent."

"You're right," the carpenter replied. "My brother doesn't know the first thing about building a home. It's fortunate he can afford to hire others to build a house for him."

B. C. Forbes suggested that "whether we find pleasure in our work or whether we find it a bore depends entirely upon our mental attitude towards it, not upon the task itself."

The same can be said of finding importance in what we do. It all depends on how we choose to see it. Maybe that is why Booker T. Washington, in *Up From Slavery,* advised his readers that "there is as much dignity in tilling a field as in writing a poem."

## NOT UNTIL WEDNESDAY

Several years ago, an eager young man desired a part-time job to help make his way through Stanford University. As he stood before Louis Janin one Friday morning, he was told there was only a stenographer position available. "I'd love it!" exclaimed the excited young man. "However, I can't start until next Wednesday."

Bright and early on Wednesday morning, the young man reported for duty. "I like your promptness and enthusiasm," Janin assured the lad. "I do have one question. Why couldn't you start until Wednesday?" "Well, you see, sir," the young man replied. "I had to find a typewriter and learn how to use it."

The young man committed to learning what needed to be learned was Herbert Hoover.

"No difficult or simple job ever gets done until someone decides *right now* to do what it takes to get the job done.

Unfortunately, too many people stand by ready to carry the stool when there is a piano to be moved."

*Herbert Hoover*

## NO REASON BREEDS NO PRODUCTIVITY

Millions of bees were transported from the cold Midwest climate to a tropical island. Immediately, the bees followed their instinct to gather honey for the winter. However, winter didn't come and soon the bees became lazy. The honey went untouched, but the people didn't. With no specific reason to produce, the honey bee's time was spent flying about stinging people.

*So it is with employees. The absence of clear expectations and performance goals will produce little more than trouble and frustration.*

## NOT JUST FOR THE BIRDS

Mankind might do well to study the work habits of the birds. Their example provides inspiration to aspiring executives, new college graduates, or people desiring growth and achievement in their professional lives.

Although an unpopular fowl, the blackbird serves his family well. Beginning its day around 2:30 A.M., the blackbird doesn't punch out until 7:30 that evening. During the course of its day (seventeen hours), it will set over one hundred meals before its young.

The thrush maintains a comparable life-style. Arising at 2:30 A.M., it feeds two hundred mouths six times in a span of nineteen hours. At 9:30 each night, the thrush finally stops.

One flying friend sleeps in until 3:00 A.M. and carries on until 9:00 P.M. The extra sleep gives the titmouse the energy necessary to feed its young (said to be a total of over four hundred meals daily) during the eighteen-hour day. Being a finicky eater, the titmouse must find enough caterpillars to feed those hungry mouths.

*Those are pretty impressive workdays, not to mention impressive accomplishments. People with a gusto for succeeding make the eight-*

*hour day an exception rather than the rule. They find their work so exciting and challenging that time is of little interest. What does have meaning to them is accomplishment.*

## ALTERED DREAMS

An airplane navigator noticed his flight approaching a picturesque lake in the mountains. "You know," he told his crew, "when I was a young lad, I fished on a lake like that. I would sit in the boat and every time a plane flew by wished I was directing it. Now, I look on the lake and wish I was fishing."

### I Can Do Something

I am but one,
But I am one.
I cannot do everything,
But I can do something.
What I can do
I ought to do.
And what I ought to do,
With God's help,
I will do.

*Anonymous*

### All V.I.P.'s

All have a share in the beauty
All have a part in the plan;
What does it matter what duty
Falls to the lot of man?
Someone must blend the plaster
And someone must carry the stone;
Neither the man nor the master
Ever has builded alone.
Making a roof from the weather
Or building a house for a king,
Only by working together have men
Ever accomplished a thing.

*Anonymous*

## WHICH BONE ARE YOU?

William Wilkerson writes of four types of bones that tend to exist in every organization.

First, there are the *wishbones*. These individuals spend most of their time wishing others would do the work. Ironically, if they spent as much time working as they do wishing, valuable work would get done.

Then, we have the *jawbones*. Needless to say, these people spend a lot of time talking about the work that needs to be done but never getting anything done.

The *knucklebones* love to knock what everyone else is doing. These people usually quit working as soon as they find a job. Reason? They pour all their efforts into criticizing others.

The productive bones are the *backbones*. They get the work done and aren't concerned with who gets the credit.

## WORK

If you find yourself longing for the good old days, you might read over the list of rules for white-collar workers posted in 1872 by a carriage manufacturing company in New York:

1. Office employees each day will fill lamps, clean chimneys, and trim wicks.

2. Each clerk will bring a bucket of water and a scuttle of coal for the day's business.

3. Make your pens carefully. You may whittle nibs to your individual taste.

4. Men employees will be given an evening off each week for courting purposes, or two evenings if they go to church regularly.

5. After thirteen hours of labor in the office, the employees should spend the remaining time reading the Bible or other good books.

6. Every employee should lay from each pay a goodly sum of his earnings for his declining years so that he will not become a burden on society.

7. The employee who has performed his labors faithfully and without fault for five years will be given an increase of five cents per day in his pay, providing profits from the business permit

*Anonymous*

## JUST YOU AND ME

I have run across some absolutely irrefutable statistics that show exactly why you are tired, and it's no wonder you are tired. There are not as many people working as you may have thought . . . at least according to the survey just completed. The population of this country is 200 million. Eighty-four million are over 60 years of age, which leaves 116 million to do the work. People under 20 years of age total 75 million, which leaves 41 million to do the work.

There are 22 million people employed by the government, which leaves 19 million to do the work. Four million are in the armed forces, which leaves 15 million to do the work. Deduct 14,800,000, the number of people in state and city offices, which leaves 200,000 to do the work. There are 188,000 in hospitals, asylums, etc., so that leaves 12,000 to do the work.

Now, it may interest you to know that there are 11,998 people in jail, so that leaves just 2 people to carry the load. That's just you and me—and I am getting tired of doing everything myself.

*Anonymous*

# Worry

*As a rule, men worry more about what they can't see than about what they can.*

**JULIUS CAESAR**

50

Some of your hurts you have cured,
And the sharpest you still have survived,
But what torments of grief you endured
From evils that never arrived!

*Ralph Waldo Emerson*

Worry is an old man with bended head carrying a load of feathers which he thinks are lead.

*Anonymous*

Worry is holding in your mind that which you don't want to happen. Remember: If you think it is and it isn't, it will become an is even though it isn't

*Anonymous*

Worry tries to cross a bridge before you come to it.

*Anonymous*

A day of worry is more exhausting than a day of work.

*Anonymous*

The word "fear" appears over four hundred times in the Bible.

*Glenn Van Ekeren*

Nothing in life is to be feared. It is only to be understood.

*Marie Curie*

Within you lies a power greater than what lies before you.

*Anonymous*

These then are my last words to you: Be not afraid of life. Believe that life is worth living, and your belief will help create the fact.

*William James*

There are two days in the week about which and upon which I never worry: One . . . is yesterday . . . and the other day I do not worry about is tomorrow.

*Robert J. Burdette*

Worry is wasting today's time cluttering up tomorrow's opportunities with yesterday's troubles.

*Anonymous*

If you think too much and fail to take action, fear makes its home within you.

*Anonymous*

## FAITH IS LETTING GO

A college student was studying for exams at a friend's apartment until after midnight. Bidding his friend good night, the young man began the two-mile walk across the dark, empty campus to his home. As he approached the midpoint of his hike, he suddenly felt uneasy, with an eerie feeling of impending doom. As he picked up his pace, his heart pounded with a rush of adrenaline. His fears were not unfounded, for just as he passed the darkest thicket of bushes, two men jumped him. They forced him to the ground, gagged and blindfolded him. There in the darkness, the assailants dragged the young student to their waiting car and robbed him of everything he had. The robbers then drove to a secluded wooded area and forced him out of the car. Still blindfolded and gagged, the young man was then brutally dragged deeper into the woods, where the men tied a rope over a limb of a huge tree. They forced their struggling victim to grasp the end of the rope, and then gave him a violent shove, swinging him clinging to the end of the rope.

"Hang on for your life," they shouted at the blindfolded student, "or you will be dashed to pieces on the rocks below! You are swinging over a ragged cliff that drops hundreds of feet below!" Then they left him. The frightened student could not yell and could not see. His soul was filled with horror at the thought of the deadly fall, and he clutched frantically at the swaying rope. His strength steadily failed. At last he could hold on no longer. The end had come. His fingers relaxed their convulsive grip, and he fell—six inches, to the solid earth at his feet! He was not swinging over a dangerous cliff as the men had told him. It was only a ruse of the robbers to gain time to escape. When the young man let go of the rope, he fell not to his death, but to his safety!

*Sometimes, faith is not clinging; faith is letting go.*

## PRISONERS OF FEAR

A new prison in British Columbia was completed with much of the labor done by the prisoners themselves. The new modern structure was to replace the old Fort Alcan prison that for hundreds of years had housed many prisoners. After the prisoners were moved into their new quarters, they spent long and physically tiring days stripping the old prison of lumber, electrical appliances, and plumbing to be used for the needy miners nearby. Under the supervision of the prison guards, the inmates then proceeded to tear down the old prison walls.

While dismantling the jail walls, they were shocked and infuriated to find that although mighty locks were attached to the heavy doors and two-inch steel bars covered the windows, the walls had been made out of paper and clay painted to resemble iron. It was obvious to all the prisoners that during their imprisonment in the old prison, a mightly heave or a hard kick would have easily knocked out the wall, allowing them to escape. For years, they had huddled in their locked cells, thinking escape was impossible. Nobody had ever tried it because they thought it was impossible.

*Many of us are prisoners of fear and simply do not attain our goals because we do not try to reach them. How do we know if we* can *or* can't *if we don't try?*

## CAN WORRY KILL YOU?

The expression "worried to death" has more truth in it than you might think.

There is a story about Nick Sitzman, a strong, young bull-of-a-man, who worked on a train crew. It seemed that Nick had everything: a strong healthy body, ambition, a wife and two children, and many friends. However, Nick had one fault. He was a notorious worrier. He worried about everything and usually feared the worst.

One midsummer day, the train crew were informed that they could quit an hour early in honor of the foreman's birthday. Accidentally, Nick was locked in a refrigerator boxcar, and the rest of the workmen left the site. Nick panicked.

He banged and shouted until his fists were bloody and his voice was hoarse. No one heard him. "If I can't get out, I'll freeze to death in here," he thought. Wanting to let his wife and family know exactly what had happened to him, Nick found a knife and began to etch words on the wooden floor. He wrote, "It's so cold, my body is getting numb. If I could just go to sleep. These may be my last words."

The next morning the crew slid open the heavy doors of the boxcar and found Nick dead. An autopsy revealed that every physical sign of his body indicated he had frozen to death. And yet the refrigeration unit of the car was inoperative, and the temperature inside indicated fifty-five degrees. Nick had killed himself by the power of his fear.

*Fear can be paralyzing as well as fatal.*

### FEAR BREEDS FEAR

A young college student was fighting a terrible Iowa blizzard on his way home for Christmas vacation. He became so exhausted straining to see the road through the swirling, blinding snow that he knew he had to stop.

He pulled into the first town and wearily tramped into a small hotel. "Sorry, sir," he was told by the clerk. "There isn't a room to be had. The weather is bad, and everyone on the road seems to have stopped here." The traveler found another run-down motel. It didn't matter what the place was like. He had to get some sleep.

"Full up!" the proprietor said as he slammed the door against the cold blast of air.

At the last place displaying a "No Vacancy" sign, he sat down. His body ached with weariness. He pleaded with the clerk, "I don't care where you put me. If there's space on the floor, I'll sleep there."

"We have a small area that was a storage closet, and I guess we could squeeze a rollaway bed in it."

They moved in a small cot and the young student flopped down on it, grateful for some rest. But he couldn't sleep. The room was closed in, and he suffered from claustrophobia. There were no lights in the tight space, and he began to feel his way around the room, groping to find a window or transom to let in some air.

The walls seemed to move in on him, and his throat became tight with fear. He had to find a window. He began groping again, and his hands finally felt a window—but the window was nailed shut! Panic gripped his chest. He had to have air or he would die. He took off his shoe, and swinging as hard as he could, broke out the bottom pane of the window. With a weary, relieved sigh, he fell on the cot and fell sound asleep.

The next morning he opened his eyes and discovered that the window that had given him openness and fresh air was not a window to the outside at all. During a remodeling process, it had been sealed in with a solid brick wall. Nothing had changed in his situation except what he had perceived in his mind. His fears were creations of his own imagination, leading to a solution that he thought solved his dilemma.

*One thing to remember about fear and worry is that, for the most part, they are creations of our imaginations.*

## ONLY ON WEDNESDAY

I read about a man who handled worry in a creative fashion. There seemed to be so many things to worry about, he decided to set aside one single day each week to worry. As worries occurred, he would write them down and put them in his worry box. Then, on Worry Wednesday, he read through each worry. To his amazement, most of the things he was disturbed about had already settled themselves or had been taken care of in some other way. Thus, he learned there was seldom a justifiable reason to worry.

## WORRY

A couple started off their ride to visit a friend. The morning air was pleasant, and they enjoyed themselves until they happened to remember a certain bridge which was very old and probably unsafe. "I shall never dare to go over that bridge," exclaimed the wife, "and we can't get across the river any other way." "Oh," said the man, "I forgot that bridge. It is a bad place; suppose it should break through and we should fall into the water and be drowned!" "Or," said the woman, adding to his complaint, "suppose you should step on a rotten plank and break your leg. What would become of me and the baby?" "I don't know," responded the husband. "What would become of any of us, for I couldn't work, and we should all starve to death!" So the lugubrious talk ran on until they reached the spot where the old bridge had stood—and lo, they discovered that since they had been there, it had been replaced with a new one! All their anxiety had been worse than useless.

*King's Business*

## OVERCOMING THE EIGHT PERCENT

Recently, I saw a worry survey that says 40 percent of the things we worry about never happen, 30 percent are in the past and can't be helped, 12 percent concern the affairs of others that aren't our business, 10 percent are about sickness, either real or imagined, and 8 percent are worth worrying about. Even the 8 percent worth worrying about aren't really worth the energy of worry. Putting faith in action, those doubts, fears, and worries can be overcome and the attainment of goals achieved.

So really, 0 percent of the things we worry about are really worth the effort.

## FEELING GOOD BUT FEELING BAD

It is significant that the English word *worry* is derived from an Anglo-Saxon word that means *to strangle* or *to choke*. Worry cuts off the air supply that allows us to *carpe diem* (Latin for *seize the moment*). People get so busy worrying about yesterday or tomorrow, that they miss today. We become like the old woman who said, "I always feel bad when I feel good, because I just know that I'll feel bad after a while." Worry chokes the opportunity to seize the moment and makes us susceptible to a life of feeling bad.

## TRUST YOUR BUOYANCY

While walking along the edge of the Dead Sea one day, a man lost his balance and tumbled into a deep section of water. Unable to swim, the man became panic-stricken. In desperation, he began to thrash about, fighting the elements of the massive sea. After a few minutes, he was completely exhausted and felt he could do no more. Crying out to God for help, he expected death to open its door. What a pleasant surprise awaited him. His physical exhaustion forced him to relax, and he began to float. In his fear, he had forgotten that the Dead Sea is so full of salt and other minerals that if people lie still, they will quickly come to the surface. All the man needed to do was to trust himself to the buoyancy of the water.

## TWO THINGS NOT TO WORRY ABOUT

In my life, I have found there are two things about which I should never worry. First, I shouldn't worry about the things I can't change. If I can't change them, worry is certainly most foolish and useless. Second, I shouldn't worry about the things I can change. If I can change them, then taking action will accomplish far more than wasting my energies in worry. Besides, it is my belief that, nine times out of ten, worrying about something does more danger than the thing itself. Give worry its rightful place—out of your life.